Corpus Linguistics and Variation in English

LANGUAGE AND COMPUTERS: STUDIES IN PRACTICAL LINGUISTICS

No 75

edited by
Christian Mair
Charles F. Meyer
Nelleke Oostdijk

Corpus Linguistics and Variation in English

Theory and Description

Edited by
Joybrato Mukherjee and Magnus Huber

Rodopi

Amsterdam - New York, NY 2012

Cover image: www.morgueFile.com

Cover design: Inge Baeten

The paper on which this book is printed meets the requirements of "ISO 9706:1994, Information and documentation - Paper for documents - Requirements for permanence".

ISBN: 978-90-420-3495-2
E-Book ISBN: 978-94-012-0771-3

Printed in The Netherlands

Contents

Introduction: Corpus linguistics and variation in English

Joybrato Mukherjee and Magnus Huber

Justus Liebig University, Giessen

The present volume contains a selection of papers presented at the 31st Annual Conference of the International Computer Archive of Modern and Medieval English (ICAME) in Giessen, Germany in May 2010. The overarching conference topic was 'Corpus linguistics and variation in English'. Although papers and posters from all areas of English corpus linguistics were of course welcome, the conference topic indicated a particular focus at the 31st ICAME Conference on research activities and projects that place special emphasis on the compilation, annotation and – most importantly – the analysis of computer corpora in order to capture the multi-dimensional variability of the English language, depending on a range of factors that cause variation in language, e.g. language contact, genre and style, region and time.

The papers and posters that were presented at the 31st ICAME Conference were characterized by a very high quality and introduced a number of innovative and original research ideas as well as new methodological approaches. Thus, it does not come as a surprise that a large number of the conference contributions qualified for the Conference proceedings. After a strict peer-reviewing process, we were left with some forty papers. We decided to group them into two volumes: The present volume includes all the papers that are based on the five plenary lectures at the 31st ICAME Conference and 13 further papers which combine theoretical considerations and/or methodological innovations with descriptive case studies. The second volume of the Conference proceedings is available electronically in the *eVarieng* online series, published under the auspices of the Varieng Research Unit of the University of Helsinki, Finland (see http://www.helsinki.fi/varieng/journal/index.html). The *eVarieng* volume carries the subtitle 'Focus on non-native Englishes' as it includes all the papers that are concerned with variation in postcolonial second-language varieties of Englishes, learner Englishes and English as a lingua franca.

As can be seen in the five plenary papers included in the present volume, all our keynote speakers provided the conference participants with very distinct perspectives from various linguistic subdisciplines on the conference topic 'Corpus linguistics and variation in English': The paper by **Stefan Th. Gries** highlights the importance of quantitative-statistical methods for the description of variation in English, picking up on current debates in the corpus-linguistic community; **Michaela Mahlberg** provides a hands-on practical introduction to the corpus-based analysis of stylistic variation, a research area at the interface between linguistics and literary studies; **Miriam Meyerhoff** shows that even modest corpora of lesser known languages can be used to shed light on processes of variation and change in contact variants of English such as English-based creoles in postcolonial contexts; **Edgar W. Schneider** uses a range of specialised and historical corpora to discuss the evolution of Southern vernacular forms of American English; and **Elizabeth C. Traugott** makes it clear that corpus resources are indispensable tools for the analysis of historical change in general and grammaticalisation processes in particular. All five plenary papers provide rich and thought-provoking theoretical and methodological discussions above and beyond the actual case studies that they include.

The other papers in the present volume, too, combine theoretical and/or methodological considerations with a corpus-based description of actual language use. They also illustrate the enormous range of corpus-based work in English linguistics. **Gisle Andersen** investigates the proactive manifestation of listenership in business negotiations. **Marina Bondi and Corrado Seidenari** analyse the use of evaluative language in blog comments, highlighting significant features of an increasingly important web genre. **Doris Dant**'s study based on the *Corpus of Contemporary American English* (COCA) confirms that *The Chicago Manual of Style*, in spite of being the most influential style guide in the United States, is not always in line with variation in linguistic reality. **Hans Martin Lehmann and Gerold Schneider** discuss various kernel issues related to dependency treebanks and how they can be used to analyse syntactic variation. Wright's *English Dialect Dictionary* (EDD) is at the heart of **Manfred Markus**'s paper who shows that – and how – the EDD can be used as a corpus. **Hagen Peukert** discusses statistical ways of making meaningful text-type predictions for a given text on the basis of the analysis of the text-internal distribution of phonemes. New ways of detecting lexicogrammatical routines and degrees of predictability of lexical choices at the level of *n*-grams are explored by **Thomas Proisl**. Using various diachronic and synchronic corpora of British English, **Paula Rodríguez-Abruñeiras** traces the development of the exemplifying markers *for example* and *for instance*, which also reveals features of a process of grammaticalisation. The Irish component of the *International Corpus of English* (ICE) is used by **Patricia Ronan** to describe and categorise the variable functions of *would* as a pragmatic softener. The transitive *out of -ing* pattern in American English is analysed by **Juhani Rudanko** along the lines of construction grammar. **Stefania Spina** focuses on methodological issues that are relevant to the compilation of a corpus of television news, e.g. genre distinctions. From a more theoretical perspective, **Michael Stubbs** looks at the relationship between (naturally occurring) texts and (artificially constructed) corpora, making it clear, *inter alia*, that texts and corpora relate to fundamentally different conceptions of context. Finally, **Turo Vartiainen and Jefrey Lijffijt** use a parsed version of the *British National Corpus* (BNC) to analyse the heterogeneous group of premodifying *-ing* participles.

We have abstained from grouping the papers in the present volume into smaller sections, as we felt that this would create artificial topical distinctions. Instead, we have arranged all the 18 papers in a strictly alphabetical order.

We are very grateful to a number of people without whom the present volume would never have materialised. First and foremost, we would like to thank our joint teams in Giessen who supported us beyond the call of duty in organising the 31st ICAME Conference in May 2010. The conference was also supported and sponsored by various institutions, in particular the German Research Foundation (DFG) and our home institution, Justus Liebig University, Giessen. We are particularly grateful to all the contributors for having chosen the present volume as the outlet for their research. We are also very grateful to the reviewers of all the paper and poster submissions for the conference as well as the reviewers of the papers that were handed in for the present volume after the conference. Special thanks are due to Dilini Algama, Sandra Feller, Christopher Koch, Mirjami Körtvelyessy and Marie-Christine Vogel for taking care of all the steps involved in the production of the final camera-ready manuscript. Sandra Götz in particular invested a lot of time and energy in the final proof-reading and editing rounds. Just like the highly memorable 31st ICAME Conference in Giessen, the present Conference proceedings are also a product of successful teamwork; all remaining errors and infelicities are our responsibility alone.

Joybrato Mukherjee and Magnus Huber
Giessen
December 2011

Listenership in polylogic discourse

Gisle Andersen

Norwegian School of Economics and Business Administration

Abstract

This study investigates how listenership is manifested in a particular discourse setting, namely simulated business negotiation. The study is based on material recorded on video from a corpus of negotiations between international business students. There is a special focus on the interactional placement of backchannels. This refers to the direction of backchannelling between the two teams as well as possible trajectories of listenership signals between the individual interlocutors. The data shows that backchannels are used not only as indicators of listenership across the negotiation table, signalling comprehension vis-à-vis speakers from the opposite team, but also to support co-team members' utterances and that the pragmatic functions of individual tokens crucially depend on the context of use.

1. Introduction

In pragmatics and discourse studies, there has been a bias towards studies of the role of speakers in conversation, and the role of the listener has been given less attention. Nevertheless, corpus-based studies have amply demonstrated that listeners contribute actively by signalling comprehension, agreement, positive or negative evaluation and other attitudinal meanings using a variety of linguistic and non-linguistic means. Previous research has mainly focused on auditory realisations, for example backchannels such as *mm*, *mhm* or *uh-huh*, attitudinally salient interjections like *wow* or *damn*, discourse markers like *oh*, *yes/yeah* and *okay*, lexical repetitions, etc., while visual response tokens such as head nods or eye movements are less frequently accounted for (Yngve 1970; Stenström 1984; Tottie 1991; Stenström 1994; Holmes and Stubbe 1997; Gardner 1998; Stubbe 1998; McCarthy 2002; Heintz 2003; McCarthy 2003; Andersen 2009; Kjellmer 2009; Bjørge 2010). Most comparative studies of listenership have looked at how it is manifested across regions or cultures or compared native and non-native speaker groups, studies which show, for example, that Americans use more backchannels than German speakers (Heintz 2003), and that American and British usage differs in some respects but not in others (Tottie 1991; McCarthy 2002). To some extent, there has also been a focus on gender differences (Holmes and Stubbe 1997). Most of our current knowledge about listener activities stems from investigations of interactional patterns in everyday conversation, although Bjørge (2010) is a notable exception. Less is known about the role and practise of listenership in institutional conversational settings, where the communication serves a particular academic or professional purpose. There has also been a bias towards the study of conversations between two people. According to Kerbat-Orecchioni (2004), there is "a deep-rooted tendency to associate interaction with interaction between two people, considered as the prototype of all interaction" (Kerbat-Orecchioni 2004: 2). The notion of *polylogue* describes multi-participant interaction involving three or more speakers.

There is therefore a need for studies which show how listenership is practised in polylogues. This paper investigates how listenership is manifested in simulated business negotiations (Bjørge 2010). I investigate the role of response tokens realised as minimal listener responses (backchannels) or non-minimal (lexical) responses that contribute as acknowledgements of receipt of information, as a means of keeping the communication channel open and as signals of attitudinal meanings. I focus particularly on the *interactional placement* of backchannels, which refers to the direction of backchannelling in terms of possible trajectories of listenership signals between the individual interlocutors in a discussion between two groups of speakers. The manifestation of listenership can be expected to differ according to speech genre, and business meetings are supposedly different from everyday conversation. In LSP contexts, the spoken discourse is used to achieve some professional goal, such as reaching an agreement about a business issue. Business negotiation involves arguments, counter-arguments, proposals and counterproposals, and there is a fine interplay between the conflicting and shared interest of two parties (Firth 1995). Negotiation can be technically construed as a group interaction in which two teams with conflicting interest meet, but which does contain monologue-like sequences, in which the opposing team is being informed, and also dialogue-like sequences between pairs of speakers. These characteristics – the underlying conflicting interests of the two parties and the need for the subtle management of information – can be expected to have bearings on the interactional behaviour of negotiators, including the way they use backchannels and other response tokens.

The paper is organised as follows. Section 2 describes the corpus data that this study is based on. Section 3 gives a brief qualitative survey of how speakers express listenership and of the functional range of response tokens used, focussing in particular on what seems to be genre-specific usage types. Section 4 provides quantitative results which show the main tendencies of interactional placement, that is who is signalling active listenership and to whom. Finally, Section 5 gives some concluding remarks.

2. Data

The NHH (Norges Handelshøyskole; Norwegian School of Economics and Business Administration) negotiation corpus provides transcribed video recordings of negotiations performed by NHH students who play out roles as businesspeople aiming at reaching an agreement with an opposing team. The students partake in an oral task organised as a negotiation scenario. The purpose of the assignment is to train negotiation skills as well as English language and communication skills, and to raise intercultural awareness. The data are further described in the paper by Bjørge (2010), who initiated this corpus collection. The current study is based on a subset of recordings of Norwegian students at the bachelor level. The students are intermediate-advanced learners of English who take a course in Intercultural Business Communication. The assignment is an obligatory activity, in which the students must engage actively in order to get credits for the course. The data have been transcribed and annotated according to an adapted version of the conventions of the ELFA corpus.[1]

The two sessions studied here are each of approximately 45 minutes' duration (approx. 11,000 words). The negotiation scenario concerns the ficticious sale of silicon wafers needed for the production of solar cell panels between a Norwegian producer and a Chinese buyer. The students had 30 minutes preparation time and were instructed to plan the negotiation, distribute participant roles and determine their team's bargaining position. The overall aim of the task is to reach an agreement with the other team concerning negotiable factors such as price, amount, repeat orders, transportation costs, means of transportation and insurance costs. The teams are also instructed to follow conventional phases of negotiation, specifically the introduction (relationship-building), information exchange, concession and agreement/summary phase (Beamer and Varner 2008: 326ff.).

3. The functions of response tokens in polylogues

This section describes types of use of response tokens that seem to be at least potentially specific to this particular genre. Tottie describes two basic functions of backchannels, the supportive function, which is to signal "understanding and agreement" (Tottie 1991: 256) and the regulative (interactional) function, "to encourage the speaker to continue his turn" (ibid.). The supportive function can be illustrated by (1).

(1) B2 one of the reasons that we say that this del= this shipment will be a little bit delayed is because we think about the transportation costs, [and]
A2 **[yeah]**
B1 we're also very conscious about the environment, so the plane, or air shipment is something that we prefer would not happen

A2's *yeah* serves to signal understanding at different levels, in terms of the propositional meaning of the speaker's utterance, as well as the acknowledgement of receipt of a new topic in the discourse, namely transportation costs. The regulative function can be illustrated by (2).

(2) A1 well what we need here is 156 millimetres of multicrystalline wafers so, what can you tell me about [what you have here]
B1 [well basically] erm we produce different kinds of silicon wafers

A2 **-mm**

B1 er the multicrystalline silicon wafers that you're talking about is what we are mostly producing, we are actually, we have a market share of 20 per cent (A1 nods) and we

A2's *mm* serves to signal his (and his team's) interest in the production of silicon wafers, and it is used to encourage B1 to elaborate, which she does.

As several authors have pointed out, e.g. Tottie (1991), listener signals are often also fortified with attitudinal meanings, signalling involvement of various types – such as a positive or negative evaluation – and of various strengths – ranging from scepticism or weak doubt to enthusiastic agreement (Andersen 2001: 63ff.). A pertinent example is (3).

(3) A3 [yeah we can] see that but we also think that it would be er interesting for you to erm get into the Chinese market

B2 **absolutely**, [**yes**]

A3 [and er], in that way erm, maybe this could be like a product for you to see how that would wo- would work and that you would benefit from actually lowering the price

A2 **\mm**

B2's *absolutely yes* provides a signal of enthusiastic agreement, more so than would be possible with a mere *mm*. This observation illustrates a general characteristic of the category of items we are dealing with here, namely the lack of interchangeability of different forms. Although we may postulate that response tokens like *yeah, yes, okay* and *mm* have a core meaning of signifying agreement and understanding at a basic level, each has its own specialised functions. Besides, *okay* signals acknowledgement and receipt of information which is more involved than a mere *mm* would be.

(4) B2 we have used a lot of er resources for our production and, er technology through this process and we er have tested these new solar wafers both in space, er near space and on ground terrestrial markets both in very humid climates, (A2 nods) cold climates, er so we think our product is very capable of handling almost every condition

A1 **ok\ay**

A3 and you also think that your product can handle the fact that we are so many people in our country, so

In this context, in example (4), *okay* seems to have a specialised function of marking *acceptance*, that is, the hearer accepts the guarantee about the product's quality and finds no reason to question it. In other cases, *okay* may signal the acknowledgement of information that counts as a new offer, a new negotiation item that has been introduced, or a new stage in the negotiation. There seems to be a general flavour of acceptance conveyed by *okay* that is not conveyed by *yeah/yes* or *mm*.

Another important point to be noted is that one and the same marker may serve different functions according to discourse context.

(5) A1 so how, is there anything you can give us like before say November?
B1 that's kind of erm, it's a month to November so I guess we have to say that that's not happening but if we are really doing our best, I can
B2 if you would er repeat orders, if you would keep this that it wouldn't be a once, er that you would have orders during next year we would be able to
A2 /**yeah**
B2 erm postpone some other deliveries
B1 [**yeah**]
B2 [and put] you first in line

The two highlighted *yeah*s in (5) exemplify the same form occurring as response tokens; nevertheless the two instances invite very different pragmatic inferences. A2's *yeah* carries a neutral signal of understanding and acceptance of the type 'okay, I accept what you say', directed towards a proposal that is being made by a member of the other party. On the other hand, B1's *yeah* is part of a collaborative proposal and provides a more emphatic signal akin to 'that's very true indeed', adding support to and underlining the coherent views of the members of team B. In other words, a response token may be directed towards something uttered by a speaker of the other team or one's own team. The latter type serves to emphasise the team-internal consensus. Another notable factor is that, in polylogue, more than one interlocutor may respond simultaneously to what was said. Example (6) illustrates such collective backchannelling.

(6) A3 and when will it be here then?
B2 the first one as we said in December and the last shipment probably in the end of March
A2 but yo= you said erm that you had capacity problems
B1 **yeah**
B2 **yes**
A2 but suddenly now when we say we want maybe twenty thousand it's no problem

Arguably, this type of use has both team-internal as well as team-external functions, as it serves to confirm what speaker A2 said about capacity problems, as well as signalling internal consensus between team members. In other contexts, the whole team may be engaged in collective backchannelling.

One interesting sequence in the data has a special status. Example (7) shows what is clearly a turning point in one of the negotiation sessions.

(7)	B1	er we see that there's an amazing growth and that you are obviously the market leader here, so I guess we might reduce the price, to,
	B2	this would, we could reduce it to thirteen hundred and I think that would be our final [offer]
	B1	[but then] I guess we have to get a bigger quantity, you have to get a bigger quantity from us, you have to order more than just the fifteen thousand
	B2	or that we make a, sign a contract for future er [involvement]
	A1	(nods)
	B1	[yeah]
	B2	in each other's companies
	B1	[cos]
	A2	[I think] thirteen hundred is a reasonable price
	A1	**(nodding) yeah**
	A3	**yeah**, we can accept that, [**yeah** (**nodding**)]
	A1	[**yeah**]

This extract encompasses the resolution of the difficult price issue and represents the height of the drama, as it were. A cluster of response tokens signal strong internal consensus, in this case with regard to price. Another type of clustering can be observed in the summary phase, which in both sessions can be identified by an introductory statement of the type *so what are we agreeing on here.*

(8)	A2	erm so what are we agreeing on here
	B2	er we're agreeing on fifteen thousand
	A1	(nods) /**mhm**
	B2	er of the multicrystalline
	A2	[/**mhm**]
	A1	[**yes**]
	B1	one fifty six, [millimetres]
	A1	[**yeah**]
	A2	/**yeah**
	A1	that's right
	B2	er, at a price of thirteen hundred per unit
	A2	/**mm**

As is evident, the summary takes the form of a series of initiation-response pairs in a back-and-forth manner, each pair representing one of the items negotiated. (The summary continues beyond what is seen in (8).)

The next extract shows how the negotiators of team A take part in a joint strategy to convince the other team to accept a five year warranty.

(9) A2 but Silicon Valley is a lot more stable climate, and China is a great variety in climate and er there's a large market for you here, so
B1 [**that's true**]
A2 [er if you] could give us five year we might have a deal, I think
A3 or, if you think about it, if we go back to the quantity, and you see that we were willing to buy two hundred thousand in quantity, that is the same as your total production today
A1 <u>mm</u>, it will increase one hundred [percent]
A3 [er <u>yeah</u>], so we will increase your entire production with one hundred percent
B2 **yes**
A3 isn't that very lucrative for you
B2 [but if it's possible]
A1 [then it's only fair]
A2 and you should be able to er to trust your product to give a warranty for five years
A1 <u>yeah</u>, and when we're buying this quantity I think it's only fair that we receive the five years
A2 and if the product is good, then it won't be a cost for you
B1 [**well that's true**]

Example (9) illustrates how response tokens serve different functions according to which team the responder represents. B1 and B2's team-external responses *(well) that's true* and *yes* are clearly very defensive and seem to have a flavour of 'that's *admittedly* true'. In fact, team B are forced to admit that receiving an order from team A would radically increase their market share. On the other hand, the team-internal response tokens, A1's *mm*, A3's *yeah* and A1's *yeah* (underlined) seem to serve a highly specialised function as they contribute to putting increased pressure on the opposite team. It seems that in such a joint argumentation sequence, the response tokens add to the pressure placed upon team B, at the same time signalling the consensus of team A.

Finally, example (10) represents an interesting case where *mm* comes after a long monologue by speaker B3, a sequence which is notable for its lack of backchannels from the opposite team (during which, in fact, A1 is looking in his papers and making notes).

(10) B3 (after long monologue)
if you are able to reduce so much in China that will, er, be very good for the whole world, erm, yes, and as we have understood, China, the population in China is increasing, and the more people the more pollution
B2 (nods) **mm**
B3 so if we can manage to, er, yeah, make these solar cell panels to be used in China that will help the total environment in the world very much

It seems that B2's *mm* is not principally regulative or aimed at triggering B3 to continue, but rather it serves to express *empathy* towards a co-team member over the lack of conversational support from the other side during the long monologue. This and the above examples show that, even when it comes to team-internal backchannelling, we must acknowledge functional variability and the need to specify functions in order to fully account for response tokens in polylogue.

4. Who backchannel(s)? The interactional placement of backchannels

In a recent article, Kjellmer (2009) asks the question "Where do we backchannel?" In the context of the current study, it might also be pertinent to ask the question "Who backchannel(s), and where?" As seen from examples (5-10) in Section 3, the functional characteristics of response tokens are crucially dependent on the relation between the listener and the speaker. I therefore propose to study listenership with respect to the *interactional placement* of response tokens, that is to say, the direction of backchannelling between the two teams (seller → buyer or vice versa), as well as who responds to whom, to see if individual contributions are evenly distributed or if there are particular channels between pairs of team members that are particularly prone to backchannel use. In principle, in a polylogic spoken discourse involving a handful of people, any listener can respond to what any speaker says. However, since we are dealing with negotiation scenarios involving two opposite teams, the main route of the information exchange is between the two teams. One would therefore expect response tokens to be used mainly across the negotiation table, in other words for indicating listenership towards something said by a speaker from the opposite team, as opposed to speakers from one's own team. The hypothesis is therefore that team-internal response tokens are less common than team-external response tokens. However, other factors may also affect the degree to which speakers use response tokens, such as

a) the physical placement of speaker/listener, assuming that a longer distance reduces the likelihood of using a response token;
b) the role of speakers as representing either the seller or the buyer team; although generally perceived as of equal status, one party (seller) has a more pronounced task of convincing the other, and this bias could have bearings on use of response tokens;
c) the role played by the individual speakers such as that of team leader;
d) the language proficiency of speaker and listener, assuming that the most active participants use and trigger most response tokens.

In principle, all of these factors could be tested, but a fully fledged multifactorial testing of these parameters is beyond the scope of the present study.

4.1 Response tokens within and across teams in Session 1

In Figures 1 and 2 below, the arrows indicate the occurrence of response tokens, so that the arrows between A2 and A3 in Figure 1 indicate that speaker A2 responded with a backchannel to something that A3 said, and vice versa.

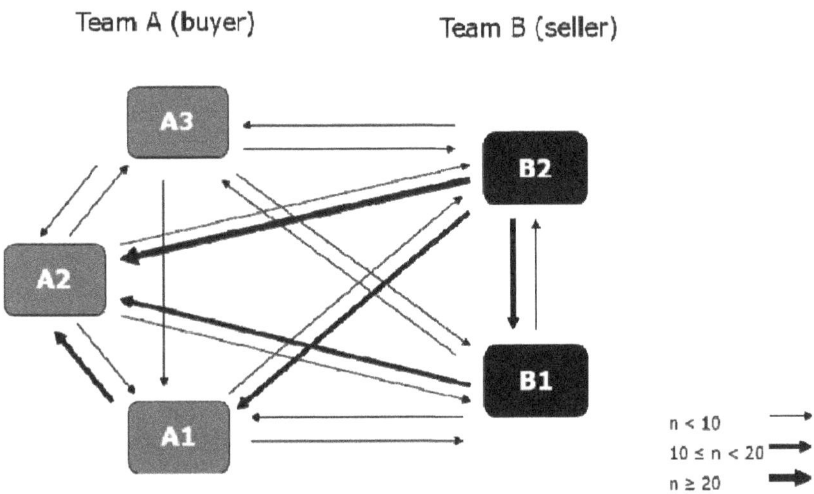

Figure 1. Response tokens within and across teams in Session 1

The thickness of the arrows is meant to signify the number of response tokens. Figure 1 shows that, in Session 1, in accordance with my initial assumption, it is indeed the buyer team members (A1-3) who use response tokens the most, accounting for about 78 per cent of the cross-table response tokens, as shown by the heavier arrows pointing from Team B to Team A, and not the other way round. The significance of team-internal response tokens is seen from the remarkable fact that 26 per cent of the response tokens are responses to own team members' utterances. We also note that all five speakers use response tokens. Interestingly, virtually all possible speaker combinations occur. Only one out of 20 possible speaker/listener combinations does not incur any response tokens, namely A1→A3; in other words, speaker A3 never backchannels anything said by speaker A1. The fact that the combinations A1↔A2 and A2↔A3 readily occur provides at least circumstantial evidence that physical distance may play a role, since speakers A1 and A3 are the non-adjacent members of team A. The two team leaders (CEOs), in this case speakers A2 and B2, take a leading role on behalf of their respective teams, and they are indeed also the most active listeners in each group, suggesting that individual roles may be relevant and that active speakers are also active listeners.

4.2 Response tokens within and across teams in Session 2

The data from Session 2 generally support these observations. This session involves one more speaker. Therefore the picture is a bit more complex, and the number of backchannels is more thinly distributed across the different speaker pairs in the polylogue, as seen from the lower number of heavy arrows.

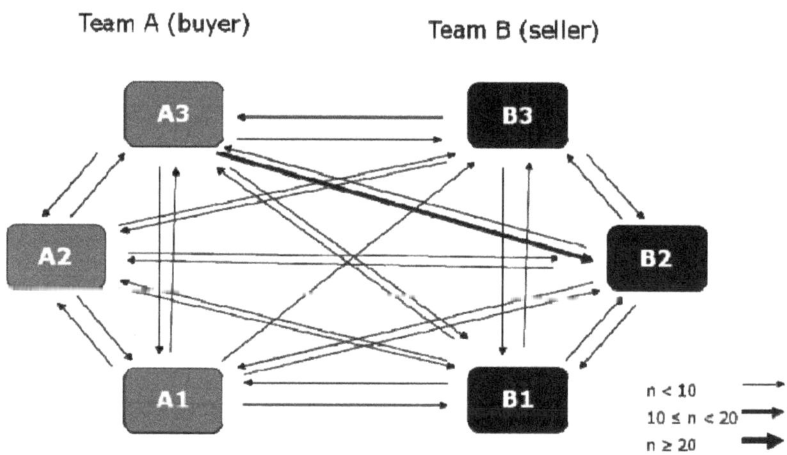

Figure 2. Response tokens within and across teams in Session 2

Here it is in fact the speakers from the seller team (B1-3) who use response tokens the most, accounting for about 72 percent of the cross-table response tokens. So we cannot unequivocally conclude that the team role as seller or buyer has a conspicuous effect on response tokens production, but investigation of more data is needed. Here, an even higher proportion of the response tokens are team-internal, specifically 33 per cent. In this case, all six speakers use response tokens and virtually all possible speaker combinations occur. Only one out of 30 possible speaker/listener combinations does not have any response tokens, namely B3→A1. Again, this suggests that physical placement may play a role, since speakers A1 and A3 are at a maximal distance apart. Again, the two team leaders, in this case A2 and B2, are the most active listeners in each group.

5. Concluding remarks

This paper has shown that in polylogic business negotiations, response tokens are used with significant functions both team-externally and team-internally. From an interactional perspective, business negotiation must be described not just as a bilateral affair between two sides, but must be accounted for in terms of the complexity of the multidimensional communicative space in which the interaction is performed. The most important observations that can be drawn from this study are the following:

- Response tokens are not restricted to signalling understanding and agreement across the negotiation table but are also salient between members of the same team.
- The pragmatic function of individual forms crucially depends on whether an item is used team-internally or team-externally.
- All participants in the data use response tokens, and active speakers are also active listeners.
- There seem to be types of uses that are genre-specific, such as collective backchannelling showing team-internal consensus, backchannel clusters in the agreement phase and serial backchannelling in the summary phase.

Finally, the most important implication of this study is that it is highly problematic to include all response tokens into the same category (in quantitative corpus-based studies or elsewhere), as the items studied here are notoriously multifunctional.

Note

1 <http://www.uta.fi/laitokset/kielet/engf/research/elfa/corpus.htm> (17.10.2010)

References

Andersen, G. (2001), *Pragmatic Markers and Sociolinguistic Variation.* Amsterdam: John Benjamins.

Andersen, G. (2009), 'Responses in Academic and Professional Discourse.' Panel discussion at the *11th International Pragmatics Conference*, Melbourne.

Beamer, L. and I. Varner (2008), *Intercultural Communication in the Global Workplace.* Boston, MA: McGraw-Hill.

Bjørge, A.K. (2010), 'Conflict or cooperation: The use of backchannelling in ELF negotiations', *English for Specific Purposes*, 29: 191-203.

Firth, A. (ed.) (1995), *The Discourse of Negotiation.* Oxford: Pergamon.

Gardner, R. (1998), 'Between speaking and listening: The vocalisation of understandings', *Applied Linguistics*, 19: 204-224.

Heintz, B. (2003), 'Backchannel responses as strategic responses in bilingual speakers' conversations', *Journal of Pragmatics*, 35: 1113-1142.

Holmes, J. and M. Stubbe (1997), 'Good listeners: Gender differences in New Zealand conversation', *Women and Language*, 20: 7-14.

Kerbat-Orecchioni, C. (2004), 'Introducing polylogue', *Journal of Pragmatics*, 36: 1-24.

Kjellmer, G. (2009), 'Where do we backchannel? On the use of *mm*, *mhm*, *uh huh* and such like', *International Journal of Corpus Linguistics*, 14: 81-112.

McCarthy, M. (2002), 'Good listenership made plain: British and American non-minimal response tokens in everyday conversation', in: R. Reppen, S.M. Fitzmaurice and D. Biber (eds.), *Using Corpora to Explore Linguistic Variation*. Amsterdam: John Benjamins. 73-90.

McCarthy, M. (2003), 'Talking back: "Small" interactional response tokens in everyday conversation', *Research on Language and Social Interaction*, 36: 33-63.

Stenström, A.-B. (1984), *Questions and Responses in English Conversation*. Lund: Lund University Press.

Stenström, A.-B. (1994), *An Introduction to Spoken Interaction*. London: Longman.

Stubbe, M. (1998), 'Are you listening? Cultural influences on the use of supportive verbal feedback in conversation', *Journal of Pragmatics*, 29: 257-289.

Tottie, G. (1991), 'Conversational style in British and American English: The case of backchannels', in: K. Aijmer and B. Altenberg (eds.), *English Corpus Linguistics*. London: Longman. 254-271.

Yngve, V. (1970), 'On getting a word in edgewise', in: Chicago Linguistic Society (ed.), *Papers from the 6th Regional Meeting, Chicago Linguistic Society*. Chicago, IL: Chicago Linguistic Society. 567-577.

and now I'm finally of the mind to say i hope the whole ship goes down...: Markers of subjectivity and evaluative phraseology in blogs

Marina Bondi and Corrado Seidenari

University of Modena and Reggio Emilia

Abstract

The paper is part of a research project on evaluative meanings in Italian and English web-logs. Web-logs may be regarded as increasingly popular, virtual arenas where information (including news) is produced, shared and – crucially – commented on evaluatively. Our focus here is on how bloggers evaluate the news in English and in Italian. Looking at business, politics and sport news on dedicated web-logs, we investigate the phraseology most frequently employed in comments on a piece of news. The data for our study are taken from the Business, Politics and Sport sections of a blog corpus that collects texts dating from September 2008 to September 2009: in all 3,042,023 running words. Our methodology is adapted from Gledhill's (2000) study on Salient Grammatical Words (SGW). We start with an overview of the keyword lists extracted from the blog corpus, looking at potential markers of the nature and structure of news blogs. We then focus on markers of subjectivity, draw their collocational profile, identify evaluative uses in context, and, following Hunston (2008) and Groom (2010), explore the semantic sequences they are characterized by. Markers of subjectivity are found to be involved in similar semantic sequences in the two languages, though characterized by different syntactic patterns and collocational profiles. The analysis confirms the importance of evaluation in blogs, as well as the key role of semantic sequences in a contrastive analysis of patterns.

1. Introduction

Web-logs (or blogs) are web-pages in which the author's entries (posts) are listed usually in reverse chronological order. Typically, a thread of comments posted by the audience is attached to each post.

As a new, increasingly popular Internet medium, blogs have attracted the attention of a number of researchers in the area of social sciences, discourse analysis (Myers 2010) and in the field of Computer Mediated Communication in particular (Baron 2008; Halavais 2002; Krishnamurthy 2002).

Blogs, although very different in their content, form and audience, have been often likened to online diaries or personal journals. For instance, Herring et al. (2005) report that more than 70% of the 203 blogs randomly selected for their study about the blog as a genre are "of the personal journal type (...), in which authors report on their lives and inner thoughts and feelings". Accordingly, self-expression seems to play a central role in bloggers' motivation to write. In a study about blogging as a social activity by Nardi et al. (2004), informants mentioned "expressing opinions to influence others", "seeking others' opinions" and "releasing emotional tension" among the five main reasons why they choose to blog. According to Baron (2008: 110), "(o)ver time, blogs have evolved from strictly current events sites to arenas for more varied self-expression".

As a sort of repository for people's opinions and emotions, blogs are increasingly coming under the scrutiny of the computational research community as well. It has been recognized fairly soon that the new medium "offers a unique look into people's reactions and feelings towards current events" (Balog et al. 2006: 207). Automatic mood and opinion detection systems have been developed for commercial purposes to exploit the blogosphere as the "aggregate voice of millions of potential consumers", as a vast repository for commentaries, opinions, views, moods, and attitudes (Mishne and Glance 2006).

In our view web-logs may be regarded as virtual arenas where content (including news) is produced, shared and – crucially – commented on evaluatively. In other words bloggers and blog commenters, in discussing the wide range of issues that are debated on in blogs, show a strong tendency to evaluate and show (or imply) their attitude to them.

Accordingly, the underlying assumption of the present research is that in blog posts (and comments especially) the discursive function of evaluation is central. In this sense a corpus of blogs may be seen as a functionally principled collection that provides a suitable starting point to try to make sense, at least for the text type in question, of how attitudinal meaning is expressed in actual use.

Broadly similar approaches to evaluation, using 'functionally *ad-hoc*' corpora, have been proposed in the study of EAP. For example, Hunston (2005) compiled a corpus of a special kind of research article: the "conflict articles"; Römer (2008) collected a corpus comprising reviews of publications from the discipline of linguistics.

The outline of the paper is as follows: in Section 2 we present our data, a corpus of business, politics and sport blogs in English and Italian. An overview of our methodology is briefly presented in Section 3. Section 4 is devoted to the analysis of the data and to the discussion of some provisional results. Finally, in Section 5, we explore further directions in our research and draw some conclusions.

2. Data

The data for the present study are taken from a section of the BLOG corpus. The BLOG corpus collects texts dating from September 2008 to September 2009: in all 3,042,023 running words. The corpus is made up of 2 comparable sub-corpora: English blogs (1,459,575 words, 71 blog sources) and Italian blogs (1,582,448 words, 65 blog sources).

Each sub-corpus is organized according to 6 macro-categories derived with minor adaptations from *Technorati* (<http://technorati.com/blogs/directory>), one of the most popular blog directories on the web. The macro-categories are:

BUSINESS, ENTERTAINMENT, SCIENCE & TECHNOLOGY, LIFESTYLE, POLITICS and SPORT.[1] Further 24 micro-categories are adapted from the 50 available at <http://technorati.com>.

For every micro-category, a sample of approximately 60,000 words was collected from 3 different blog sources (approx. 20,000 words each). In view of the specific focus of the research, only blogs with an average of 10 or more comments per post were included in the sample. However, for 8 micro-categories (7 for Italian and 1 for English) we were able to find just two blogs that met such requirement: in this case the sources contributed 30,000 words each.

As we wanted to be able to analyze separately the author's entries from their comment-threads and every single comment from each other, the beginning and the end of each post, comment thread and single comment are marked with the relevant tag. No linguistic tagging is added. Furthermore, to be able to retrieve the texts in their original web context, every post and its comment-thread are tagged with their own perma-link.

In the present paper we focus on a subset of the whole corpus, including 'news' blogs. By news-blogs we mean blogs that are typically more news-oriented than the average of the blogosphere. Accordingly, the NEWS blog corpus is made up of the BUSINESS, POLITICS and SPORT sections of the blog corpus, i.e. the sections collecting those blogs that in our opinion are more news sensitive. The NEWS blog corpus consists of 1.2m words, about 600,000 words each for the English and Italian sub-corpus.

The choice of a subset is not only due to the fact that a smaller corpus is easier to manage when looking at frequent phenomena. The specific nature of the subcorpora included was also a determining factor. Within the wider corpus, news blogs were characterized by more balanced forms of reference, as against marked use of subjectivity in the other components. This made news blogs ideal territory for an analysis of core elements of evaluation.

3. Methods

In the present paper, we propose to explore the discourse of news web-logs focusing on evaluative phraseology. Whereas lexical-semantic approaches to evaluation have tended to analyze overtly evaluative lexis, alternative approaches within corpus linguistics attempt an account of evaluative meaning from a phraseological perspective. A discussion of evaluative phenomena from a phraseological point of view is found, for example, in Channel (2000), Francis (1993, 1995), Hunston (2011), Hunston and Francis (2000), Hunston and Sinclair (2000), Römer (2008), to name but a few.

The corpus-driven approach proposed for our research is adapted from Groom (2007), whose method is borrowed and re-adapted from Gledhill's (2000) work on the research article genre. Gledhill proposes an alternative approach to keyword analysis (Scott 2008): his focus is on grammar keywords rather than on lexical keywords.

We start with an overview of the keyword-lists obtained comparing our corpora with reference corpora of general English and general Italian, the BNC and the CORIS/CODIS. Then we concentrate on grammar keywords, or "salient grammatical words" (SGW) in Gledhill's own terminology and identify those that are candidates for being involved in evaluative patterns, typically markers of subjectivity. By drawing their collocational profile, we examine in context their recurrent phraseology in terms of grammar patterns and preferred lexis.

Such an approach is not dissimilar to that of local grammars (see Hunston and Sinclair (2000) for a local grammar approach to evaluation), that provide a reliable framework for the mapping of relevant *ad-hoc* semantic roles onto pattern elements. Following Hunston (2008) and Groom (2010), however, we try to analyze such structures – and their relation to the semantics of evaluation – in terms of semantic sequences, "recurring sequences of words and phrases that may be very diverse in form and which are therefore more usefully characterised as sequences of meaning elements rather than as formal sequences" (Hunston 2008: 271).

4. Analysis

Subjectivity markers score at the very top of the keyword lists produced by comparing our BLOG corpora with BNC and CORIS/CODIS: *I* (1st), *my* (4th), *I'm* (12th), *am* (30th), *mi* (7th), *io* (12th), *me* (16th). We took this to be an indication of the high degree of subjectivity we were expecting to find in our data. Accordingly, we decided to take a closer look at such word forms in the two NEWS sub-corpora devised for the present study.

We drew a collocational profile for each of the 7 selected items to give an idea of their preferred pattern of occurrence. Then we had a look at the number of evaluative instances for each node that are accounted for by the patterns. Finally we made an attempt to subsume the different patterns in more abstract, recurrent semantic sequences.

In the remainder of this section we present in turn (1) a brief sketch of each collocational profile and (2) a schematized representation of the evaluative semantic sequences in which they are incorporated.

4.1 Collocational profiles and patterns

English

I (5,560; 101.5 pttw)
I is, obviously enough, followed by a verb form most times (96%). *think* is the most frequent R1 collocate (494).

L1	*but*	(252)	*and*	(251)	*that*	(116)	*as*	(114)	*if*	(84)	*so*	(80)
R1	*think*	(494)	*am*	(301)	*have*	(292)	*don't*	(290)	*would*	(228)	*was*	(220)
R2	*the*	(291)	*that*	(248)	*to*	(212)	*a*	(150)	*it*	(146)	*think*	(140)

The collocational profile seems to suggest the following as a prototypical pattern on the right of *I*: a verb, most probably *think*, then either a determiner (*the*, *a*) or the pronoun *it* on the one hand, or, on the other hand, a particle like *that* or *to*.

An inspection of the evaluative concordances confirms this pattern. A clause is frequently projected by the verb form, either implicitly or explicitly by means of *that* or *to*. In a random sample of 575 occurrences (10.3% of the total),[2] these are the patterns most frequently found: *I* **v** (***that***) (179; 31.1% – *I think that*); *I* **v n/prep** (60; 10.4% – *I expect* X *to*; *I agree with*);[3] *I* **v *to*-inf**; *I* v ***wh*/*if*** (20; 3.4% – *I hate to*; *I wonder how*/*if*).

I'm (579; 10.5 pttw)
I'm is, proportionally, almost twice as frequent in NEWS as in BNC.[4]

L1	*but*	(33)	*and*	(25)	*so*	(12)	*what*	(9)	*maybe*	(8)	*that*	(8)
R1	*not*	(105)	*sure*	(50)	*a*	(36)	*just*	(18)	*glad*	(16)	*in*	(14)
R2	*to*	(43)	*sure*	(32)	*that*	(30)	*the*	(22)	*a*	(21)	*for*	(17)

A prototype pattern would be as follows: *I'm*, then an adjective (most times), and finally preferably either *to* or *that* or a determiner.

As is the case with *I*, the evaluative concordances show that frequently a clause is projected (implicitly or explicitly) by the predicative complement following *I'm*. The patterns most commonly attested are: *I'm* **adj** (***that***) (130/579; 22.4% – *I'm surprised that*); *I'm* **adj/n** (72; 12.4% – *I'm serious*/*a fan*); *I'm* **adj prep** (50; 8.6% – *I'm OK with*); *I'm* **prep** (27; 4.6% – *I'm for*); *I'm* **adj *wh*/*if*** (20; 3.4% – *I'm curious if*); *I'm* **adj *to*-inf** (14; 2.4% – *I'm glad to*).

am (351; 6.4 pttw)
am is, proportionally, roughly twice as frequent in NEWS as in BNC. *am* is obviously preceded by *I* as a norm (301 times over 351).

L2	*and*	(14)	*that*	(14)	*but*	(11)	*as*	(7)	*if*	(7)	*now*	(6)
R1	*not*	(40)	*a*	(23)	*sure*	(19)	*I*	(13)	*afraid*	(9)	*glad*	(8)
R2	*that*	(23)	*to*	(20)	*a*	(17)	*the*	(15)	*of*	(10)	*about*	(9)

The collocational profile and the analysis of the evaluative concordances suggest for *am* an analysis similar to the one for *I'm*. The patterns found are: *am* **adj** (***that***) (69/351; 19.6%); *am* **adj/n** (47; 13.3%); *am* **adj prep** (33; 9.4%); *am* **adj *to*-inf** (10; 2.8%) *am* **prep** (7; 1.9%); *am un*/*sure* ***wh*/*if*** (6; 1.7%).

my (1,015; 18.5 pttw)
The co-text around *my* is admittedly not strongly patterned. *in* and *of* are the only items co-occurring with *my* with relatively high frequency in a single position (119 and 73 times on L1).

L1	*in*	(119)	*of*	(73)	*on*	(38)	*to*	(31)	*and*	(21)	*for*	(21)
R1	*opinion*	(27)	*own*	(23)	*point*	(18)	*first*	(17)	*mind*	(16)	*favorite*	(15)
R2	*is*	(71)	*and*	(38)	*of*	(27)	*to*	(25)	*for*	(21)	*that*	(19)

In a random sample of 339 concordances (just over 1/3 of the total) an evaluative predicative construction is attested for by about one line for every five. In this loose pattern *my* is typically followed by a noun, or by an adjective and then a noun, and usually a form of the verb BE is in the near surrounding, either on the right or on the left (68/339; 20%). Frequent patterns are: **(link-v)** *my* **(adj) n (link-v)** (29/339; 8.5% – *my favourite team is*; *is my cup of tea*); *my* **n BE** (***that***) (28; 8.2% – *my point is that*); **(S) prep** *my* **n (S)** (13; 3.8% – *to my knowledge*).

Italian

mi (2,025; 33.8 pttw)
mi (nearly twice as frequent in NEWS as in CORIS) is the accusative and dative clitic form of *io* (*I*).

L1	*non*	(273)	*che*	(161)	*e*	(81)	*ma*	(45)	*io*	(42)	*se*	(34)
R1	*sembra*	(210)	*pare*	(102)	*sono*	(86)	*ha*	(77)	*è*	(57)	*chiedo*	(56)
R2	*che*	(178)	*di*	(108)	*un*	(49)	*a*	(43)	*il*	(38)	*per*	(33)

The collocates suggest a prototypical pattern as follows: *mi*, a verb (most probably *sembra* – lit. 'it appears' – 10.3% of the times) and then a conjunction (*che* – 'that' – 8.7%; *di* – to – 5.3%; or *a* – 'to' – 2.1%) or a determiner (*un* – 'a/an' – 2.4% and *il* – 'the' – 1.8%). In a random sample of 292 concordances,[5] the following are the patterns most commonly found: *mi* **v n/prep** (55; 18.8% – *mi piace* 'I like'; *mi dispiace per* 'I'm sorry for'); *mi* **v** (***che***) (50; 17.1% – *mi sa che* 'I guess that'); *mi* **v adj/n** (33; 11.3% – *mi sembra stupido/un rischio* 'it seems stupid/a risk to me'); *mi* **v *di*-inf** (13; 4.4% – *mi va di* 'I feel like'); *mi* v ***wh/if*** (15; 5.1% – *mi chiedo se* 'I wonder if'); *mi fa* **inf/n** (15; 5.1% – *mi fa ridere/schifo* 'it makes me laugh/sick'); *mi* **v inf** (14; 4.7% – *mi duole* 'I regret'): (tot. 66.2%).

io (1,057; 17.6 pttw)
io (*I*, but note that Italian is a pro-drop language: *io* and *I* are therefore not fully comparable) is more than twice as frequent in NEWS as in CORIS.

L1	*anch*	(66)	*che*	(50)	*anche*	(37)	*ma*	(36)	*se*	(18)	*e*	(15)
R1	*non*	(142)	*sono*	(85)	*mi*	(42)	*ho*	(35)	*credo*	(27)	*dico*	(23)
R2	*che*	(77)	*ho*	(28)	*sono*	(27)	*un*	(27)	*di*	(18)	*l*	(17)

The most probable pattern: *io*, a verb (most probably *sono* – 'am' – or a cognitive verb) and finally either a conjunction (*che* or *di*) or a determiner or a pronoun. The most frequent patterns on a random sample of 300 concordances: *io* **v** (***che***) (45; 15% – *io credo che* 'I believe that'); *io* **v n/prep** (43; 14.3% – *io amo/spero in* 'I love/hope for'); *io* **link-v adj/n/prep** (40; 13.3% – *io sono fiducioso/un* *esperto/per* 'I am confident/an expert/for'); *io* **v** ***di*-inf** (*io suggerisco di* 'I suggest to'; *io* **v** ***wh/if*** (11; 3.6%): (tot. 49.8%).

me (731; 12.2 pttw)
me is the tonic accusative form of *io*: it is proportionally more than twice as frequent in NEWS as in CORIS.

L1	*secondo*	(210)	*per*	(177)	*a*	(133)	*come*	(32)	*da*	(31)	*non*	(25)
R1	*non*	(54)	*è*	(49)	*la*	(31)	*lo*	(31)	*il*	(22)	*ne*	(21)
R2	*che*	(31)	*è*	(23)	*il*	(17)	*sono*	(15)	*non*	(14)	*un*	(14)

The prototype pattern is: a preposition on L1 (*secondo* – 'according to' – + *per* – 'for' – + *a* – 'to' – 71.1%) a verb on the right (frequently a link-v: *è* – 'is' – + *sono* – 'am' – + *sembra* + *pare* – 'it appears' –, 126/731 in R1 and R2) and then the conjunction *che* (4.2% in R2) or a determiner (*il* + *un*; 4.2% in R2). The most frequent patterns on a random sample of 246 concordances are: *per/secondo me* **link-v adj/n** (63; 25.6%); **(S)** *secondo/per me* **(S)** (60; 24.3%);[6] *a me* **v** ***che*** (13; 5.2% – *a me pare che* 'I think that'); *a me* **v n** (23; 9.3% – *a me piace* 'I like').

4.2 Semantic sequences

The surface complexity evidenced by the different profiles and patterns presented hides the fact that evaluative meaning is made through sequences of meaning elements that remain fairly stable across the sample.

Two major evaluative sequences seem to emerge from our data. In the first a cognitive, communicative or speech process is made explicit. This element of the sequence, the one typically more devoid of lexical meaning, seems to function as a marker for the actual evaluation taking place toward the end of the sequence. The sequence accounts for over one every ten occurrences of *I*, *I'm*, *am* and *my* (232/1,844; 12.5%); and for about one every three occurrences of *io*, *mi* and *me* (291/838; 34.7%).

In the second sequence, the act of evaluation is generally instantiated in the stretch of text reporting the cognitive process. Then the sequence goes on with the reference to an entity or process that constitutes the object of the evaluation. The sequence accounts for more than one occurrence every three of *I*, *I'm*, *am* and *my* (666; 36.1%); and for about one every four occurrences of *io*, *mi* and *me* (231; 27.5%).

Table 1. Sequences with cognitive processes

item (I, io,...)	**cognitive marker (secondo/per me)**	**entity/process evaluated + evaluation**
(...) i	think	funding shifted from offshore dollar deposits to the sale of dollar denominated securities (...)
(…) I'm	under the impression	their financial resources are considerably less (…)
(…) I am	aware that	there is unfortunately a utterly fantastic amount of corruption within our justice system
I	find	the global warming debate numbing
in my	opinion	the MLS produces an exciting soccer (...)
My	initial reaction is	disgust (…)
Mi (I)	pare che (think that)	in questo congresso si sia sentito di tutto, (…) (we have heard incredible things in this congress)
io (I)	non ho paragonato (did not compare)	button ai grandi campioni del passato (…) (to the great champions of our past)
Ma nemmeno io (…) (I)	avrei immaginato (would not have imagined)	uno spettacolo di così stupefacente bellezza. (such an incredibly beautiful sight)
A me (I)	sembra che (think)	voi (you)siate tutti impazziti! ('ve all gone mad)
	Secondo me	ce la può fare! (he can make it!)
	(...) per me	la destra (the right) è messa peggio. (is in a worse shape)

The data shows that each sequence has its own preferred patterns. Sequence 1 seems to favour **v (*that*)**-patterns (67.2% for EN items; 28.8% for IT items). **adj (*that*)**-pattern within predicative constructions is dominant in Sequence 2 for English items (29.8%), whereas **v n/prep** is decidedly the preferred pattern by Sequence 2 for Italian items (104/231; 45%). However, as apparent from the list in 4.1 and from the instances in the table above, there is a fairly high degree of variation and the patterns cannot be said to belong in a sequence exclusively.

Table 2. Sequences with evaluative processes

item (I, io,...)	**evaluation**	**entity/process evaluated**
(…) I	can't believe	you voted for Cap and Trade (…)
(…) I	really don't care any longer to	hear the opinions of "a senior economist" you met in Davos.
I'm	in favor of	restitution of pieces with major cultural significance, (…)
I am	all for	Obama (...) working with Republicans and getting some sane policies through.
(For all) my	disgust at	the antediluvian obscurantism of the Taliban (…)
(...) mi (I'm)	stupisco che (surprised that)	l'Occidentale non lo abbia evidenziato (...) (the Occidentale did dot emphasize that)
(…) Io (I)	avrei preferito (would have preferred)	il buono vecchio Lamar (…) (good old Lamar)
(...) mi (I)	dispiace per (am sorry for)	Briatore.
(...) io (I)	sono molto sorpreso in positivo (am quite impressed)	dalla prestazione di Liuzzi. (by Liuzzi's performance)
A me (I'm)	non interessa affatto (not interested at all in)	essere politically correct (being politically correct)

entity/process evaluated	**item**	**evaluation**
Ten mintues with Blair in the ring with the gloves	would be my	idea of heaven.
Leggere i giornali oggi (Reading the newspapers today)	mi	spaventa (frightens me)

5. Conclusion

The analysis of grammatical keywords, with their collocational profile and the semantic sequences they create, confirmed the inherently evaluative nature of blogs, as well as the key role of markers of subjectivity in the genre. Whether in Italian or in English, blogs were found to be characterized by evaluative patterns involving first person pronouns and adjectives as subjectivity markers. These contributed to very similar semantic sequences in the two languages, involving a wide range of lexical realizations of semantic categories such as 'cognitive/ communicative/speech process', 'entity/process evaluated', 'evaluation'.

Methodologically, the study confirmed the relevance of SGWs to an analysis of the generic features of texts, as well as the importance of combining pattern analysis with semantic sequences in drawing up a 'local' grammar.

Notes

1 This was *Technorati*'s classification at the beginning of the text collection, in January 2009, with the only difference that the section 'Technology' became 'Science & Technology' in our corpus. Today *Technorati*'s set of classes is slightly different.

2 i.e. a random sample of 600 concordances minus 25 instances with *am*, analyzed separately.

3 This includes instances of other patterns, e.g. *I* **v n** *to*; *I* **v n n**, etc.

4 *I'm* is counted as a single form, there is no overlapping with *I*.

5 i.e. a random sample of 300 concordances minus 8 instances with *io*, analyzed separately.

6 *secondo me* and *per me* (roughly: 'according to me') are syntactically and semantically complete phrases functioning as sentence adverbials. They preferably collocate with link-verbs in predicative constructions.

References

Balog, K., G. Mishne and M. de Rijke (2006), 'Why are they excited? Identifying and explaining spikes in blog mood levels', in: *Proceedings of the 11th Conference of the European Chapter of the Association for Computational Linguistics: Posters and Demonstrations (EACL '06)*. Stroudsburg, PA. 207-210. <http://acl.ldc.upenn.edu/E/E06/E06-2031.pdf> (21.09.2011).

Baron, N.S. (2008), *Always on: Language in an Online and Mobile World*. Oxford: Oxford University Press.

Channell, J. (2000), 'Corpus-based analysis of evaluative lexis', in: S. Hunston and G. Thompson (eds.), *Evaluation in Text: Authorial Stance and the Construction of Discourse*. Oxford: Oxford University Press. 38-55.

Francis, G. (1993), 'A corpus-driven approach to grammar: Principles, methods and examples', in: M. Baker, G. Francis and E. Tognini-Bonelli (eds.), *Text and Technology: In Honour of John Sinclair*. Amsterdam: John Benjamins. 137-156.

Francis, G. (1995), 'Corpus-driven grammar and its relevance to the learning of English in a cross-cultural situation', in: A. Pakir (ed.), *English in Education: Multicultural Perspectives*. Singapore: Unipress.

Gledhill, C. (2000), *Collocations in Science Writing*. Tübingen: Gunter Narr.

Groom, N. (2007), *Phraseology and Epistemology in Humanities Writing.* Unpublished Ph.D. dissertation, University of Birmingham.

Groom, N. (2010), 'Closed-class keywords and corpus-driven discourse analysis', in: M. Bondi and M. Scott (eds.), *Keyness in Texts*. Amsterdam: John Benjamins. 59-78.

Halavais, A. (2002), 'Blogs and the "Social Weather"'. Paper presented at *Internet Research 3.0*, Maastricht.

Herring, S., L.A. Scheidt, S. Bonus and E. Wright (2005), 'Weblogs as a bridging genre', *Information, Technology & People*, 18: 142-171.

Hunston, S. (2005), 'Conflict and consensus: Construing opposition in applied linguistics', in: E. Tognini-Bonelli and G. Del Lungo Camiciotti (eds.), *Strategies in Academic Discourse*. Amsterdam: John Benjamins. 1-15.

Hunston, S. (2008), 'Starting with the small words: Patterns, lexis and semantic sequences', *International Journal of Corpus Linguistics*, 13: 271-295.

Hunston, S. (2011), *Corpus Approaches to Evaluation: Phraseology and Evaluative Language*. Abingdon: Routledge.

Hunston, S. and G. Francis (2000), *Pattern Grammar: A Corpus-driven Approach to the Lexical Grammar of English.* Amsterdam: John Benjamins.

Hunston, S. and J.McH. Sinclair (2000), 'A local grammar of evaluation', in: S. Hunston and G. Thompson (eds.), *Evaluation in Text: Authorial Stance and the Construction of Discourse*. Oxford: Oxford University Press. 74-101.

Krishnamurthy, S. (2002), 'The Multidimensionality of blog conversations: The virtual enactment of September 11'. Paper presented at *Internet Research 3.0*, Maastricht.

Myers, G. (2010), *Discourse of Blogs and Wikis*. London: Continuum.

Mishne, G. and N. Glance (2006), 'Predicting movie sales from blogger sentiment', in: N. Nicolov, F. Salvetti, M. Liberman and J.H. Martin (eds.), *AAAI 2006 Spring Symposium on Computational Approaches to Analysing Weblogs (AAAI-CAAW 2006)*. <http://www.aaai.org/Papers/Symposia/Spring/2006/SS-06-03/SS06-03-030.pdf> (15.09.2011).

Nardi, B., D.J. Schiano and M. Gumbrecht (2004), 'Blogging as social activity, or, would you let 900 million people read your diary?', in: J. Hersleb and G. Olson (eds.), *Proceedings of the ACM Conference on Computer Supported Cooperative Work (CSCW '04)*. New York, NY: ACM Press. 222-231. <http://dl.acm.org/citation.cfm?id=1031643&CFID=42667825&CFTOKEN=41268861> (15.09.2011).

Römer, U. (2008), 'Identification impossible? A corpus approach to realisations of evaluative meaning in academic writing', *Functions of Language*, 15: 115-130.

Scott, M. (2008), *WordSmith Tools* (Version 5.0). Oxford: Oxford University Press.

Using COCA to evaluate *The Chicago Manual of Style*'s usage prescriptions

Doris R. Dant

Brigham Young University, Provo

Abstract

By querying the Corpus of Contemporary American English and subjecting the results to statistical analysis, this study examined usage prescriptions in the most detailed style manual in the United States – The Chicago Manual of Style. *The results lead to five recommendations. One, about half of the prescriptions are valid across all the registers and should be retained as they are. Two, in some cases, significant variations among registers should be acknowledged. Three, some prescriptions should be modified. Four, a few prescriptions should be eliminated for all registers due to widespread disregard. Five, a few prescriptions are universally observed and are no longer needed. The mean for each written register ranges from 86.1% to 88.6%. The median percent of total for all of the preferred written variants tested in this study ranges from 92.4% in the academic register to 95.5% in the newspaper register, indicating that* Chicago*'s prescriptions match actual educated usage half the time. These results carry significant implications for future editions of style manuals.*

1. Introduction

To be published in English in the West, scholars and other authors must usually yield to their editors on questions of language usage. The editors typically base their decisions on the distinctions found in style or usage manuals. These in turn are prepared by experts that Kretzschmar labels "self-appointed guardians of linguistic propriety" (2009: 272). One such, Bryan A. Garner, wrote a lengthy chapter on grammar and usage for *The Chicago Manual of Style*, one of the two best-selling style manuals on Amazon. In an unusually candid description of his guiding principles, Garner says, "In the end, the actual usage of educated speakers and writers is the overarching criterion for correctness. But while actual usage can trump the other factors, it isn't the only consideration" (2009: xviii; Garner lists nine other considerations, including simplicity, concision and conservatism). In spite of this emphasis on educated usage, Garner's chapter in *Chicago* has been criticized for being arbitrary and out of touch with the language.

Because of *Chicago*'s status as the most comprehensive style manual for US English, as the oldest continuously published style manual in the United States (1906 to the present), and as the only style manual used in the four primary printed registers of fiction, magazines, academic texts, and, to a lesser extent, news, such criticisms need to be addressed. Thus to test Garner's prescriptions in

Chicago, I compared hundreds of them to the actual usage sampled by the Davies's *Corpus of Contemporary American English* (COCA). This paper focuses primarily on those prescriptions that were investigated via bipartite queries in COCA and categorizes the results into five recommendations: (1) retain certain prescriptions as they are, (2) acknowledge significant differences among registers, (3) refine some of the prescriptions in other ways, (4) drop a few prescriptions because they are usually disregarded, and (5) drop a few others for the opposite reason: They are observed throughout the corpus.

2. Methodology

In *Chicago*, Garner says that the goal for his chapter is "to stay within the mainstream of literate language as it stands today" (2003: 196). He determined that mainstream by gathering examples from what he and others read, supplemented by searches in the Nexis (global) and Westlaw (US) databases (2009). These tools have now been surpassed by COCA, a structured corpus of texts from the spoken, fiction, news, magazine, and academic registers that at over 400 million words is large enough to sample infrequent words. The only large corpus of US English that is updated regularly (semiannually), COCA has developed into a monitor corpus suitable for a study such as this. Additionally, COCA covers twenty years, considered by Nevalainen and Raumolin-Brunberg to be "the basic unit of contemporaneous writing" (2003: 53).

Although *Chicago* is designed for edited texts, I will include COCA's speech register in this study to serve as a counterpoint to the written texts. In interpreting these findings, one should remember that the spoken texts are taken from TV and radio talk shows, where the speakers may have monitored their speech more than they might have otherwise.

To compare related variants, I totalled their frequencies in each register, then determined the percent of the total in that register contributed by each variant. The percent of total allows a comparison of one variant to another while at the same time permitting a valid comparison of usage across the registers, which are close in size to each other but not equal.

Chicago's usage sections are an amalgam of advice on colligational variants, grammatical variants, lexical distinctions, wordiness, spelling, and gender bias. Fortunately, the application of percent of total applies equally well to all these issues.

A major decision required setting the cut-off points for my recommendations. To be sound, the cut-offs needed to be based on stages of change or degrees of acceptance or prestige. Heller and Macris (1967) proposed four stages in the development and integration of usage variants. Garner (2009) adopted these stages and added one more. But neither system statistically defines the boundaries. In their grammar, Biber et al. (1999) use percentages as ranges when discussing the occurrence of regular and irregular verbs. They do not label these ranges. For objective definitions, one must turn to studies of language change where Nevalainen and Raumolin-Brunberg (2003: 55) applied ranges of percentages to Labov's stages of speech changes (1994: 79-83), cf. Table 1.

Table 1. Comparison of five representations of the stages in language change

Heller, Macris (usage)	**Garner** (usage)	**Biber et al.** (grammar)	**Labov** (speech)	**Nevalainen, Raumolin-Brunberg** (language)
Innovation	Innovation of a variant	<10%	Incipient	<15%
Free variation	More common but still unacceptable	10% - 25%	New and vigorous	15% - 35%
Subtraction or addition begins	Commonplace but avoided by the careful	25% - 50%	Mid-range	36% - 65%
Resolution	Virtually universal, opposed by a few	50% - 25%	Nearing completion	66% - 85%
	Universally adopted except by "eccentrics"	75% or 85%	Completed	>85%

The completed stage corresponds closely with the overall mean for *Chicago*'s preferred variants in each of the written registers of COCA: Fiction and academic – 86%; magazines – 89%, and news – 87%. To err on the side of generosity toward *Chicago*, I split the difference between Biber et al.'s and Nevalainen and Raumolin-Brunberg's top categories. Thus for a prescription to qualify for my first recommendation – to be retained as it is – the preferred form must account for 80 percent of the total occurrences of the related variants in all the written registers.

3. Results

Submitting many of *Chicago*'s prescriptions to queries in COCA revealed that half of those prescriptions are supported by the actual practice of educated editors and authors (see the concluding Table). All the prescriptions were divided into five categories, depending on the applicable recommendation I make for each. The recommendations include making no changes, dropping some prescriptions, and modifying others.

3.1 Retain most prescriptions as they are

The first set of prescriptions is by far the largest group, accounting for almost half of the prescriptions included in this study (see Table 2). These are the prescriptions where the preferred form occurs at least 80 percent of the time in all the written registers. Because they represent usages that are currently settled, I recommend that these prescriptions be retained as they are.

Table 2. Prescriptions to retain, no modifications needed

accompanied **by**, *not* with	**actually**, in actual fact
affirmative, in the	**all right,** alright
altogether, all together	amount, number
appraise, apprise	**as for**, as far as
based **on** *or* **in**, *not* upon	**before, in preparing for**, preliminary to
before, previous to	**before, until**, prior to
binding **on**, *not* upon	breach, breech
circumstances under the, in the	climactic, climatic
close, proximity, close proximity	compendious, voluminous
comply **with**, *not* to	**couple**, couple of
depend **on**, *not* upon	**doubtless,** doubtlessly
drag: **dragged**, *not* drug	dream: dreamed *Amer.*, dreamt *Brit.*
equivalent **to** *or* **in**, *not* with	excerpt **from**, *not* of
feel bad, feel badly	**finish, make final,** finalize
first, firstly; **second**, secondly; etc.	**help**, help to
independent **of**, *not* from	instill **in, into**, *not* with
later, subsequently	**notwithstanding**, not withstanding
orient, orientate	**outside**, outside of
over, unduly, overly	pair: *singular, not plural*
pendant, pendent	personally: *not with* I *for opinions*
phenomenon: *plural* phenomena	**pleaded**, pled
preferable **to**, *not* than	**regardless**, irregardless
regrettably, regretfully: *syn. for* unfortunately	staunch, stanch

Note: Where one alternative is preferred over another, *Chicago*'s preferred form is in bold face in this and the other summary tables. For the other paired terms, *Chicago* recommends maintaining the traditional distinctions.

For example, *Chicago* favors the colligational variant *depend on* (versus *depend upon*). Curiously, *depend on* is more popular in all the other registers, including the spoken register, than it is in the academic register (see Table 2). However, even in the academic register, it occurs 81 percent of the time, as can be seen in the following table.

Table 3. Lemmas of *depend(s) on* (preferred) versus *depend(s) upon*

Variants	Spoken	Fiction	Magazine	Newspaper	Academic
depend on	87%	89%	89%	92%	81%
depend upon	13%	11%	11%	8%	19%

A grammatical variant preferred by *Chicago* that fits in this category is *feel bad* (versus *feel badly*). Again, academic usage is significantly lower than that in the other printed registers (see Table 4). Perhaps this fact may be attributed to the frequently commented upon academic penchant for multisyllabic words (for example, see Nida 1992).

Table 4. Lemmas of *feel(s) bad* (preferred) versus *feel(s) badly*

Variants	Spoken	Fiction	Magazine	Newspaper	Academic
feel bad	87%	96%	96%	92%	85%
feel badly	13%	4%	4%	8%	15%

A final example is the distinction between *amount* (preferably used with mass nouns) and *number* (used with count nouns). Table 5 shows the rarity of *amount of* followed by a plural noun. When *amount of* does occur, its collocate is often a noun plural in form but singular in meaning (a word such as *resources* or *savings*). If these occurrences were deleted, the percent of total would be even lower. The reverse search, the one looking for *number of* in the context of a singular, or mass, noun, produced virtually no valid tokens. Because the tagger does not distinguish between a singular noun used as an adjective and one used as a noun, the hits were typically in the form of 'number of adult males'.

Table 5. *Number of* (preferred) versus *amount of* in the context of a plural noun

Variants	Spoken	Fiction	Magazine	Newspaper	Academic
number of	94%	96%	95%	95%	97%
amount of	6%	4%	5%	5%	3%

In forty-six instances, *Chicago*'s prescription is supported by COCA. These prescriptions can therefore stand without modification.

3.2 Acknowledge differences among registers

Another category of prescriptions should, in my opinion, be modified to acknowledge significant differences among the registers (see Table 6). This information would (1) enable writers and editors to make the choices appropriate to their register; (2) remind editors that an author's choice, while not *Chicago*'s preferred form, might still be appropriate for a specific register; (3) inform editors that because in their register both variants are used about equally, the editors perhaps should not impose one or the other upon writers; or (4) alert the editors in a particular register to the vigorous growth of the disparaged variant.

Table 6. Prescriptions with significant differences among registers

center on, upon, *not* around	cohabit, *not* cohabitate
criteria, criterion (*use* criterion *as the singular*)	peroration, oration (*maintain traditional distinctions*)
determine whether (*preferred*), determine if (*use only in speech*)	loathe, loath (*maintain traditional distinctions*)
shortly, soon, *not* in the near future	despite, *not* in spite of
in regard to, *not* in regards to	different from, *not* different than
off, *not* off of	impose on, *not* impose upon
dissent from or against, *not* dissent to *or* dissent with	

A particularly dramatic example of a prescription in this category is *pair*, which *Chicago* prefers to be treated as a singular rather than plural noun (see Table 7). Representative queries for *pair*, in which *pair of* is followed by a plural noun and by either *is* or *was* versus *are* or *were,* reveal that in fiction *pair* is singular 55 percent of the time, but it is plural 45 percent of the time. According to Nevalainen and Raumolin-Brunberg's (2003) criteria, both variants are in the mid-range. Given this degree of flux, fiction editors might allow either variant, particularly in dialog, since usage in dialog might account for this statistic. In contrast, writers and editors in the academic field should use only singular verbs with *pair.*

Table 7. *Pair* as a singular (preferred) versus plural noun in *pair of* [plural noun]

Variants	Spoken	Fiction	Magazine	Newspaper	Academic
pair s. n.	82%	55%	70%	69%	87%
pair pl. n.	9%	45%	30%	31%	13%

For the prescription preferring *different from* to *different than*, writers and editors find themselves in a different situation (see Table 8). Here academic use of the preferred form is considerably greater than that in newspapers. Newspaper editors and writers should be alerted to the vigorous growth of *different than* in their register.

Table 8. *Different from* (preferred) versus *different than*

Variants	Spoken	Fiction	Magazine	Newspaper	Academic
different from	53%	83%	88%	74%	92%
different than	47%	17%	12%	26%	8%

A relatively rare lexical item, *peroration*, is proscribed when a writer is referring to a "rousing speech or writing" (*Chicago* 2003: 225). For that, *oration* is *Chicago*'s word of choice. But as Table 9 shows, only in the academic register is *peroration* merely an incipient variant. Elsewhere it is a vigorous usage, particularly in magazines.

Table 9. *Oration* (preferred) versus *peroration* in reference to a rousing text

Variants	**Spoken**	**Fiction**	**Magazine**	**Newspaper**	**Academic**
oration	67%	75%	69%	79%	94%
peroration	33%	25%	31%	21%	6%

In all, thirteen prescriptions have percents of total for the preferred variant that dip below 80 percent in at least one written register. In those instances, *Chicago* should acknowledge the differences among the registers.

3.3 Refine *Chicago* in other ways

A third set of prescriptions require modification other than or in addition to attention to the differences among registers (see Table 10). Sometimes *Chicago*'s view does not reflect actual usage. Sometimes there is no mainstream variant. Sometimes the denigrated variant has overtaken the preferred variant. In each of these cases, refining the prescription would notify writers and editors that usage is unsettled and the choices are more flexible than may have been thought to be.

Table 10. Prescriptions requiring other forms of modification

center **on**, upon, *not* around	**chair**, chairman, chairwoman, chairperson
coalesce into	court-martial, courts-martial
data	enamored **of**, *not* with
get	**half**, half of
illegible	infringe **on**, *not* upon
intense	**life-and-death**, *not* life-or-death
question whether, question of whether, question as to whether	sneak: *p.* **sneaked**, *not* snuck
spit: *p.* **spat**, *not* spit	

Chicago considers *snuck* a verb form appropriate only for "dialect and tongue-in-cheek usages" (2003: 229). However, in fiction and magazines it is in the mid-range stage, and even in newspapers and academia it is a vigorous variant (see Table 11). Indeed, in tracking it over the last twenty years, COCA reveals that it has grown in general use from 37 percent of total to 56 percent, while *sneaked* dropped from 63 percent of total to 44 percent. Of course, the acceptance of *snuck* on TV talk shows (74 percent of total) accounts for much of this growth. This increase in prestige should be noted by *Chicago*.

Table 11. *Sneaked* (preferred) versus *snuck*

Variants	Spoken	Fiction	Magazine	Newspaper	Academic
sneaked	26%	55%	59%	73%	67%
snuck	74%	45%	41%	27%	33%

Chicago prefers *question whether* over the two related variants but views *question of whether* as second best. *Question as to whether* – being unduly wordy – is to be avoided. However, in spite of the economy of *question whether*, in COCA it is the form that comes in second (see Table 12). *Chicago*'s evaluation should be revised to recognize editors and authors' clear preference for *question of whether*. Notably, however, the two preferred forms account for over 80 percent of the total in three of the written registers, a statistic that clearly supports *Chicago*'s denigration of *question as to whether*.

Table 12. *Question whether* (preferred) versus *question of whether* (next best) and *question as to whether*

Variants	Spoken	Fiction	Magazine	Newspaper	Academic
question whether	28%	24%	36%	51%	33%
question of whether	61%	65%	61%	47%	62%
question as to whether	11%	12%	3%	2%	5%

Another modification needed in *Chicago* concerns *life-and-death* versus *life-or-death* (see Table 13). *Chicago* states, "Logic aside (life and death being mutually exclusive), the first phrase is the standard idiom" (2003: 221). Yet in no register does *life-and-death* achieve 80 percent of total, and in newspapers both variants are in the midrange. Again, the academic register teams up with the spoken register to be the two that are the fondest of the illogical form. *Chicago* should allow either form.

Table 13. *Life-and-death* (preferred) versus *life-or-death*

Variants	Spoken	Fiction	Magazine	Newspaper	Academic
life-and-death	74%	67%	65%	59%	73%
life-or-death	26%	33%	35%	41%	27%

3.4 Drop due to widespread disregard

For a prescription to qualify for the fourth recommendation – to drop the prescription due to widespread disregard – in all the written registers the denigrated form must account for at least 40 percent of the total occurrences of the related variants, putting it in the mid-range stage. Seven prescriptions belong in this category (see Table 14).

Table 14. Prescriptions to drop because of high level of disregard

absolve from, of	acquit **of**, *not* from
anxious **about**, *not* to	bestow **on**, *not* upon
contingent **on**, *not* upon	dissimilar **to**, *not* from
dive: *p.* **dived**, *not* dove	

Chicago states that *anxious* should be used with *about* and should appear only in the context of a concern; it should not be used with *to*. Because it has the least support in COCA of all the tested prescriptions, this prescription is intriguing. In four of COCA's registers, the proscribed form *anxious to* appears in over 80 percent of the total occurrences (see Table 15). In the exception, the academic register, it hovers at 74 percent. As can be seen above in Sections 3.1-3.3, several preferred forms do not reach the level of use maintained by this proscribed form. Accordingly, *anxious to* should receive accepted status or, minimally, the prohibition against it should be dropped, but neither has happened. The prescription is repeated – unchanged – in the recently released sixteenth edition of *Chicago* (2010).

Table 15. The preference in COCA for *anxious to* (proscribed) versus *anxious about*

Variants	**Spoken**	**Fiction**	**Magazine**	**Newspaper**	**Academic**
anxious about	13%	10%	25%	19%	26%
anxious to	87%	90%	75%	81%	74%

3.5 Drop, always observed in COCA

Four prescriptions occur 100 percent of the time in all the registers and therefore belong in the final stage of language change (see Table 16). Given that no tokens of the denigrated forms appeared in either the spoken or written texts, these prescriptions should be dropped. They are of no concern to the editors and authors of COCA's written texts. The space these prescriptions occupy could be allotted to usage issues that are in earlier stages.

Table 16. Prescriptions to drop because they were always observed in COCA

go: *ppt.* **gone**, *not* went	inhere **in**, *not* within
protuberance, *not* protruberance	stationary, stationery [distinguish between these words]

4. The final test of arbitrariness

Overall, a significant number of *Chicago*'s prescriptions are adhered to in the COCA texts. The median percent of total for all of the preferred written variants tested in this study ranges from 92.4 percent in the academic register to 95.5 percent in the newspaper register (see Table 17). These high percentages demonstrate that at least half of *Chicago*'s prescriptions are not arbitrary but are reflections of actual educated usage.

While lower than the median because of the presence of outliers, the mean in each written register is nonetheless above my cut-off of 80 percent for acceptable prescriptions. It slightly surpasses Nevalainen and Raumolin-Brunberg's (2003) cut-off of 86 percent for the completed stage of change.

Table 17. Overall use of preferred variants, as percent of total tokens

Statistic	Spoken	Fiction	Magazine	Newspaper	Academic
Mean	78.2%	86.4%	88.6%	86.8%	86.1%
Median	87.6%	95.0%	95.0%	95.5%	92.4%

Critics may argue that these figures are to be expected because COCA is a collection of edited texts for which writers and editors have consulted *Chicago*'s guidelines. There are several related responses to this objection: Although popular, *Chicago* is only one among several style manuals, especially in academia. Manuals disagree with each other on specific usage items (VanOrnum, Dant and Auger 2010) as well as on what should be included (Heller and Macris 1967). Furthermore, the standard described by usage manuals is not a fixed phenomenon. Prescriptions suddenly appear or disappear, possibly a result of individual experts attempting to influence language change "with their own ideas" (Kretzschmar 2009: 272). Additionally, the possibility exists that the list of prescriptions is so long that editors focus on those variants they see as most significant or aggravating. This topic needs further study. If all of *Chicago*'s prescriptions were slavishly followed, an even higher degree of adherence would have been uncovered.

Because of this level of variability in usage presentation and application and because of Garner's own desire to reflect mainstream educated usage, an evaluation of *Chicago*'s prescriptions via queries in COCA is a valid exercise that can provide editors and authors with current information about the practices of their peers and the loci of consensus within their own registers.

References

Biber, D., S. Johansson, G. Leech, S. Conrad and E. Finegan (1999), *Longman Grammar of Spoken and Written English*. Harlow: Pearson Education.

Garner, B.A. (2009), *Garner's Modern American Usage*. 3rd edition. New York, NY: Oxford University Press.

Heller, L.G. and J. Macris (1969), 'English usage and modern linguistic theory', *American Speech*, 42: 131-135.

Kretzschmar, W. (2009), *The Linguistics of Speech*. New York, NY: Cambridge University Press.

Labov, W. (1994), *Principles of Linguistic Change. Volume 1: Internal factors*. Cambridge, MA: Blackwell.

Nevalainen, T. and H. Raumolin-Brunberg (2003), *Historical Sociolinguistics: Language Change in Tudor and Stuart England*. New York: Longman.

Nida, E. (1992), 'Sociolinguistic implications of academic writing', *Language in Society*, 21: 477-485.

The Chicago Manual of Style: The Essential Guide for Writers, Editors, and Publishers. (2003), 15th edition and (2010), 16th edition. Chicago, IL: University of Chicago Press.

VanOrnum, S., D.R. Dant and J. Auger (2010), 'A corpus-based evaluation of usage advice from the *CSE* and *Chicago* style manuals'. Paper presented at the 53rd Annual Council of Science Editors Meeting, Atlanta, GA, May 2010.

Corpus linguistics, theoretical linguistics, and cognitive/ psycholinguistics: Towards more and more fruitful exchanges

Stefan Th. Gries

University of California, Santa Barbara

Abstract

This article discusses my version of corpus linguistics, its relation to what I think are neighboring fields (mainly cognitive and psycholinguistics), how corpus linguistics can and should enter into more mutually beneficial relations with these fields, and the from my perspective most promising contemporary cognitive and psycholinguistic approach that provides a natural point of connection to corpus-based approaches.

"Resistance is futile!" (The Borg)

1. Corpus linguistics and (more) theoretical approaches

The relation between corpus linguistics (CL) and linguistic theory has traditionally been somewhat problematic. I think there are several reasons for this: corpus linguists differ as to what they think CL is: a tool, method(ology), discipline, theory, paradigm, framework; there are some things that make CL appear less attractive to the observer from theoretical linguistics; and some corpus linguists have a rather inflexible gate-keeping attitude towards what the field is (supposed to look) like that, ultimately, impedes progress rather than advances it.

1.1 Within corpus linguistics: What we think corpus linguistics is and has been

As for the former, some consider CL a theory, for instance Leech (1992: 106), Stubbs (1993: 2f.), Tognini-Bonelli (2001: 1), Teubert (2005: 2). Others consider CL a methodology, such as McEnery and Wilson (1996), Meyer (2002), Bowker and Pearson (2002), McEnery, Xiao and Tono (2006: 7f.), Hardie (bcd).[1] The latter two positions are particularly worth quoting here:

> corpus linguistics is a whole system of methods and principles of how to apply corpora in language studies and teaching/learning, it certainly has a theoretical status. Yet theoretical status is not theory in itself. (McEnery, Xiao and Tono 2006: 7f.)

> As a corpus linguist I consider myself primarily a methodologist and CL primarily a methodology, to be applied to whatever theory seems most appropriate for the task at hand. (Hardie, bcd)

Yet other corpus linguists (e.g. Aarts 2002; Teubert 2005; Williams 2006) use even other labels such as *discipline* or what I would call a methodological commitment: "[CL] is rather an insistence on working only with real language data taken from the discourse in a principled way and compiled into a corpus" (Teubert 2005: 4).

It is probably worth pointing out that whether scholars attribute the status of theory to CL or not often somewhat coincides with where they are on the continuum of corpus-driven and corpus-based linguistics. Corpus-driven linguists

- aim to build theory from scratch, completely free from pre-corpus theoretical premises;
- base theories exclusively on corpus data;
- often reject corpus annotation (as a pre corpus theoretical commitment), going so far so as to resort to absurdly unfounded generalizations such as "[c]ognitive linguists like to work with annotated language data. But annotations presume presupposed categories not validated by corpus evidence" (Teubert 2010: 355) – Teubert *knows* that all – all! – annotation cognitive linguists use is not validated by corpus evidence??

Corpus-driven linguistics, in essence, means 'bottom-up'. The following quote by Teubert (2005: 4) is instructive in this context:

> While corpus linguistics may make use of the categories of traditional linguistics, it does not take them for granted. It is the discourse itself, and not a language-external taxonomy of linguistic entities, which will have to provide the categories and classifications that are needed to answer a given research question.

Corpus-based linguistics, on the other hand, approaches corpus data from the perspective of moderate corpus-external premises, with the aim of testing and improving such theories, and often uses corpus annotation.

I'm more of a corpus-based linguist and, agreeing with Hardie and McEnery's (2010) stance, consider CL "a major methodological paradigm in applied and theoretical linguistics" Gries (2006a: 191). Why? Here I will mention two reasons... First, I agree with Jan Aarts, who, although he coined the term *corpus linguistics*, also is

> reported as commenting that the term was coined with some hesitation 'because we thought (and I still think) that it was not a very good name: it is an odd discipline that is called by the name of its major research tool and data source'. (Taylor 2008: 179)

Put differently, I don't accord CL the status of a theory just as I don't think there is a linguistic theory called experimental linguistics or self-paced reading time linguistics even though, just like results from CL, results from self-paced reading times may call into question units/structures/processes assumed in the kind of formal linguistics that (some of) CL was a reaction against.

Second, with the exception of, maybe, Sinclair and Mauranen's (2006) Linear Unit Grammar, I have yet to see what I consider a truly corpus-driven approach, at least within corpus linguistics (cf. below). Even corpus-linguistic studies that consider themselves corpus-driven are often not as corpus-driven as they could or claim to be. This can be seen on at least three different levels. First, from a theoretical perspective on the lexical/grammatical level, a truly corpus-driven approach would, strictly speaking, require a complete distributional analysis of the corpus (with maybe some machine-learning algorithm, neural network, or recursive association rules approach) to initially identify the linguistic units manifested in the data (similar, but more advanced to, say, C.C. Fries's well-known approach). And while some corpus linguists make statements to that effect (cf. Teubert's "Corpus linguists still don't know what a morpheme, a word, a phrase or a pattern is", bcd),

- many corpus-driven studies at least start out from the notion of a word;
- Bill Louw (bcd) has studied *all sorts of*, but my guess is he has not used a bottom-up or even replicable algorithm such as Kita et al.'s (1994) cost criteria, lexical gravity, or some other *n*-gram statistic to identify *all sorts of* as a unit – he has decided that *all sorts of* is a unit on the basis of corpus-external or pre-corpus criteria;
- POS are not uncommon in so-called corpus-driven studies (cf. Xiao 2009: 995; Linear Unit Grammar at least starts out without POS);
- even Halliday (2005: 174), revered by many corpus-driven linguists, writes "a corpus-driven grammar is not one that is theory-free," referring to Hunston and Francis (2000) and Tognini-Bonelli (2001).

Xiao (2009: 995) summarizes the problems of corpus-driven linguistics persuasively: "applying intuitions when classifying concordances may simply be an implicit annotation process, which unconsciously makes use of preconceived theory", and this implicit annotation is "to all intents and purposes unrecoverable and thus more unreliable than explicit annotation".

The second level on which corpus driven work is often less corpus-driven as is assumed is concerned with the more concrete perspective of the lexical/grammatical level. For example, many corpus-driven studies look at *n*-grams, where *n* is arbitrarily defined as one number (currently, *n*=4 is en vogue), but most studies do not

- check whether that number is indeed the best number for all *n*-grams; as one of rather few laudable exceptions, Biber (2009) checks for 5-grams;
- check whether it would not indeed be better to have different *n*'s for different *n*-grams: obviously, 3-grams may miss *according to*, 4-grams may miss *in spite of*, 5-grams may miss *on the other hand*, 6-grams may

miss *as a matter of fact*, and 7-grams may miss *be that as it may* (cf. Kita et al. 1994; Mason 2006; as well as Gries and Mukherjee 2010 on varying-length *n*-grams);

- even consider discontinuous *n*-grams, e.g., those constituted by idioms such as *run a/the risk* (e.g. Nagao and Mori 1994).

The third and final level is concerned with the notion/level of the register. Of course, corpus linguists of all persuasions often study words and constructions in corpora that come with divisions into modes (speaking vs. writing), registers, or sub-registers. However, for any given phenomenon, the register distinctions that a researcher chooses to take into account – often out of convenience – may not be most useful from a truly bottom-up perspective, which is why more seriously corpus-driven/bottom-up approaches are required (cf. Gries 2006b, 2010b; Gries et al. 2011).

With regard to this division of corpus-driven vs. corpus-based linguistics, Xiao (2009) states "the distinction between the two is overstated" and that "the corpus-based approach is better suited to contributing to linguistic theory". As to the former, I disagree – if anything, it is *under*stated given that truly corpus-driven work is probably a myth at best. However, to some degree I can understand how, at the time, the issue of corpus-based vs. driven was a useful distinction to raise awareness of the larger issues involved in, and following from, that distinction (Tognini-Bonelli, personal communication). The latter, I find interesting because in effect it says that corpus-driven linguistics, where scholars use corpus-driven characteristics to argue for corpus linguistics as a theory, is in fact less suited to contributing to linguistic theory than corpus-based linguistics, which often views corpus linguistics as a method(ology) 'only'.

1.2 From within corpus linguistics: What we think/say we and others do

Turning to what we and scholars from other disciplines see from, and think about each other, I think there are some things that make corpus linguistics less attractive to the observer from theoretical linguistics. These include some corpus linguists' rather unusual

- ideas about potentially relevant neighboring disciplines;
- ways of defending their perspective(s);
- sometimes narrow and prescriptive views about the nature of the discipline (above and beyond the above issues).

I don't have the space to discuss all of these issues in detail so some examples must suffice. As for (1), Teubert (2010: 395) characterizes the relation between NLP and cognitive linguistics (CogLing) as follows: NLP is one of CogLing's "illegitimate offspring[s]". This statement is, I regret to say, simply completely absurd. I fail to see any connection between these fields other than that Teubert does not want CL to be like either of them, and neither do, I think, most members of these two disciplines. I don't see cognitive linguistics papers in *Computational Linguistics* or the many different proceedings in which computational linguists publish, nor do I see NLP papers in *Cognitive Linguistics*. As another example, Teubert (2010: 398) flatly asserts, brushing aside 30 to 40 years of psycholinguistic research on speech production, "[w]hen we speak, we do not turn thought into language". As a final example, consider Mason's (2007: 2) argument in favor of Linear Unit Grammar (in an otherwise very interesting paper):

> Formal approaches to the description of sentence structure furthermore take for granted a hierarchical (phrase) structure [...]. However, language is not produced in that way, but instead is a linear sequence created in stops and starts. A hierarchical structure thus cannot account for the fact that the beginning of an utterance is already produced before the whole sentence has been completely worked out. Similar issues apply for the reception of language. Unlike the hierarchical, a linear approach is more closely related to the way most language is received. Processing usually begins before a complete sentence has been heard or read, and quite often the remaining parts of a sentence can be predicted with high accuracy before its completion.

Not only does this excerpt appear to assume that we do turn thoughts into language, *pace* Teubert, it also betrays a serious misunderstanding of psycholinguistic approaches to language production and comprehension: an incremental approach to language production and comprehension of the type that Mason's last sentence appears to represent does by no means require abandoning a largely hierarchical view of language structure (cf. Hawkins's (1994, 2005) or Kempen's (passim) work on incremental production). A looser definition of constituency may be useful to increase the range of units that are manipulated in comprehension and production to include (linear) multi-word units etc., but that does not mean such units cannot still be analyzed hierarchically.

As for (ii), discourse with and about (more) theoretical linguistics is often characterized by a strange us vs. them gate-keeping warfare that

- involves people's inability to read, as when multiple commentators in the bootcamp discourse (examples include Wynne and of course Louw) fail to understand from my postings on the corpora list or the publicly posted syllabus of the bootcamp that maximally one sixth of the bootcamp was devoted to statistical tests;
- argues against strawmen, as when Teubert states that "[l]inguistics is the study of real, human language, not the development of useful gadgets simulating the use of language", something that I think just about every participant in the bootcamp discourse (including me) would subscribe to; in fact, in a recent interview (Gries, forthcoming), I argued that precisely

for such reasons the term *computational linguistics* is, to my mind, sometimes used inappropriately:

- "I want to call something ___ *linguistics*, if its ultimate goal is to increase our understanding of (the use of) human language, or even the linguistic system's place in the larger domain of human cognition, and I want to call something ___ *computing* if its ultimate goal is not concerned with understanding (the use of) human language but its computational application or implementation. For example, for me, developing a talking ticketing machine for the airport parking lot (a useful gadget, I presume) falls under the heading of natural language processing, but I would not call it ___ *linguistics* (even if frequency data from corpora are used to tweak how the machine parses its input), but, if pressed, would call it *linguistic computing*".
- Similarly, when Williams (2010: 403) states, "[a]s Lou Burnard and Chris Tribble so ably pointed out, those who teach and translate are not to be looked down on", I am wondering who this is an argument against – nobody defended a position where teachers and translators are to be looked down on. Finally, Williams' (2010: 402) agreement with "Firth who refuted all mentalism in favour of building models from what we really see rather than from introspective 'knowledge' of what we think might be happening", 'argues' against only a ridiculous caricature of what cognitive linguistics of the kind I have been and will be arguing for is like (cf. below Sections 2.1 and 3).
- uses geographical labels in place of arguments (as when agendas are simply labeled as "transatlantic", which I guess means 'bad');
- contrasts (good) old-fashioned Sinclairian core corpus linguistics with those who "piss into" Sinclair's canonical corpus linguistics tent,[2] who use corpora in "a seemingly inappropriate, toolbox-like, inherently non-Sinclairian way" (Mukherjee, bcd, characterizing the viewpoint he opposes);
- couches interdisciplinary discourse in terms of "hijacking" (Teubert 2010: 356) and "takeover bid[s]" (Williams 2010: 407) or Wynne's condescending (2010: 427) "people who *think* that they are doing corpus linguistics" (my emphasis).

Not only has this kind of discourse never helped anything, but it can also, as Hardie and McEnery argue persuasively, effectively constitute re-writing the history books in how "it elides the methodologist tradition completely from history, and describes the field of corpus linguistics as if it rested solely on the accomplishments of neo-Firthian scholars and the philosophers from whom they draw inspiration" (Hardie and McEnery 2010: 388); Mukherjee's discussion of this type of "corpus dogmatism" is similarly right on target.[3]

As for (iii), some gatekeepers of corpus linguistics have a narrower view of the field, or a more prescriptive attitude towards the field, than the actual and healthily diverse field would appear to support. These are some examples from Teubert:

- "corpus linguistics looks at phenomena which cannot be explained by recourse to general rules and assumptions" (Teubert 2005: 5) – well, I know many corpus linguists who are interested in explaining phenomena this way, esp. since "general rules and assumptions" do not rule out probabilistic rules and assumptions.
- "When linguists come across a sentence such as 'The sweetness of this lemon is sublime.', their task is [...] to look to see if other testimony in the discourse does or does not provide supporting evidence" (Teubert 2005: 10) – this comment and others reveal what Mukherjee (2010: 373) characterizes as a "fixation" on meaning in discourse at the cost of meaning in the mind (although everything in discourse was at one point of time filtered through at least one mind; cf. below). And seeing if there is more evidence in the discourse about a lemon's sweetness appears to me as something for the hypothetical *Journal of Taste and Smell Research*, not the hypothetical *Journal of Corpus Linguistics*.
- Teubert (2005: 2f.) states that "[c]orpus linguistics looks at language from a social perspective. It is not concerned with the psychological aspects of language" (my emphasis), but on the other hand, he writes (ibid.: 7): "Linguistics is not a science like the natural sciences whose remit is the search for 'truth'. It belongs to the humanities, and as such it is a part of the endeavour to make sense of the human condition. Interpretation, and not verification, is the proper response to the quest for meaning".

Not only do I not see how blanking out the very thing that makes us human – mind/*Geist* – helps in the endeavour to make sense of the human condition, I will also outline below many ways in which cognitive approaches to language are not only compatible with much recent work in corpus linguistics, but also provide a framework into which corpus-linguistic results can be integrated elegantly.

1.3 Taking stock...

Now, all of this must not distract from the facts that CL in its present form is a young discipline, but has left quite a mark on linguistics in general and theoretical linguistics in particular. However, I think CL can benefit from more interaction because many take the above delimitation(s) of the field too literally and often develop tools/methods that may appear useful when applied with the we-never-talk-about-anything-other-than-the-discourse(s) perspective but that hardly get validated against anything outside the discourses.

For example, there are 20+ measures of dispersion but few corpus linguists try to determine which are best in which circumstances (exceptions include Lyne 1985 and Gries 2008, 2009). For example, there are many different ways to generate *n*-grams, but few corpus linguists try to determine which of these ways result in something corresponding to something outside of the narrow confines of the discourses. For example, there are 30-something measures of collocational strength, but not only do few corpus linguists try to determine which are best when (Evert and Krenn 2005 and Wiechmann 2008 are laudable exceptions), there are now also corpus linguists who pretty much argue for trying different ways to modify existing measures and pick whatever yields results that intuitively (!) appear best and then sell that functionality as part of an unvalidated commercial web-based package. These facts are troubling because such validations are so necessary as studies differ with regard to which, say, measures of attraction yield the best results: Krug (1998) finds string frequency to be most predictive; Gries et al. (2005, 2010) find $p_{\text{Fisher-Yates}}$ to yield good results; Wiechmann (2008) gets the best results with (the theoretically maybe problematic measure) *Minimum Sensitivity* and $p_{\text{Fisher-Yates}}$. Thus, do we as corpus linguists just go on using *MI* (or *t* or …) just because we're supposed to focus on the discourse only and because the WordSketch engine makes that easy? Don't we care there are psycholinguistic results available that bear on our choice of statistics?

Obviously, I think we should and, thus, CL would benefit from applying corpus methods outside of CL and its discourses proper because that would increase CL's visibility in the field of linguistics as a whole and in particular with disciplines that have often independently arrived at similar findings or conclusions, but also because external validation would streamline corpus-linguistic research enterprises. In fact, Butler (2004) argues for a "greater awareness in corpus linguistics of the need for a more powerful and cognitively valid theory" (Hoey 2005: 7). However, if that is so, which theory should CL turn to?

By now it has become obvious that I disagree with most of Teubert's opinions, which is why one can turn to him to guess which theory I have in mind for CL. Here are some instructive quotes:

- "For me, corpus linguistics and cognitive linguistics are two complementary, but ultimately irreconcilable paradigms" (2005: 8).
- "Corpus linguistics localises the study of language, once again, firmly and deliberately, in the *Geisteswissenschaften*, the humanities" (2005: 13).
- "Corpus linguistics looks at language from a social perspective. It is not concerned with the psychological aspects of language" (2005: 2f.).

Adding up all this brings me to a psycholinguistically informed, (cognitively-inspired) usage-based linguistics which should be located, firmly and deliberately, in the social/behavioral sciences.[4] And in some sense, that is the logical choice. First, as we are talking about the humanistic perspective and the *Geisteswissenschaften*, is not illuminating the cognitive system(s) that ultimately give rise to discourse(s) telling us much more about the 'human condition' than interrelations between text files? We can't seriously be in the *Geisteswissenschaften* if the one thing we *a priori* blank out is *Geist*?!

Second, at some point in time, going cognitive is necessary: things only enter into discourse when a speaker has processed them and 'decided' to utter them and, thus, make them part of the discourse, and the way a hearer processes input is also determined by that hearer's internal structure. As Maxwell (bcd) put it:

> I would have thought that meaning was not inherent in any corpus, nor in some community's use of language, but could only be understood (bad term, but I can't think of another) with reference to the individual minds of the people using that language (cf. Washtell, bcd, for a similar statement)

Thus, a psycho- and cognitive-linguistically informed usage-based linguistics it is. But how does this field relate to what's happening in CL?

2. Corpus linguistics and one particular (more) theoretical approach

2.1 Corpus linguistics and cognitive linguistics/psycholinguistics: Some commonalities

If one takes a look at some such frameworks (cf. Gonzálvez-García and Butler (2006) for an excellent discussion of different cognitive/functional models), many commonalities between CL and (newer) developments in psycholinguistically informed, (cognitively-inspired) usage-based linguistics emerge. In fact, many notions and results in CL not only have immediate psycholinguistic and/or cognitive-linguistic relevance, but can also be explained in a more illuminating way once we open our eyes to and explore the large body of evidence that other disciplines have to offer.

For example, when we corpus linguists talk about token frequencies,

- cognitive linguists become interested because, on the whole, token frequencies correlate with degree of entrenchment (Schmid 2000) or phonetic reduction and development of new forms (Fidelholtz 1975);
- psycholinguists become interested because, on the whole, token frequencies correlate with ease/earliness of acquisition (Casenhiser and Goldberg 2005); lexical decision tasks, word naming, picture naming (Howes and Solomon 1951; Forster and Chambers 1973).

When we in corpus linguistics talk about type frequencies,

- cognitive linguists become interested because type frequencies are correlated with (morphological) productivity and language change (type frequency: Bybee 1985; rule reliability: Albright and Hayes 2003);
- psycholinguists become interested because type frequencies are correlated with the productivity of, say, constructions in first/second language acquisition.

When corpus linguists talk about dispersion, which they do too rarely, cognitive and psycholinguists become interested because dispersion has implications for psycholinguistic experiments (Gries 2009) and learning/acquisition (cf. Simpson and Ellis 2005; Ambridge et al. 2006; Schmidtke-Bode 2009).

When corpus linguists argue against a strict separation of syntax and lexis, cognitive linguists agree, and many psycholinguists have long assumed that words and syntactic patterns are represented as qualitatively similar nodes in a network where, in production, lexical and syntactic nodes are activated when they fit the semantic/pragmatic meaning to be communicated.

When corpus linguists talk about the Idiom Principle ("a language user has available to him or her a large number of semi-preconstructed phrases that constitute single choices, even though they might appear to be analysable into segments" (Sinclair 1991: 110), cognitive linguists become interested because it reminds them of Langacker's (1987: 57) unit, which is

> a structure that a speaker has mastered quite thoroughly, to the extent that he can employ it in largely automatic fashion, without having to focus his attention specifically on its individual parts for their arrangement [...] he has no need to reflect on how to put it together

as well as Langacker's (1987: 42) rule-list fallacy, which states

> [t]here is a viable alternative: to include in the grammar both the rules and instantiating expressions. This option allows any valid generalizations to be captured (by means of rules), and while the descriptions it affords may not be maximally economical, they have to be preferred on grounds of psychological accuracy to the extent that specific expressions do in fact become established as well-rehearsed units. Such units are cognitive entities in their own right whose existence is not reducible to that of the general patterns they instantiate.

When corpus linguists talk about words and patterns, psycholinguists become interested because when something attains unit status it can prime and be primed (both lexically and syntactically), and cognitive linguists become interested because Hunston and Francis's (2000) patterns are very similar to Goldberg's (2006) constructions. Compare the following two widely-cited quotes:

> The patterns of a word can be defined as all the words and structures which are regularly associated with the word and contribute to its meaning. A pattern can be identified if a combination of words occurs relatively frequently, if it is dependent on a particular word choice, and if there is a clear meaning associated with it. (Hunston and Francis 2000: 37)

> Any linguistic pattern is recognized as a construction as long as some aspect of its form or function is not strictly predictable from its component parts or other constructions recognized to exist. In addition, patterns are stored as constructions even if they are fully

> predictable as long as they occur with sufficient frequency. (Goldberg 2006: 5)

When corpus linguists talk about concordances, collocations, *n*-grams, colligations – i.e., anything having to do with co-occurrence information – psycholinguists become interested because such co-occurrence information

- helps children discern phonotactic patterns (Saffran et al. 1996);
- can predict reading times (MacDonald 1993) and gaze duration (McDonald et al. 2001);
- helps subjects recognize frequent 4-grams faster (when 1-gram and 2-gram frequency is controlled) (Snider and Arnon, forthcoming);
- language production and comprehension have been shown to be highly item-specific, which is just another way of saying context-bound (e.g. lexically-specific reduction or priming effects).

In a twist whose irony is probably underappreciated, many of these approaches are more corpus-driven than much self-proclaimed corpus-driven work, as when Reddington et al. (1998) and Mintz et al. (2002) apply bottom-up cluster algorithms to corpus data to explain children's recognition of parts of speech.

Also, in conformity with Teubert's social perspective, Croft (2009) and others have been arguing for a cognitive sociolinguistics and the first papers, volumes, and conferences focusing on such issues can now be found. The theory of Construction Grammar even explicitly allows for such a connection: "the function pole in the definition of a construction indeed allows for the incorporation of factors pertaining to social situation, such as e.g. register" (Goldberg 2003: 221). There is also increasingly more work in CogLing relying on corpora. There were several theme sessions on corpora and/or frequency effects in cognitive linguistics at cognitive linguistics conferences, and more than half of all papers in the next proceedings of the American version of the CogLing conference use corpora. Similarly, more and more psycholinguistic work utilizes corpora, as can be seen by searching for the words *corpus*/*corpora* on, say, the website of the *Journal of Memory and Language*.

2.2 Taking stock again…

Given the above, it becomes clear that CL is much concerned with things having immediate psycholinguistic and/or cognitive-linguistic relevance, but it becomes just as clear that, to a considerable degree, it is linguists outside of CL that apply our methods, demonstrate their relevance to notions/data outside of the 'discourses', and validate some of the suggestions we've made. It follows that not only can CL benefit from relating to more of what happens in these 'irreconcilably different' disciplines, but that these disciplines have developed theories and models that allow us to move from the purely descriptive approach for which corpus linguists are often criticized to explanation, prediction, and the embedding into a larger context, or theory, or model. The kind of cognitive-linguistic/psycholinguistic model many of the above studies come with is an exemplar-based approach, which I need to briefly outline.

3. Exemplar-based models and their relation to CL

We have seen above that infants are very good at keeping track of distributional characteristics of the ambient language such as bigram probabilities (phonemes), phonological characteristics that help distinguish between open- and closed-class words or nouns and verbs, trigram probabilities (words), and phrasal boundaries as defined by function words. Obviously, distributional knowledge is ultimately knowledge based on frequencies of occurrence, frequencies of co-occurrence, and dispersion characteristics – but how is that acquired and represented? The main assumptions of exemplar-based models in linguistics are as follows.

Speakers/listeners encounter (aspects of) tokens/exemplars and 'place them' into a multidimensional memory space/network such that the location of that token is determined by the values it exhibits in the dimensions of the memory space. This is probably easiest to conceptualize for phonemes, because many of the dimensions with regard to which phonemes are described are inherently quantitative, such as their formant frequencies: a vowel sound will be placed at a location in the multidimensional space that corresponds to its perceived F_1, F_2, etc. frequencies. More generally, phonemes are "associated with a distribution of memory traces in a parametric space, in this case a cognitive representation of the parametric phonetic space" (Pierrehumbert 2003: 185).

Figure 1 represents a three-dimensional snapshot of a speaker's truly n>3-dimensional memory space, where percepts of some linguistic units are indicated as points whose locations are based on the three dimensions *x*, *y*, and *z*, and whose grey-shading reflects their positions on the *z*-axis. While the representation in merely three dimensions is of course a simplification, it is plain to see that, for example, the points make up two categories on the dimension represented on the *x*- and the *y*-axis: there is a category with low *x*- and high *y*-values and a category with high *x*- and low *y*-values. At the same time, these two categories appear to fall into two categories along the *z*-axis: low/dark values and high/light values. If the speaker whose memory system is represented in Figure 1 now perceives another linguistic unit of the type represented in Figure 1 – for example, a unit with the values x=0, y=12, z=-8, then a new (dark) point will be inserted at these coordinates and strengthen the representation of the category with low *x*- and *z*-values and high *y*-values. This also implies that exemplars which are similar/dissimilar to each other are in close proximity/at a distance from each other respectively, and categorization of a new exemplar proceeds on the basis of multidimensional spatial proximity to clouds of already memorized exemplars. In other words, "each instance redefines the system, however infinitesimally, maintaining its present state or shifting its probabilities in one direction or the other" (Halliday 2005: 67) and "it is usual that each learning event updates a statistical representation of a category independently of other learning events" (Ellis 2002: 147).

Two important qualifications are in order. First, the above does not imply that speakers/listeners remember each token and everything about each exemplar: while speakers do not immediately categorize tokens to discard all more detailed information, (aspects of) memories of individual exemplars may still not be accessible because they may

- decay or be subject to generalization/abstraction as well as reconstruction (Ellis 2002: 153; Abbot-Smith and Tomasello 2006: 275);
- never make it into long-term memory: the fact that "we normally don't remember things we encounter only once or twice (unless they are particularly striking, or highly significant for personal reasons)" (Dąbrowska 2009: 207) implicitly facilitates the identification of typical contexts.

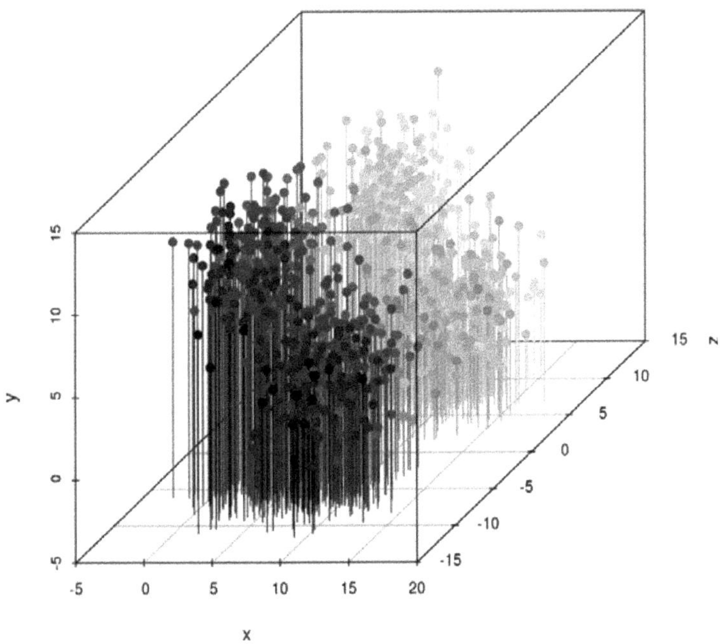

Figure 1. A three-dimensional representation of the *n*-dimensional memory space of a fictitious speaker of a language *L*

Second, this approach is not restricted to quantitative dimensions, such as formant frequencies. For example, in the case of words and constructions, it means that constructional slots are associated with distributions of words that occur in these slots and that in turn make up a (usually semantically fairly coherent) category. Even more generally, these kinds of effects are not restricted to phonemes or lexical items – quite the contrary: the distributional aspects to be remembered are numerous and involve phonetic, phonological, prosodic, morphemic, lexical (co-)occurrence as well as extra-linguistic/contextual aspects including utterance and situational context (such as the incongruity implication of the WXDY construction), sociolinguistic speaker factors, and information concerning register/mode, where I follow Biber (1995: 9) and understand register as a situationally/communicatively-defined category.

It may be useful to discuss the notion of register in this context a bit. Not only is register currently a hot topic in corpus linguistics, it is also an extremely complex and multifaceted notion and one that has repercussions for very many linguistic phenomena: depending on whom we talk to, we adjust our articulatory effort(s), lexical choices, syntactic complexity, etc. As Halliday (2005: 66) put it, "[r]egister variation can in fact be defined as systematic variation in probabilities; a register is a tendency to select certain combinations of meanings with certain frequencies". It seems counterintuitive, though, to assume that our cognitive systems have a different multidimensional space of the type schematically represented in Figure 1 for each register, especially since the number of registers we engage in, or are otherwise exposed to, is considerable. It is therefore worth mentioning at least briefly how something like register can be realistically integrated into this type of approach.

My take on this is that corpus-linguistic work contributes a very useful perspective on this. Biber's work on multidimensional variation provides the most instructive perspective and avoids the risk of postulating different knowledge/memory spaces for different registers. As is well known, Biber's approach to register variation is based on co-occurrence frequencies of many features from different linguistic levels of analysis; lexical, syntactic/ grammatical, semantic features, etc. Quite obviously, Biber's approach is therefore based on exactly the kind of information that is the foundation of exemplar-based models. Thus, the most straightforward way to include register information is in the form of the co-occurrence patterns of linguistic features with and within usage events in very much the same way that speakers store usage events with some contextual information (e.g., again, the incongruity implication of the WXDY construction), and in that case, what we call registers are clusters, or factors, that emerge from these co-occurrences and others. Alternatively, one could go a step further and postulate that the multidimensional space, in addition to the dimensions we already assume it to comprise (e.g. the three in Figure 1), also has dimensions such as the dimensions of variation identified in, say, Biber (1988).

The appealing aspects of this model, its implications, and the ways in which it is compatible with corpus work are manifold. On a theoretical level, it helps explain first language acquisition without recourse to largely untestable parameters, but also without a "meta-grammar" of the type mentioned by Maxwell (2010: 379) etc., a topic about which much of corpus linguistics proper has had little to say. It is compatible with our knowledge that speakers/listeners store immense amounts of probabilistic information, and the assumption of clouds of remembered exemplars can model all kinds of frequency effects:

- high frequencies of (co-)occurrence correspond to dense clouds with many different points in close proximity;
- categorization and prototype effects follow from the multidimensional structure of an exemplar cloud (e.g. exemplars in the 'middle' of a more densely populated area exhibit the prototype effect of first associations, faster recognition, etc.);
- the model can explain how, given their different exposure to language and, hence, different multidimensional spaces, even native speakers of a language can differ considerably in their command of the language and their judgments: "each speaker of a language has their own grammar, derived from the individual's linguistic experience. These grammars will obviously be similar and to a large extent overlapping, but they will not be identical". (Mason 2007: 2; cf. also Dąbrowska, submitted);
- the model can unproblematically account for register, sociolinguistic, and other contextual effects.

On a methodological level, this kind of model also forces us to turn (more) towards multidimensional approaches, which can be multidimensional in two senses: multidimensional$_1$ meaning that many different dimensions of variation are included in our analyses; multidimensional$_2$ meaning that co-occurrence information from as many different dimensions is included (cf. Gries 2010c). An example of an approach that is multidimensional$_1$ is the Behavioral Profile approach; examples for approaches that are multidimensional$_1$ and multidimensional$_2$ are association rules or multifactorial classification/ regression approaches, where model selection processes are used to determine which dimensions for which data are available should be retained (i.e., for which dimensions we need to rotate our multidimensional space to see another important difference). This implies the use of, for instance, more

- general(ized) linear models as in studies of alternation phenomena (Gries 2003; Szmrecsanyi 2005; Bresnan et al. 2007; Arppe 2008; Janda et al. 2010, etc.).
- more mixed-effects models (at least once these have been developed well enough), because they allow us to model all sorts of effects specific to speakers, writers, files, words, constructions, etc.
- more bottom-up and/or multivariate approaches in exploratory studies, in the parlance of an exemplar-model approach, to determine which (meaningful) dimensions emerge when the space is compressed and rotated; this includes principal component/factor analyses (Biber's multidimensional approach being the most fitting example); cluster analyses (as in Divjak and Gries 2006); correspondence analysis (as in Glynn 2008); multidimensional scaling (as in Croft and Poole 2008), etc.

4. Wrapping up

In this position paper, I tried to make a few minor proposals, which included the proposal to maybe rethink the contrast of corpus-driven and corpus-based linguistics, and to definitely rethink the us vs. them hijacking warfare. However, my main focus was something else: first, I hope I have been able to

- discuss some reasons why some part of theoretical linguists and some part of CL have so far not yet entered into the kind of fruitful relation I would like to see more of;
- convey my thoughts on why I think that this (only slowly narrowing) gap should be closed at a much faster pace;
- show that much of CL is extremely compatible with recent developments in cognitive linguistics/construction grammar as well as psycholinguistic approaches based on exemplar models, and that these theories can (i) help us answer *why*-questions in a much more revealing way than the humanistic hermeneutic-circle meaning-in-discourses is negotiated-by-the-community way upheld by some as well as (ii) inform corpus linguistics in terms of research questions we may want to ask next, methods from these areas that we can learn from a lot to improve the ways in which we pursue our questions, and findings that help us select which of the methods we have developed are most useful in which contexts. (Recent work especially in the domain of corpus-based SLA research is most instructive in this respect, cf., e.g., Ellis and Ferreira-Junior 2009).

Williams (2010: 402) claims that "Firth refuted all mentalism", but, well, Firth maybe *argued against* mentalism, but certainly did not *refute* it, and I for one am not willing to settle for a corpus linguistics that tries to sell, or dignify, pointing to (repeated) co-occurrences in discourses as 'explanation'. Is it not better to be able to explain distributions in corpora – e.g., reduced pronunciations of words – with reference to generally-known cognitive mechanisms regarding learning, habitualization, and articulatory routines than to what else happens in the discourse? Should we not explain repetitions of syntactic patterns based on implicit learning mechanisms that may ultimately lead to a unified approach towards syntactic and lexical priming and are attested in many other phenomena, too, rather than just point to repetition effects in discourses. Don't we want to explain constructional choices such as Particle Placement with reference to cognitive mechanisms of online sentence production rather than just catalog which verbs prefer which construction? Is it not better to be able to explain changes in diachronic corpora – e.g., the development of *going to* as a future marker in English – with reference to generally-known effects of automatization as a result of frequency of occurrence than to what else happens in the discourse? I think the answer is always "Yes!".

On that basis, my main focus is the proposal for us corpus linguists to assume as the main theoretical framework within which to explain and embed our analyses a psycholinguistically informed, (cognitively-inspired) exemplar/usage-based linguistics. Thankfully, I am not alone in this. There are some linguists who have assumed at least somewhat similar positions already (Schönefeld 1999; Schmid 2000; Mukherjee 2004; Butler 2004, for instance), but the major breakthrough I think is needed in order for corpus linguistics to shed its 'purely-descriptive' label has not yet happened. The from my point of view most important arguments in a very similar spirit are from Miller and Charles (e.g. 1991) as well as Hoey (e.g. 2005).

For example, Miller and Charles's work on near synonymy and antonymy (e.g. Miller and Charles 1991) involves the notion of a contextual representation, which is "a mental representation of the contexts in which the word occurs, a representation that includes all of the syntactic, semantic, pragmatic, and stylistic information required to use the word appropriately", but even more fitting is one of my favorite quotes from Hoey (2005: 11):

> the mind has a mental concordance of every word it has encountered, a concordance that has been richly glossed for social, physical, discoursal, generic and interpersonal context. [...] [A]ll kinds of patterns, including collocational patterns, are available for use.

It's time to finally recognize this connection between corpus linguistics, cognitive linguistics and psycholinguistics...

Notes

1 This paper is a revised and much extended version of Gries (2010a). In citations, I use "bcd" to refer to the bootcamp discourse on the CORPORA list in the summer 2008 that followed the announcement of my Quantitative Corpus Linguistics with R bootcamp (cf. <http://listserv.linguistlist.org/cgi-bin/wa?A1=ind0808&L=corpora> (14.09.2011)). Much of this article takes issue with Teubert's position, which is solely due to the facts that (i) he was for many years the editor of what probably is the flagship journal of the discipline, (ii) like Louw, he has been being very vocal with regard to his position, but (iii) unlike Louw, his position is comprehensible.

2 This quote is from a 'review' considered anonymous of two book manuscripts submitted to the Benjamins SCL series in 2003/2004.

3 Curiously, Teubert (bcd 2010: 354) even argues against a particular software that I have come to be associated with on the grounds that "it does not matter what kind of strings of information are processed. It could be language, but it could also be DNA sequences or the ciphers behind the '3' in the number pi" – as if that wasn't true of any concordance such as MicroConcord (which is used by Louw, but runs on DOS and seems unable to output more than 1500 matches (<http://www.lexically.net

/software/index.htm> (14.09.2011)) or uses non-ASCII characters (<http://www.athel.com/order/engsoft.html#mcc> (14.09.2011)).

4 I use the term *usage-based* here as meaning 'linking use (as in 'found in corpora'), synchrony, diachrony' and in terms of Langacker's (1987: 494) statement that "[s]ubstantial importance is given to the actual use of the linguistic system and a speaker's knowledge of this use" (cf. Gonzálvez-García and Butler 2006 for more discussion).

References

Aarts, J. (2002), 'Does corpus linguistics exist? Some old and new issues', in: L.E. Breivik and A. Hasselgren (eds.), *From the COLT's Mouth... and Others': Language Corpora Studies in Honour of Anna-Brita Stenström.* Amsterdam: Rodopi. 1-19.

Abbot-Smith, K. and M. Tomasello (2006), 'Exemplar-learning and schematization in a usage-based account of syntactic acquisition', *The Linguistic Review*, 23: 275-90.

Albright, A. and B. Hayes (2003), 'Rules vs. analogy in English past tenses: A computational/experimental study', *Cognition*, 90: 119-61.

Ambridge, B., A. Theakston, E.V.M. Lieven and M. Tomasello (2006), 'The distributed learning effect for children's acquisition of an abstract grammatical construction', *Cognitive Development*, 21: 174-93.

Arppe, A. (2008), *Univariate, Bivariate, and Multivariate Methods in Corpus-based Lexicography: A Study of Synonymy*. Unpublished Ph.D. dissertation, University of Helsinki.

Biber, D. (1988), *Variation Across Speech and Writing*. Cambridge: Cambridge University Press.

Biber, D. (1995), *Dimensions of Register Variation: A Cross-Linguistic Comparison.* Cambridge: Cambridge University Press.

Biber, D. (2009), 'A corpus-driven approach to formulaic language in English: Multi-word patterns in speech and writing'. Plenary talk held at Corpus Linguistics 2009, University of Liverpool.

Bowker, L. and J. Pearson (2002), *Working With Specialized Language: A Practical Guide to Using Corpora.* London: Routledge.

Bresnan, J., A. Cueni, T. Nikitina and R.H. Baayen (2007), 'Predicting the dative alternation', in: G. Bouma, I. Krämer and J. Zwarts (eds.), *Cognitive Foundations of Interpretation.* Amsterdam: Royal Netherlands Academy of Arts and Sciences. 69-94.

Butler, C.S. (2004), 'Corpus studies and functional linguistic theories', *Functions of Language*, 11: 147-86.

Bybee, J.L. (1985), *Morphology: A Study of the Relation Between Meaning and Form.* Amsterdam: John Benjamins.

Casenhiser, D.M. and A.E. Goldberg (2005), 'Fast mapping of a phrasal form and meaning', *Developmental Science*, 8: 500-508.

Croft, W. and K.T. Poole (2008), 'Inferring universals from grammatical variation: Multidimensional scaling for typological analysis', *Theoretical Linguistics*, 34: 1-37.

Croft, W. (2009), 'Toward a social cognitive linguistics', in: V. Evans and S. Pourcel (eds.), *New Directions in Cognitive Linguistics*. Amsterdam: John Benjamins. 395-420.

Dąbrowska, E. (2009), 'Words as constructions', in: V. Evans and S. Pourcel (eds.), *New Directions in Cognitive Linguistics*. Amsterdam: John Benjamins. 201-223.

Dąbrowska, E. (submitted), 'Individual differences in native language attainment: A review article'.

Divjak, D.S. and St.Th. Gries (2006), 'Ways of trying in Russian: Clustering behavioral profiles', *Corpus Linguistics and Linguistic Theory*, 2: 23-60.

Ellis, N.C. (2002), 'Frequency effects in language processing and acquisition', *Studies in Second Language Acquisition*, 24: 143-88.

Ellis, N.C. and F. Ferreira-Junior (2009), 'Constructions and their acquisition: Islands and the distinctiveness of their occupancy', *Annual Review of Cognitive Linguistics*, 7: 187-220.

Evert, S. and B. Krenn (2005), 'Using small random samples for the manual evaluation of statistical association measures', *Computer Speech and Language*, 19: 450-66.

Fidelholtz, J.L. (1975), 'Word frequency and vowel reduction in English', *Chicago Linguistic Society*, 11: 200-213.

Forster, K.I. and S.M. Chambers (1973), 'Lexical access and naming time', *Journal of Verbal Learning and Verbal Behavior*, 12: 627-635.

Glynn, D. (2008), 'Multivariate construction grammar: A quantitative approach to constructional semantics'. Paper presented at the conference of the German Cognitive Linguistics Association, University of Leipzig.

Goldberg, A.E. (2003), 'Constructions: A new theoretical approach to language', *Trends in Cognitive Sciences*, 7: 219-224.

Goldberg, A.E. (2006), *Constructions at Work: On the Nature of Generalization in Language*. Oxford: Oxford University Press.

Gonzálvez-García, F. and C.S. Butler (2006), 'Mapping functional-cognitive space', *Annual Review of Cognitive Linguistics*, 4: 39-96.

Gries, St.Th. (2003), *Multifactorial Analysis in Corpus Linguistics: A Study of Particle Placement*. London: Continuum.

Gries, St.Th. (2006a), 'Introduction', in: St.Th. Gries and A. Stefanowitsch (eds.), *Corpora in Cognitive Linguistics: Corpus-based Approaches to Syntax and Lexis*. Berlin: de Gruyter. 1-17.

Gries, St.Th. (2006b), 'Exploring variability within and between corpora: Some methodological considerations', *Corpora*, 1:109-151.

Gries, St.Th. (2008), 'Dispersions and adjusted frequencies in corpora', *International Journal of Corpus Linguistics*, 13: 403-437.

Gries, St.Th. (2009), 'Dispersions and adjusted frequencies in corpora: Further explorations', in: St.Th. Gries, S. Wulff and M. Davies (eds.), *Corpus*

Linguistic Applications: Current Studies, New Directions. Amsterdam: Rodopi. 197-212.

Gries, St.Th. (2010a), 'Corpus linguistics and theoretical linguistics: A love-hate relationship? Not necessarily…', *International Journal of Corpus Linguistics*, 15: 327-343.

Gries, St.Th. (2010b), 'Bigrams in registers, domains, and varieties: A bigram gravity approach to the homogeneity of corpora', in: M. Mahlberg, V. González-Diaz and C. Smith (eds.), *Proceedings of Corpus Linguistics 2009*, University of Liverpool. <http://ucrel.lancs.ac.uk/publications /cl2009/404_FullPaper.doc> (14.09.2011).

Gries, St.Th. (2010c), 'Behavioral profiles: A fine-grained and quantitative approach in corpus-based lexical semantics', *The Mental Lexicon*, 5: 323-346.

Gries, St.Th. (forthcoming), 'Methodological and interdisciplinary stance in corpus linguistics', in: G. Barnbrook, V. Viana and S. Zyngier (eds.), *Perspectives on Corpus Linguistics: Connections and Controversies*. Amsterdam: John Benjamins.

Gries, St.Th., B. Hampe and D. Schönefeld (2005), 'Converging evidence: Bringing together experimental and corpus data on the association of verbs and constructions', *Cognitive Linguistics*, 16: 635-676.

Gries, St.Th., B. Hampe and D. Schönefeld (2010), 'Converging evidence II: More on the association of verbs and constructions', in: J. Newman and S. Rice (eds.), *Empirical and Experimental Methods in Cognitive/Functional Research*. Stanford, CA: CSLI. 59-72.

Gries, St.Th. and J. Mukherjee (2010), 'Lexical gravity across varieties of English: An ICE-based study of *n*-grams in Asian Englishes', *International Journal of Corpus Linguistics*, 15: 520-548.

Gries, St.Th., J. Newman and C. Shaoul (2011), '*N*-grams and the clustering of genres', *Empirical Language Research*, 5. <http://ejournals.org.uk/ELR/ article/2011/1> (10.11.2011).

Halliday, M.A.K. (2005), *Computational and Quantitative Studies*. London: Continuum.

Hardie, A. and T. McEnery (2010), 'On two traditions in corpus linguistics, and what they have in common', *International Journal of Corpus Linguistics*, 15: 384-394.

Hawkins, J.A. (1994), *A Performance Theory of Order and Constituency*. Cambridge: Cambridge University Press.

Hawkins, J.A. (2005), *Efficiency and Complexity in Grammars*. Oxford: Oxford University Press.

Hoey, M. (2005), *Lexical Priming: A New Theory of Words and Language*. London: Routledge.

Howes, D.H. and R.L. Solomon (1951), 'Visual duration threshold as a function of word probability', *Journal of Experimental Psychology*, 41: 401-410.

Hunston, S. and G. Francis (2000), *Pattern Grammar: A Corpus-driven Approach to the Lexical Grammar of English*. Amsterdam: John Benjamins.

Janda, L., T. Nesset and R.H. Baayen (2010), 'Capturing correlational structure in Russian paradigms: A case study in logistic mixed-effects modeling', *Corpus Linguistics and Linguistic Theory*, 6: 29-48.

Kita, K., Y. Kato, T. Omoto and Y. Yano (1994), 'A comparative study of automatic extraction of collocations from corpora: Mutual information vs. cost criteria', *Journal of Natural Language Processing*, 1: 21-33.

Krug, M. (1998): 'String frequency: A cognitive motivating factor in coalescence, language processing, and linguistic change', *Journal of English Linguistics*, 26: 286-320.

Langacker, R.W. (1987), *Foundations of Cognitive Grammar. Volume I: Theoretical Prerequisites*. Stanford, CA: Stanford University Press.

Leech, G.N. (1992), 'Corpora and theories of linguistic performance', in: J. Svartvik (ed.), *Directions in Corpus Linguistics: Proceedings of Nobel Symposium 82*. Berlin: de Gruyter. 105-122.

Lyne, A.A. (1985), *The Vocabulary of French Business Correspondence*. Geneva: Slatkine-Champion. 101-124.

MacDonald, M.C. (1993), 'The interaction of lexical and syntactic ambiguity', *Journal of Memory and Language*, 32: 692-715.

Mason, O. (2006), *The Automatic Extraction of Linguistic Information from Text Corpora*. Unpublished Ph.D. dissertation, University of Birmingham.

Mason, O. (2007), 'From lexis to syntax: The use of multi-word units in grammatical description', in: C. Camuali, M. Constant and A. Dister (eds.), *Proceedings of Lexis and Grammar 2007*. <http://infolingu.univ-mlv.fr/Colloques/Bonifacio/proceedings/mason.pdf> (14.09.2011).

Maxwell, M. (2010), 'Limitations of corpora', *International Journal of Corpus Linguistics*, 15: 379-383.

McDonald, S., R. Shillcock and C. Brew (2001), 'Low-level predictive inference in reading: Using distributional statistics to predict eye movements'. Paper presented at the 7th Annual Conference on Architectures and Mechanisms for Language Processing, Saarbrücken.

McEnery, T. and A. Wilson (1996), *Corpus Linguistics*. Edinburgh: Edinburgh University Press.

McEnery, T., R. Xiao and Y. Tono (2006), *Corpus-based Language Studies: An Advanced Resource Book*. London: Routledge.

Meyer, C.F. (2002), *English Corpus Linguistics: An Introduction*. Cambridge: Cambridge University Press.

Miller, G.A. and W.G. Charles (1991), 'Contextual correlates of semantic similarity', *Language and Cognitive Processes*, 6: 1-28.

Mintz, T.H., E.L. Newport and T.G. Bever (2002), 'The distributional structure of grammatical categories in the speech to young children', *Cognitive Science*, 26: 393-424.

Mukherjee, J. (2004), 'Corpus data in a usage-based cognitive grammar', in: K. Aijmer and B. Altenberg (eds.), *Corpus Data in a Usage-based Cognitive Grammar*. Amsterdam: Rodopi. 85-100.

Mukherjee, J. (2010), 'Corpus linguistics versus corpus dogmatism – pace Wolfgang Teubert', *International Journal of Corpus Linguistics*, 15: 370-378.

Nagao, M. and S. Mori. (1994), 'A new method of *n*-gram statistics for large number of *n* and automatic extraction of words and phrases from large text data of Japanese', *Proceedings of the 15th Conference on Computational Linguistics*. 611-615. <http://dl.acm.org/ft_gateway.cfm?id=991994&type=pdf&CFID=45628901&CFTOKEN=82898916> (14.09.2011).

Pierrehumbert, J. (2003), 'Probabilistic phonology: Discrimination and robustness', in: R. Bod, J. Hay, and S. Jannedy (eds.), *Probabilistic Linguistics*. Cambridge, MA: The M.I.T. Press. 177-228.

Redington, M., N. Chater and S. Finch (1998), 'Distributional information: A powerful cue for acquiring syntactic categories', *Cognitive Science*, 22: 435-469.

Saffran, J.R., R.N. Aslin and E.L. Newport (1996), 'Statistical learning by 8-months-old infants', *Science*, 274: 1926-1928.

Schmid, H.-J. (2000), *English Abstract Nouns as Conceptual Shells: From Corpus to Cognition*. Berlin: de Gruyter.

Schmidtke-Bode, K. (2009), '*Going-to*-V and *gonna*-V in child language: A quantitative approach to constructional development', *Cognitive Linguistics*, 20: 509-538.

Schönefeld, D. (1999), 'Corpus linguistics and cognitivism', *International Journal of Corpus Linguistics*, 4: 131-171.

Simpson, R. and N.C. Ellis (2005), 'An academic formulas list: Extraction, validation, prioritization'. Paper presented at Phraseology 2005, Université catholique de Louvain.

Sinclair, J.M. (1991), *Corpus, Concordance, Collocation*. Oxford: Oxford University Press.

Sinclair, J.M. (2006), *Linear Unit Grammar: Integrating Speech and Writing*. Amsterdam: John Benjamins.

Snider, N. and I. Arnon (forthcoming), 'More than words: Speakers are sensitive to the frequency of multi-word sequences'.

Stubbs, M. (1993), 'British traditions in text analysis: From Firth to Sinclair', in: M. Baker, F. Francis and E. Tognini-Bonelli (eds.), *Text and Technology: In Honour of John Sinclair*. Amsterdam: John Benjamins. 1-46.

Szmrecsanyi, B. (2005), 'Language users as creatures of habit: A corpus-based analysis of persistence in spoken English', *Corpus Linguistics and Linguistic Theory*, 1. 113-150.

Taylor, C. (2008), 'What is corpus linguistics? What the data says', in: M. Kytö and A.-B. Stenström (eds.), *ICAME Journal* 32: 179-200.

Teubert, W. (2005), 'My version of corpus linguistics', *International Journal of Corpus Linguistics*, 10: 1-13.

Teubert, W. (2010), 'Our brave new world?', *International Journal of Corpus Linguisitcs*, 15: 354-358

Tognini-Bonelli, E. (2001), *Corpus Linguistics at Work*. Amsterdam: John Benjamins.

Wiechmann, D. (2008), 'On the computation of collostruction strength: Testing measures of association as expressions of lexical bias', *Corpus Linguistics and Linguistic Theory*, 4: 253-290.

Williams, G. (2006), 'La linguistique de corpus: Une affaire prépositionnelle', in: F. Rastier and M. Ballabriga (eds.), *Corpus en Lettres et Sciences Sociales: Des Documents Numériques à l'Interprétation*. Paris: Texto. 151-158.

Williams, G. (2010), 'Many rooms with corpora', *International Journal of Corpus Linguistics*, 15: 400-407.

Wynne, M. (2010): 'Interdisciplinary relationships', *International Journal of Corpus Linguistics*, 15: 425-427.

Xiao, R. (2009), 'Theory-driven corpus research: Using corpora to inform aspect theory', in: A. Lüdeling and M. Kytö (eds.), *Corpus Linguistics: An International Handbook*. Berlin: de Gruyter. 987-1008.

Syntactic variation and lexical preference in the dative-shift alternation

Hans Martin Lehmann and Gerold Schneider

University of Zurich

Abstract

In this paper we investigate the dative shift alternation on the basis of 580 million words annotated with a dependency parser. We explore the link between lexical and syntactic choice in a core case of syntactic variation. We show that the sheer amount of automatically parsed data permits new approaches toward studying not only lexis but also other language internal factors influencing the syntactic choice offered by the dative shift alternation. Our approach offers new possibilities by replacing intuition-based decisions inherent to traditional variationist methodology with decisions based on observation.

1. Introduction

In our experimental investigation of the dative-shift alternation we use Pro3Gres, a dependency parser with a hand-written grammar, as an instrument of observation. Mukherjee (2005) provides a detailed, corpus-based study of ditransitive verbs. The dative-shift has been investigated with variationist methodology by Bresnan and Nikitina (2009). Bresnan and Nikitina (2009) spend much of their argument on the gradience they encounter in the definition of the envelope of variaton, i.e. that the alternate form *can* be used without shift in meaning. In our paper we shift the focus to usage and observe which lexical types *do* occur in the alternate form and which form is actually preferred by a lexical type. Our approach takes the syntactic construction identified by the parser as a starting point and has a generalization over the lexical types found in the construction as its main goal.

2. Data and method

The present study is based on the automatic analysis of 580 million running words. Besides the written part of the *British National Corpus*, the data consists of a collection of news-language acquired on CD-Rom and from the internet. Table 1 provides an overview of the data. The data consists of almost 50% written language. The CNN Transcripts, which account for the other half of the data, range from written-to-be-spoken to fairly spontaneous dialogue in interviews. At this magnitude a more careful selection of data was not possible.

Table 1. Overview of the data analyzed

Source	**Abbreviation**	**word-count**
BNCW-written	bncwwri	89,774,445
The Boston Globe	bogl	37,450,270
CNN Transcripts	cnn	309,588,268
Los Angeles Times	latm	42,307,657
The Daily Mail	tdma	22,130,851
The [London] Times	tlnd	36,545,704
Times Sunday	tlns	17,696,675
The Mail on Sunday	tmos	6,302,424
USA Today	usat	18,155,419
Total		**579,951,713**

The data was syntactically analysed with Pro3Gres (Schneider 2008). For more details on the annotation chain, see Lehmann and Schneider (2010) and Lehmann and Schneider (2009). The syntactically annotated data was used for the retrieval of the dative-shift construction, as in (1) and for the prepositional construction, as in (2).

(1) I just ***show*** *the* ***prisoners*** *a* ***picture*** *of an aborted baby* and [...] (BNC:K5C:22)
(2) Mother and son were ***showing*** *Alicia's* ***picture*** *to* ***strangers*** on the park's edge when [...] (LATM99020864)

Pro3Gres makes use of a hand-written grammar. The rule for the double object construction turned out to be empirically problematic. In its standard form it restricts the construction to a set of verbs found in double object construction in the PENN treebank (Marcus et al. 1993). For verbs that do not happen to occur in the PENN treebank, this would have resulted in an observational gap. As a consequence, the class of verbs that can enter the construction could not be derived empirically. To avoid this problem we decided to reparse the data with this lexical restriction removed. In the present analysis any verb can potentially enter into a double object construction.

In addition to core-ditransitives also instances of *elect*-verbs as in (3) and benefactives, as in (4) are reported.

(3) He once **called *Clinton*** an unusually good ***liar***, a remark he has never disavowed. (LATM99004734)
(4) The woman showed her appreciation by **baking *Annabelle/Steven*** a ***cake***. (BNC.F3N.961)

In terms of lexical restrictions, the retrieval of verb-attached PPs with the help of Pro3Gres is unproblematic. The selection of prepositions requires further consideration. At first glance, a restriction of verb-attached PPs to the preposition *to* appears as the most intuitive strategy. However, the inclusion of benefactives in the double object retrieval would have skewed our observation by considering only one part of construction pairs like *bake s.o. a cake* and *bake a cake for s.o.* For this paper, we decided to restrict prepositions of verb-attached PPs to *to* and *for*. We include all constructions of *verb – object NP – verb-attached PP*, irrespective of the parser's decision on the status of the PP as complement or adjunct. All these decisions increase recall at the cost of precision, which results in many unwanted instances.

3. Results

The two retrieval patterns result in 519,682 reported double object constructions and 1,501,154 prepositional constructions. These two sets of results could form the basis for a wide range of investigations. Here we will focus on syntactic variation in the form of the dative shift alternation and lexical types as a language internal factor in this variation. The study of lexical types is only made possible by one of the main advantages of the fully automatic retrieval, which is the accessibility of a large number of observed instances.

To generalize over lexis we need to establish types. In (5) and (6) we observe the same lexical triplet *give people information* in the alternation. The lexical type abstracts from word-forms like *give* and *gave* and ignores determination and modification.

(5) The military says senior airman Ahmad al-Halabi **gave** classified ***information*** about the prison *to* ***people*** from Syria and Qatar. (CNN:20031107LDT:Dobbs)

(6) We are honor-bound to **give** ***people*** this ***information***, he says. (USAT657507)

(7) [...] the project manager at the company has been ***giving*** extremely negative ***information*** about me ***to*** prospective ***clients***. (LATM99055500)

(8) In fact she has been asked to **give** short lecture ***demonstrations*** of the exercises ***to*** two other stroke ***clubs*** in neighbouring Hayling and Emsworth. (BNC:KAD:167)

We can also establish a broader lexical type by abstracting over *people* and *clients*, assigning one type to (5), (6) and (7). Eventually, it is also possible to form a type that covers all four instances above by just focusing on the verb lemma. From here on we will refer to these three types as VOO for the full lemma triplets, VXO for the verb object pairs and VXX for the type based on verb lemma. In order to establish a minimal basis for the observation of constructional preferences we limit all types to the occurrence of at least 3 instances per construction and lexical type. This restriction is somewhat arbitrary and we are looking into a statistically motivated cut-off, the implementation of which still poses problems due to the high number of instances. Table 2 provides an overview of the consequences for the number of observations and the number of types.

Table 2. The dative-shift alternation and lexical restrictions.

lexical types	f dshift*	f pcomp*	lexical types	verb-types
VOO	40,393	9,220	634	44
VXO	296,763	253,008	4678	278
VXX	515,972	1,368,251	1850	1850
unrestricted	519,682	1,501,154	-	-

* *f_pcomp and f_dshift > 3 for each lexical type*

Requiring identity of the full lemma triplet in the set VOO sharply restricts the number of observations. Loosening this requirement by only requiring the same lemma for the verb and the direct object in the set VXO massively increases the coverage. Limiting the lexical restriction to the identity of only the verb covers the vast majority of all the instances observed in the two patterns. Even more interesting is the effect these lexical requirements have on the number of types observed. The restriction that both the dative shift construction and the prepositional complement construction have to be observed at least 3 times for each lexical type severely limits the included observations for the set VOO. Without scarceness of data we would expect the number of lexical types to be lower in the set of VXO where we abstract from the lemma of the indirect object. The opposite is the case, because many instances remain unobserved due to the limit of three instances per lexical type and construction. The set VOO includes only the tip of the iceberg and we indeed find that 580 million words are barely enough data to yield results for full lemma triplets.

We focus on lexical types that do occur in both constructions. This is in stark contrast with intuition-based judgements used in the traditional variationist framework, where we would ask if the lexical items can occur in both constructions. In addition to this desired shift to an observation-based strategy, the restriction also excludes the majority of the garbage incurred by the two retrieval patterns.

Table 3 shows an excerpt of a list of the 634 VOO lemma triplet types. The list is ordered by the preference for the dative shift. Triplets at the top show a strong preference for the double object construction, those at the bottom show a strong preference for the prepositional complement construction. The triplet *ask you question* prefers the double object construction with 99.8% and the triplet *pay it attention* prefers the prepositional complement construction *pay attention to it* with 97.6%. We also see that the column iObj is mainly populated by personal pronouns at the top and that the nouns occurring in that slot are mainly referring to human beings or entities with an associated group of human beings. It is also interesting to note that the frequency at both ends of the cline are generally higher than in the middle and that the triplets strongly preferring the dative shift are much more frequent than those showing a preference for the prepositional complement construction.

Table 3. Lemma triplets ordered according to their preference for the dative shift. 634 types observed in 580 million words.*n dshift and n to/for > 3*

lemma triplet	dshift	to	for	% dshift	iObj
ask you question	4876	3	8	99.8	you
tell you truth	1203	4	1	99.6	you
tell you story	958	3	3	99.4	you
ask him question	1089	6	1	99.4	him
show you picture	1698	13	1	99.2	you
give you number	470	3	1	99.2	you
bring you update	456	5	0	98.9	you
give them information	519	6	0	98.9	them
bring them home	502	6	0	98.8	them
ask them question	404	3	2	98.8	them
[...]		[...]			[...]
cost you price	4	0	4	50	you
send us e-mail	19	19	0	50	us
give administration mark	4	4	0	50	administration
give bush vote	5	5	0	50	bush
send them question	8	8	0	50	them
do himself damage	6	5	1	50	himself
send russia message	5	5	0	50	russia
show audience picture	4	4	0	50	audience
owe him life	7	7	0	50	him
issue us statement	9	9	0	50	us
give child drug	5	5	0	50	child
[...]		[...]			[...]
send country message	4	42	0	8.7	country
give company break	9	99	0	8.3	company
do you something	11	35	90	8.1	you
send people message	20	279	3	6.6	people
send child message	4	62	0	6.1	child
do you anything	10	49	143	5	you
send world message	5	148	0	3.3	world
do you work	4	2	121	3.1	you
pay it attention	14	587	1	2.3	it

Table 4. 955 VXO types with *give* and *to* in 580m wds. *f_pcomp and f_dshift > 3*

	dshift		to	dshift	pronX
	n		n	%	%
give X idea	4783	give idea to X	43	99.1	89
give X chance	9626	give chance to X	124	98.7	50
give X sense	6751	give sense to X	90	98.7	85
give X example	1713	give example to X	23	98.7	96
give X lead	2684	give lead to X	40	98.5	14
give X update	1247	give update to X	20	98.4	94
give X try	241	give try to X	4	98.4	24
give X call	1264	give call to X	21	98.4	89
give X perspective	1226	give perspective to X	23	98.2	90
give X glance	195	give glance to X	4	98	70
[...]		[...]			[...]
give X opposition	4	give opposition to X	4	50	25
give X lustre	4	give lustre to X	4	50	25
give X authenticity	5	give authenticity to X	5	50	30
give X customer	8	give customer to X	8	50	25
give X poignancy	6	give poignancy to X	6	50	50
give X precision	5	give precision to X	5	50	10
give X proportion	6	give proportion to X	6	50	25
[...]		[...]			[...]
give X consent	14	give consent to X	68	17.1	13
give X thank	40	give thank to X	240	14.3	15
give X effect	42	give effect to X	256	14.1	16
give X preference	19	give preference to X	119	13.8	10
give X shout-out	7	give shout-out to X	44	13.7	16
give X approval	43	give approval to X	285	13.1	11
give X condolence	7	give condolence to X	56	11.1	11
give X million	19	give million to X	163	10.4	10
give X credence	30	give credence to X	262	10.3	12
give X all	6	give all to X	61	9	16
give X lie	4	give lie to X	116	3.3	3
give X who	6	give who to X	275	2.1	10
give X rise	44	give rise to X	2343	1.8	2
give X birth	12	give birth to X	2793	0.4	4

Given the frequencies observed in Table 2 and the properties for iObj observed in Table 3, we now focus on VXO, where we reach a much greater coverage of instances.

If we list all VXO types and order them according to their preference for the dative shift we find *tell X something* with 99.6% dative shift and *pay tribute to X* with 99.4% prepositional complement constructions. We have also calculated the percentage of pronominal forms found in the slot X in both constructions. In Table 4 we present such a calculation for the lexical items *give* and *to*.

In Table 4 we can observe the VXO types with the verb *give* and the preposition *to*. The type *give X idea* prefers the dative-shift with 99.1% and *give X birth* prefers the prepositional complement construction with 99.6%. The percentage of dative-shift and the percentage of pronominal X, which is given in the last column, are clearly linked. There are however notable exceptions. Such a case is *give X lead*, in which 98.5% of the instances are realised in the dative-shift construction, but only 14% of the instances have a pronominal slot X. One of the advantages of the method presented here is the possibility of immediate inspection of cases that go against the observed general trend. A closer inspection shows that a high proportion of the instances of *give X lead* is used in sports news, where it is used as fairly fixed frame, see examples (9) and (10).

(9) Barkley made one of two free throws with 17 seconds remaining to **give** the ***Rockets*** an 87-83 ***lead***. (LATM99027779)

(10) One of the new polls, by Franklin Pierce College in Rindge and WNDS-TV, **gives** ***McCain*** a 15-percentage-point ***lead*** over Bush, with a 5 - point margin of error. (USAT662752)

There are of course possibilities for generalization. In the observed instances *lead* is almost always determined and modified, which increases the weight of the NP. The first NP slot is mainly occupied by referents to human beings or groups of human beings. Such factors have been observed and investigated by Bresnan and Nikitina (2009). The present study offers a new, inductive and observation-based strategy for exploring such possible factors. We could expand our automatic analysis to determination and modification of the observed heads.

Table 4 also shows many light verb VXO constructions like *give X try, give X call, give X approval and give X preference*, in which the meaning of *give* is bleached and which could often be reformulated as transitives – *try X, call X* – with little change in meaning. Many of these light verb types cover a high number of instances and pose a problem to a variationist analysis with a binary dependent variable.

The type *give X birth* at the bottom of Table 4 is interesting in that it shows all the 'active' forms of *be born* observed in our investigation of the lexical preferences of the passive construction (cf. Lehmann and Schneider 2009). These observed cases point to another property of the dative-shift as a case of syntactic variation. They represent asymmetries involving other syntactic paradigms with similar meaning. It seems obvious that by looking at only the dative shift alternation we ignore "ways of saying the same thing" (Labov 1969: 738) and thereby get into conflict with the principle of accountability (Labov 1969). There are also fixed frames like *give rise to X* where meaning is not stable across the alternation as in *give X (pay) rise*. Another case in point is the secondary variation between *to* and *for* constructions observed in Table 3. There are types like *do you anything* where the alternate *do anything to you* and *do anything for you* differ in meaning. However, many of the observed types with *for/to* clearly are variant forms with little shift in meaning, as can be seen in (11) and (12).

(11) Budget, [...], has already ***offered*** 20% ***discounts*** **for** ***customers*** willing to book on line. (USAT644213)

(12) [...], many tour operators ***offer*** 3% ***discounts*** **to** ***travelers*** who don't use credit cards. (LATM99072636)

Based on our data we can produce lists as in Table 4 for any verb-preposition combination. Figures 1-4 are graphic representations of four such lists. Figure 1 is based on a list without lexical restrictions and covers all VXO types. Figure 2 is a graphic representation of Table 4. Figure 3 shows VXO types restricted to the verb *offer* and the preposition *to*, while Figure 4 is restricted to the verb *show* and the preposition *to*. The horizontal x-axis is assigned to the lexical VXO types. On the vertical y-axis we plot the percentage of dative shift constructions for each VXO type. As in Table 4, the data is sorted according to this percentage and results in the decreasing, upper, darker line. The percentages of pronominal X per VXO type are plotted as the lighter dots. The lower line is a curve fit to the pronominal X percentages, which gives us a general trend for the development of pronominal X with decreasing percentage of preference for dative-shift. By simply squinting at the plotted information we can observe the connection between pronominal X and preference for the dative-shift. We also see that many lexical VXO types massively differ from the trend. For example, the dot circled in Figure 2 corresponds to *give X lead,* which we have examined above.

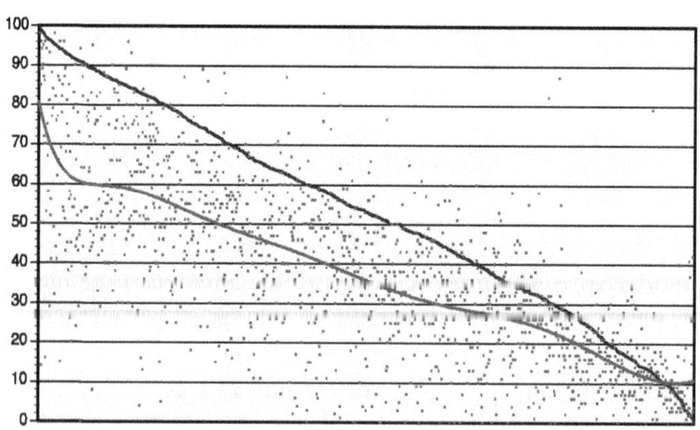

Figure 1. Verb-dObj types by preference for dative-shift

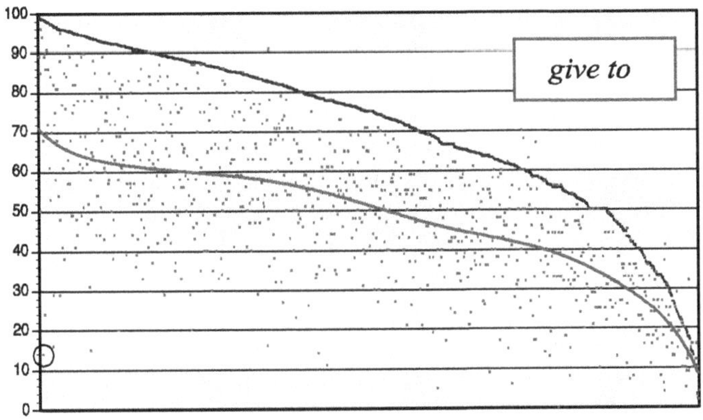

Figure 2. Verb-dObj types. Verb: *give*, prep: *to*

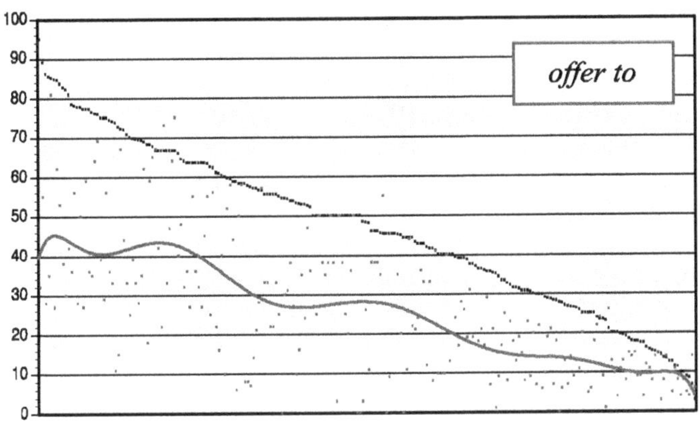

Figure 3. Verb-dObj types. Verb: *offer*, prep: *to*

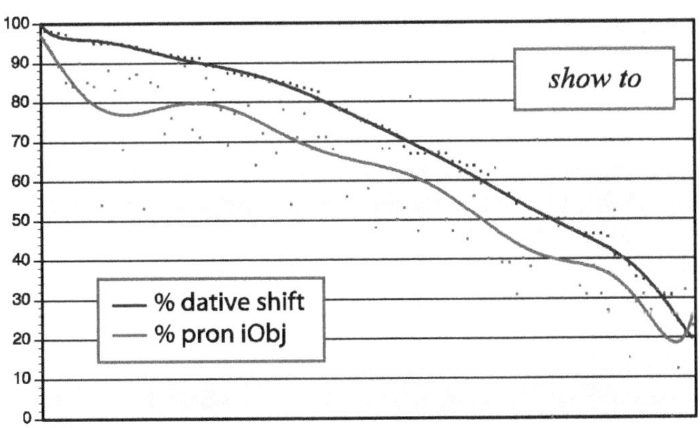

Figure 4. Verb-dObj types. Verb: *show*, prep: *to*

We have to keep in mind that the observed data in Figures 1-4 is restricted to the VXO types in which variation is actually observed based on the restriction of a minimum of three instances per variant form. What we see is the main area of variation with fixed and idiomatic VXO types that almost exclusively prefer one construction excluded. The verb *give* in Table 2 differs from the general pattern in Figure 1. It shows a higher proportion of pronominal X and a higher preference for dative-shift. In Figure 3 covering the verb *offer* we observe a more symmetric distribution of the preference for dative-shift and a lower percentage of pronominal X. We might assume that this difference is due to the generally lower frequency of the verb *offer*. However, the results for the verb *show*, which is even less frequent, display a pattern similar to *give*.

Our data also offers the possibility to look at marginal ditransitives like *flick*. Except for (13) all dative shift instances observed take *glance* as the direct object, as in (14). There are no prepositional complement constructions with *glance*.

(13) Bertie looked so scrawny that the 84-year-old Second World War veteran **flicked** ***him*** a ***piece*** of roast beef from his lunchtime sandwich. (TMOS:ASNS199912200036AE03)

(14) She **flicked** ***him*** an irritated ***glance***. (BNC:JXV:1464)

(15) With 16:38 left, Bruin guard Baron Davis found himself on his backside with ball in hand before **flicking** a ***pass*** to ***Watson***, *who made a three-point shot*. (LATM99022645)

(16) It might be a run past three players and into the penalty box before **flicking** the ***ball*** to an unmarked ***teammate***. (LATM99057212)

(15) is a borderline case in which *to Watson* could be adverbial; *where did he flick it* versus *who did he flick it to*. The instances with *glance* certainly remind of *give X glance* observed in Table 4. A closer, systematic analysis of such rare ditransitives might provide more insight into the general mechanisms at work.

4. Conclusion

The use of automatically parsed data has brought lexical types in the dative-shift alternation within reach of observation. We have presented a methodology that permits the observation of rare verbs in the alternation. We have shown that the lexical types involving different verbs exhibit specific behavior in terms of preference for the dative-shift as well as for the pronominal object.

We have employed fully automatic, error prone analysis of a huge data set and simple listing and plotting of instances and have found results similar to Bresnan and Nikitina (2009), who use manual annotation on a relatively small, carefully selected set of data and multivariate statistical analysis.

Based on our approach it will be possible to implement a systematic way of identifying problematic cases like light verbs and fixed expressions that may skew the results of a traditional variationist study. The sheer mass of observations will also permit an observation-based exploration of possible factors.

References

Bresnan, J. and T. Nikitina (2009), 'The gradience of the dative alternation', in: L. Uyechi and L. Hee Wee (eds.), *Reality Exploration and Discovery: Pattern Interaction in Language and Life*. Stanford, CA: CSLI Publications. 161-184.

Labov, W. (1969), 'Contraction, deletion, and inherent variability of the English copula', *Language*, 45: 715-762.

Lehmann, H.M. and G. Schneider (2009), 'Parser-based analysis of syntax-lexis interactions', in A.H. Jucker, D. Schreier and M. Hundt (eds.), *Corpora: Pragmatics and Discourse*. Amsterdam: Rodopi. 477-502.

Lehmann, H.M. and G. Schneider (2010), 'A large-scale investigation of verb-attached prepositional phrases', in: S. Hoffmann, P. Rayson and G. Leech (eds.), *Methodological and Historical Dimensions of Corpus Linguistics*. Helsinki: Varieng. <http://www.helsinki.fi/varieng/journal/volumes/06/> (15.09.2011).

Marcus, M., B. Santorini and M.A. Marcinkiewicz (1993), 'Building a large annotated corpus of English: The Penn Treebank', *Computational Linguistics*, 19: 313-330.

Mukherjee, J. (2005), *English Ditransitive Verbs: Aspects of Theory, Description and a Usage-Based Model*. Amsterdam: Rodopi.

Schneider, G. (2008), *Hybrid Long-Distance Functional Dependency Parsing*. Ph.D. dissertation, Institute of Computational Linguistics, University of Zurich. <http://www.zora.uzh.ch/7188/2/phd_wrapper9FINALV.pdf> (15. 09.2011).

The corpus stylistic analysis of fiction – or the fiction of corpus stylistics?

Michaela Mahlberg

University of Nottingham

Abstract

This paper argues that corpus stylistics can contribute methodologies and concepts to support the investigation of character information in fiction. Focusing on Charles Dickens, the paper looks at lexicogrammatical patterns as well as places in the literary text. It suggests that clusters, i.e. repeated sequences of words, and suspensions, i.e. interruptions of characters' speech by the narrator, can serve as textual cues in the process of characterization. These concepts are illustrated with examples for the characters Bucket and Tulkinghorn in Bleak House. *The analysis of the examples leads to an outline of challenges for corpus stylistics that result from the need to interpret features on the textual surface in relation to the effects they might have on the processing of the text by readers.*[1]

1. Introduction

The number of studies that approach literary texts with corpus linguistic methods is growing and the term 'corpus stylistics' is becoming increasingly popular. Corpus stylistics has started to be recognized as an emerging field or branch by both corpus linguists (cf. Chapelle 2011; Lindquist 2009; O'Keeffe and McCarthy 2010) and stylisticians (cf. Jeffries and McIntyre 2010; Leech and Short 2007; McIntyre and Busse 2010). It is set in the wider context of the Digital Humanities where new technologies enable new ways of conducting research and both support and challenge traditional approaches in the humanities. Part of the challenge is to assess the usefulness of innovative technologies. Any level of sophistication in the storage, presentation and manipulation of data cannot replace the need for human analysis and the identification of relevant research questions. Against this background it seems worthwhile to consider what kind of contributions corpus stylistics can make to the study of literary texts. What makes a text 'literary' is to some extent determined by its reception through the reader, who approaches the text "in a literary way" (cf. Carter 2004: 69). The enthusiasm about the application of corpus methods to the study of literary texts holds the danger of overinterpreting findings and viewing their implications as far more important than they might be in a wider critical context. Corpus methods help us to focus on salient features on the textual surface, but corpus methods alone cannot assess the relevance of those features for the process of reading a text and creating a textual world in the reader's mind. In this article I want to argue that the strengths of corpus stylistics are most apparent when it is linked to literary criticism (or stylistic approaches in a wider sense) and when findings are not presented in isolation but as part of a bigger picture, or as Carter (2010: 67) puts it: "Corpus stylistic analysis is a relatively objective methodological procedure that at its best is guided by a relatively subjective process of interpretation".

To explore the usefulness of corpus stylistic methodology, I want to focus on characterization in Dickens and in particular look at two characters from *Bleak House*: Inspector Bucket and the lawyer Tulkinghorn. I argue that clusters and suspensions provide two options of looking for character information. It will be shown that the character information found with the help of those methods can be linked to literary criticism on characterization in Dickens. Thus corpus stylistics is seen as complementing other approaches. In the final section of this article I will highlight some of the challenges that such a corpus stylistic approach has to face.

2. Extending the checklist of textual cues for character information

Culpeper (2001) views characterization as a process in which impressions of characters are formed in the reader's mind. These impressions result from the interplay of top-down and bottom-up processes in the reading of texts. The bottom-up processes draw on cues that are found in the text. Culpeper suggests a number of textual cues that can be useful starting-points for the analyst. In his list, he includes, for instance, conversational structure, conversational implicature, terms of address, dialect, syntactic features, etc. The list illustrates how stylistics can draw on a range of linguistic concepts and approaches. Corpus linguistics adds to the development of linguistic concepts. The impact of such developments is also seen in Culpeper's (2001) approach when he includes key words in his checklist. As Culpeper (2001) mainly focuses on plays, key words are suggested as a useful approach to compare the speech of different characters. Following Culpeper (2001), McIntyre (2010) illustrates how key words and key semantic domains can contribute to the study of characters in a screenplay. I want to suggest two further concepts that seem helpful additions to a checklist for character information: clusters (also briefly referred to in McIntyre 2010) and suspensions. The motivation for the inclusion of these concepts is a combination of arguments from corpus linguists and literary criticism. In the following I begin with an overview of the concepts which will then be discussed in more detail when applied to the characterization of Bucket and Tulkinghorn.

2.1 Patterns: Clusters

Clusters are repeated sequences of words, e.g. *I don't know what.* The fact that such sequences are used repeatedly suggests that they are associated with textual functions. Focusing on five-word clusters in Dickens, the following functions can be identified: clusters label or refer to characters and themes, are part of characters' speech, describe body language, introduce comments by the narrator and function in reference to time and place. Examples (1) to (5) illustrate these functions respectively, the five word clusters are in italics. As the examples show, a cluster can also be part of a larger expression with the respective function, but for the sake of brevity, I refer to the cluster as having the function.

(1) [...] and the *young lady with the black* eyes and the fur round the boots, whispered something in Emily's ear, and then [...] (*The Pickwick Papers*)

(2) [...] Thank you, Mr. Bumble, sir, *I am very much obliged* to you, I'm sure.' (*Oliver Twist*)

(3) [...] said Riderhood, when his visitor sat down, resting his chin on his hand, *with his eyes on the* ground. (*Our Mutual Friend*)

(4) Exceedingly red-eyed and grim, *as if he had been* up all night at a party which had taken anything but a convivial turn, Jerry Cruncher worried his breakfast rather than ate it, [...] (*A Tale of Two Cities*)

(5) Kit stood *in the middle of the* road [...]. (*The Old Curiosity Shop*)

Because of the functions they fulfil, clusters can be regarded as building blocks of fictional worlds. They point to settings in space and time, indicate the presence of a narrator, highlight themes, refer to characters and provide information on characters through their speech and body language. These observations are mainly based on the clusters in Dickens and would need further study for other novels. For Dickens the most important function of clusters seems to be the provision of character information which can be achieved by four out the five groups: labels, speech, body part clusters, but also *as if* clusters as illustrated in example (4). This fact might be related to the importance of characters in Dickens. In Dickens characters seem to be almost more important than plot (cf. also Kucich 1994: 403). More importantly, however, observations on clusters can be linked to the externalization of characters as will be explained below. A question about the applicability of the cluster approach to the analysis of specific texts is concerned with the frequency of the clusters. How many 'useful' clusters can be found for any one novel to draw some meaningful conclusions? Or does the usefulness of clusters lie in the cumulative picture that they provide for Dickens's novels as a whole? I will return to these questions, when I discuss two characters from the novel *Bleak House*. It will become clear that clusters alone provide only limited information and their main value lies in their consideration alongside other concepts and approaches. One such concept is the suspension.

2.2 Places: Suspensions

A 'suspension' is a span of five or more words of (narrator) text which interrupts a span of quoted speech (or thought, or writing). A suspension occurs in the same orthographic sentence as the speech it interrupts (Mahlberg and Smith 2010: 461). This definition is motivated by Lambert's (1981: 6) concept of the suspended quotation, which he describes as "a protracted interruption by the narrator of a character's speech", with 'protracted' meaning "containing at least five words". Lambert's (1981) main point about suspensions is that they reflect a hostile attitude of Dickens towards the characters he created. Leaving aside this very specific interpretation as well as technical detail as to differences between Lambert's definition and the one used here, suspensions seem to be a useful place to look for character information and specifically body language. The following is an example of a suspension (the suspension is highlighted in italics).

(6) "Once had a friend and brother serjeant of the same name," *says Mr. Bucket, offering his hand,* "and consequently feel a liking for it. Mrs. Chadband, no doubt?"

(*Bleak House*)

While the suspension interrupts the character's speech it also creates the impression of immediacy between the speech and body language. This is an important effect, as the description of body language in literature can seem lengthy compared to the time that would be taken up by the body language in the real world (cf. also Korte 1997). Also, in reality body language often accompanies speech. Thus, suspensions seem to be a useful place to create an effect of simultaneous representation. In addition to presenting body language, suspensions can also have other functions that will be illustrated in Section 3.2 below. Suspensions are not limited to Dickens, but also occur in the works of other authors. For a discussion of suspensions in *Pride and Prejudice* see Mahlberg and Smith (2010). Findings for suspensions also link in with observations by Busse (2010) on thought presentation and narrative reference to the thinker's eye. A corpus approach can aid the study of suspensions through the annotation of the text, so that concordance searches, for instance, can focus on the text in suspensions.

2.3 Interpreting the cues: Externalization of characters

John (2001) argues that characters in Dickens are externalized. She seeks to explain Dickens's approach to charaterization through his views on culture and the role of entertainment. With reference to Dickens's own writings on 'The Amusements of the People', for instance, John (2001) argues that Dickens believed in popular forms of entertainments as those best serve cultural inclusivity. John (2001) points out that for Dickens's characters the focus is not on hidden inner lives, but feelings and emotions that are displayed. Thus John (2001) draws parallels to the modes of melodrama where the ostension of character is prevalent. Although John (2001) does not explicitly discuss approaches to the representation of body language in literature, Korte's (1997) study provides support for John's argument (2001). Korte (1997) suggests a modal-functional approach to the description of body language, drawing on research on body language in the real world and linking her modal-functional categories to their functions in literary texts, such as characterization, dramatization or authentication. Korte's (1997) approach is based on the analysis of samples of texts from four different periods to identify tendencies as to the main categories of body language in each period. Because of the importance of Dickens for the 19th century, examples from his texts are naturally included to illustrate the various types of body language that Korte (1997) discusses. John's claims about Dickens's preferences for transparent characters is supported by Korte's (1997) observation on the importance of 'externalizers' in the 19th century, i.e. forms of body language that function to display relatively stable features of characters.

The interpretation of Dickens's approach to characterization as the externalization of characters is to some extent based on the observation that Dickens does not present the inner life of characters. Corpus stylistics is less suited for the discussion of what is not there than for an analysis of what is there. Unless the description of inner lives is linked to precise features that can be quantified, corpus findings cannot be interpreted as evidence of the absence of something. Additionally, Culpeper (2001) points out that while potentially any information could be relevant to the construction of character, contextual factors have an impact on how 'characteristic' behaviour is perceived to be or to what extent it is seen as being determined by its context. In the following section I want to address the question of what kind of character information clusters and suspensions can provide and how this information is to be interpreted in the textual context of the novel and the interpretative context of the externalization of character. This analysis will lead to an outline of some of the challenges that corpus stylistics is faced with.

3. Bucket and Tulkinghorn

In the following two sections I want to discuss the kind of character information that clusters and suspensions provide for Bucket and Tulkinghorn. Section 3.1 compares the two characters with regard to body language clusters that are found for them in *Bleak House*. Section 3.2 shows how concordance searches of the characters' names in suspensions reveal character information.

3.1 Clusters

The five groups of clusters illustrated above were identified by investigating clusters in a corpus of 23 texts by Charles Dickens (cf. Mahlberg 2007a). I have previously shown how viewing clusters in a single text can highlight thematic features and links between characters (cf. Mahlberg 2007b, 2007c) and how a general picture provided by clusters can serve as background for the analysis of a specific text extract (Mahlberg 2009). In the following, I want to focus on two characters in the novel *Bleak House* to examine what kind of character information clusters might provide and how this information relates to other character cues in the text. *Bleak House* contains 97 five-word clusters that occur at least five times. Most of the clusters are labels, i.e. they contain names or are otherwise specific to *Bleak House.* The three most frequent clusters are *not to put too fine, to put too fine a, put too fine a point* each occurring 15 times. They are classed as a label as they only appear in *Bleak House* (when looking at the Dickens Corpus and 19C). They are in fact part of Mr Snagsby's favourite phrase *not to put too fine a point (up)on it*. It does not seem necessary to employ the computer to find such phrases, as a major point about their existence in the novel is to be striking and noticeable. Such phrases have been described as 'tags' that can serve to identify characters and make the reader remember language or behaviour specific to a character.

Based on an initial overview of the five-word clusters in *Bleak House*, Bucket and Tulkinghorn appear as different kinds of characters. Bucket is associated with clusters such as *Sir Leicester Dedlock Baronet and, Sir Leicester Dedlock Baronet I, by Sir Leicester Dedlock Baronet, now Sir Leicester Dedlock Baronet* which show his fondness for using titles and also portray him in a comic way. Also his own title, *Inspector Bucket of the Detective*, appears among the clusters. For Tulkinghorn in contrast, there is no five-word cluster that is so strikingly associated with him. Tulkinghorn and Bucket still have sufficient similarities to enable a comparison between the two. Both are men of authority, and by virtue of their profession are associated with the law, Bucket as an inspector and Tulkinghorn as a lawyer and both are involved in discovering Lady Dedlock's secret.

If we focus on body language as character information, the five-word clusters provide different kinds of information for the two characters. Table 1 contains all five-word clusters in *Bleak House* that contain body parts or can be regarded as body language clusters because of the information they provide (*leaning back in his chair*). In addition to the frequencies of the clusters in *Bleak House*, Table 1 provides information on how often the clusters refer to Tulkinghorn (column 'T') and Bucket (column 'B'). Three of the clusters have occurrences that refer to Tulkinghorn. Bucket, in contrast does not have any body language clusters. What this information tells us is not that there is no description of body language for Bucket. It only tells us that there are no descriptions of body language that appear in repeated sequences of at least five words. Body language is in fact important for the description of Bucket, as one of his characteristic features is his use of his forefinger that is repeatedly referred to and described very pointedly in example (7):

(7) Mr. Bucket and his fat *forefinger* are much in consultation together under existing circumstances. When Mr. Bucket has a matter of this pressing interest under his consideration, the fat *forefinger* seems to rise, to the dignity of a familiar demon. He puts it to his ears, and it whispers information; he puts it to his lips, and it enjoins him to secrecy; he rubs it over his nose, and it sharpens his scent; he shakes it before a guilty man, and it charms him to his destruction. The Augurs of the Detective Temple invariably predict that when Mr. Bucket and that *finger* are in much conference, a terrible avenger will be heard of before long.

(Chapter 53)

Table 1. Body language clusters in *Bleak House*

Cluster	**BH**	**B**	**T**	**D**	**D texts**	**19C**	**19C texts**
his head against the wall	8	0	0	12	5	0	0
with his head against the	7	0	0	10	4	0	0
with his hands behind him	8	0	6	20	9	6	3
his hands in his pockets	5	0	2	90	20	13	8
with his back to the	5	0	2	43	14	22	11
leaning back in his chair	5	0	0	38	13	8	4

The body language of Tulkinghorn that is described by the clusters in Table 1 is not highlighted in the same way that Bucket's forefinger is. Instead, its meanings are defined through the contexts in which it appears. Table 1 gives some initial pointers to those contexts. The table shows the frequency of the clusters in *Bleak House*, their frequency in the whole Dickens Corpus and in a reference corpus made up of nineteenth century novels by authors other than Dickens. As the Dickens corpus and reference corpus are of similar size (about 4.5 million words each), numbers of occurrences in the corpus are not normalized. The table also contains the number of texts in the Dickens Corpus and the reference corpus in which the clusters occur. All clusters that refer to Tulkinghorn appear both in Dickens and in the reference corpus, which underlines the fact that the clusters can have different functions in different contexts. The cluster *his hands in his pockets*, for instance, which is the most frequent five-word body language cluster in Dickens can occur in contexts where it highlights exaggerated or comic behaviour as well as in contexts where it appears to add to the authenticity of a description (cf. Mahlberg 2007a). In example (8) Tulkinghorn's having his hands in his pockets is depicted as reflecting indifference, in example (9) his body language adds to show the calmness with which he conducts his conversation with Lady Dedlock.

(8) Mr. Tulkinghorn rises *with his hands in his pockets* and walks into one of the window recesses. "Now! I have no time to waste." In the midst of his perfect assumption of indifference, he directs a sharp look at the trooper, taking care to stand with his own back to the light and to have the other with his face towards it.

(Chapter 34)

(9) "My experience teaches me," says Mr. Tulkinghorn, who has by this time got *his hands in his pockets* and is going on in his business consideration of the matter like a machine. "My experience teaches me, [...]"

(Chapter 41)

The two cases of *with his back to the* refer to Tulkinghorn standing with his back to the fire/chimney-piece which was a common pose in the nineteenth century characteristic of men and associated with power as the fire was the most prominent place of the room (cf. Korte 1997: 212). The fact that Tulkinghorn is repeatedly depicted *with his hands behind him* points to him being calm, distanced and passionless. This becomes particularly apparent in example (10), where he and Krook find Nemo dead. Tulkinghorn does not show any interest when the doctor examines Nemo and discusses his cause of death with Krook. Tulkinghorn is described as standing "aloof", being "removed", his face is "imperturbable" and "inexpressive", all that he shows is his "shell".

(10) During this dialogue Mr. Tulkinghorn has stood aloof by the old portmanteau, *with his hands behind him*, equally removed, to all appearance, from all three kinds of interest exhibited near the bed – from the young surgeon's professional interest in death, noticeable as being quite apart from his remarks on the deceased as an individual; from the old man's unction; and the little crazy woman's awe. His imperturbable face has been as inexpressive as his rusty clothes. One could not even say he has been thinking all this while. He has shown neither patience nor impatience, nor attention nor abstraction. He has shown nothing but his shell. As easily might the tone of a delicate musical instrument be inferred from its case, as the tone of Mr. Tulkinghorn from his case.

(Chapter 11)

As the figures in Table 1 are relatively low, they are best interpreted as tendencies. Overall, they suggest that body language can occur with a range of different functions, appearing natural or unobtrusive or having more specific effects. This point is further supported by the distribution of the clusters *his head against the wall*/*with his head against the* which is neither related to Bucket nor Tulkinghorn. All instances of the two clusters in *Bleak House* refer to the same character (Mr Jellyby) and the body language identifies him uniquely. These clusters do not occur in the reference corpus, and their overall occurrence in the Dickens corpus as well as the distribution across chapters is lower than for the other clusters. This seems to reflect the unique function of these clusters in *Bleak House* and shows another option of highlighting character information: the body language functions in a way similar to Snagby's favourite phrase or the clusters reflecting Bucket's fondness of titles as exemplified above.

3.2 Suspensions

The concordance in Figure 1 shows the occurrences of *Bucket* in suspensions. Suspensions fall into three groups with regard to the character information that they provide. They can contain body language, the narrator's interpretation of speech or direct characterization, as illustrated by examples (11) to (13) respectively. Example (11) describes body language so that it is left to the reader to draw conclusions from this observation. In example (12) in contrast, the reader only gets the narrator's interpretation of the way in which Bucket speaks, but there is no information as to the extent to which the *very seriously* is reflected by the tone of Buckets voice, his facial expression or maybe even his posture. Example (13) is even less descriptive. In relation to Bucket's speech, the information in the suspension does not provide additional detail on how he speaks but comments on what he says. The narrator emphasizes that Buckets likes to use full titles, which the reader may have already noticed because of Bucket's repeated use of *Sir Leicester Dedlock, Baronet*. However, by making this point in a suspension and presenting it as a character trait it receives even more prominence.

(11) "[…] And Lord," says Mr. Bucket, opening his arms, "here's children too! […]"
(12) "Sir Leicester Dedlock, Baronet," returns Mr. Bucket very seriously, "I hope it may […]"
(13) "Sir Leicester Dedlock, Baronet," proceeds Mr. Bucket, who delights in a full title and does violence to himself when he dispenses with any fragment of it, "the last point in the case […]"

The initial categorization of character information in suspensions into three types provides a simplified account, as categories also overlap. Example (14) illustrates body language that is not only described but also interpreted: Bucket does not only have his head on one side, but his head is *persuasively* on one side. Additionally, the reference to his forefinger has to be seen as part of a bigger picture. Bucket's use of his forefinger is presented as a character trait and is referred to repeatedly. Its significance is explained explicitly in example (7) above. In example (14) the presence of the forefinger points to the importance of the secret conversation between Bucket and Sir Leicester. In the concordance in

Figure 1, there are five occurrence of the *(fore)finger* visible in the given context (there are more if the suspensions are viewed in full) illustrating this characteristic feature.

1	other. "I don't mind telling YOU," says	Bucket	with an engaging appearance of frankness
2	stinctly. "Now, what YOU want," pursues	Bucket,	again tapping Mr. Snagsby on the breast
3	n't what you endeavour to do," says Mr.	Bucket,	shaking hands with him and blessing him
4	ight." "You see, Mr. Snagsby," says Mr.	Bucket,	accompanying him to the door and shaking
5	ugh workman. And you needn't," says Mr.	Bucket	in a considerate and private voice, "you
6	uld speak. "Now, George," continues Mr.	Bucket,	putting his hat upon the table with an a
7	you suspect ME?" "George," returns Mr.	Bucket,	keeping his forefinger going, "it is cer
8	uld you believe it, governor," says Mr.	Bucket,	struck by the coincidence, "that when I
9	der?" "Murder!" "Now, George," says Mr.	Bucket,	keeping his forefinger in an impressive
10	thunderstruck. "Now, George," says Mr.	Bucket,	urging a sensible view of the case upon
11	sides. "Now George, old boy," says Mr.	Bucket,	taking his arm at the shop-door, "come a
12	with you, governor? And Lord," says Mr.	Bucket,	opening his arms, "here's children too!
13	ted station of society, miss," says Mr.	Bucket,	quite reddening at another narrow escape
14	YOU know life, you know, sir," says Mr.	Bucket	with a complimentary twinkle of his eye
15	rpose. "Why you see, miss," returns Mr.	Bucket,	bringing the finger into persuasive acti
16	eicester Dedlock, Baronet," returns Mr.	Bucket	very seriously, "I hope it may at one an
17	twenty-four hours. "And this," says Mr.	Bucket,	spreading it out on the table, "is in th
18	ifference. Now I think of it," says Mr.	Bucket,	warming his hands and looking pleasantly
19	s a beautiful case, you see, miss," Mr.	Bucket	goes on, glancing gravely at Sir Leicest
20	icester Dedlock, Baronet," proceeds Mr.	Bucket,	who delights in a full title and does vi
21	eicester Dedlock, Baronet," returns Mr.	Bucket	with his head persuasively on one side a
22	es!" "Now, when you're ready," says Mr.	Bucket	after awaiting his recovery, "to come to
23	r Leicester Dedlock, Baronet," says Mr.	Bucket,	and from this time forth the finger neve
24	ything(this bit of business," says Mr.	Bucket	--Sir Leicester mechanically bows his he
25	y, of course you wanted to get in," Mr.	Bucket	asserts with cheerfulness; "but for a ol
26	a menace. "Now, mademoiselle," says Mr.	Bucket	in a cool determined way, "you go and si
27	man of business, you are," returns Mr.	Bucket,	very attentive, "and consequently you're
28	ded is now in this house," proceeds Mr.	Bucket,	putting up his watch with a steady hand
29	w, Sir Leicester Dedlock, Baronet," Mr.	Bucket	begins, standing over him with one hand
30	m limb." "Bless you, darling," says Mr.	Bucket	with the greatest composure, "I'm fully
31	Don't you think any more," returns Mr.	Bucket	with admonitory finger, "of throwing you
32	er serjeant of the same name," says Mr.	Bucket,	offering his hand, "and consequently fee
33	nods. "Now, mademoiselle," repeats Mr.	Bucket,	making no demonstration except with the
34	y man." "Now I tell you what," says Mr.	Bucket,	instantaneously altering his manner, com
35	None was charged against him," said Mr.	Bucket,	coolly lifting off his hat, "but I suppo
36	out of employment, I believe," said Mr.	Bucket	apologetically for Michael Jackson, "and
37	y--" "Who has been here, you know," Mr.	Bucket	struck in, addressing the whole group wi
38	o with great speed. "My dear," said Mr.	Bucket,	jumping to his seat and looking in again
39	t's possible, Miss Summerson," said Mr.	Bucket,	pondering on it, "that her ladyship sent
40	the only amends you can make," said Mr.	Bucket,	rapidly glancing at it, "is to let me sp
41	And to hold the candle," pursued Mr.	Bucket	without correcting himself, "or hold her
42	arrow street. "Mr. Woodcourt," said Mr.	Bucket,	who had eyed him closely as we came alon
43	ce. "In consequence of which," said Mr.	Bucket,	dismissing his agreeable manner all at o
44	d so you chance to find, you know," Mr.	Bucket	went on, stooping over him with an air o
45	e. That's the drollery of it," said Mr.	Bucket	with the same lively air of recalling a

Figure 1. Concordance of *Bucket* in suspensions

(14) "Why, Sir Leicester Dedlock, Baronet," returns Mr. Bucket *with his head persuasively on one side* and his *forefinger* pendant at one ear like an earring, "we can't be too private just at present. […]"

(Chapter 54)

The forefinger is one example of how information in suspensions has to be seen in relation to a wider textual context. There are also examples in which the textual relations are more immediate. In concordance line 2, the adverb *again* points to the relationship illustrated by examples (15a) and (15b) which are a few lines apart. Here Bucket repeatedly taps Snagsby on the breast and the repetition is highlighted in the suspension. Examples (16a) and (16b) also show related examples. This time both are suspensions, corresponding to concordance lines 44 and 45 respectively. Although the wording is not exactly repeated the similarity between the suspensions is underlined through the repetition of *same*: *the same lively air* and *the same crest-fallen appearance* which emphasizes Smallweed feeling very uncomfortable in the position Buckets put him in. Example (16) not only shows the extent a suspension can take on, it also illustrates that suspensions do not necessarily contain information that refers (only) to the speaker. In suspensions the narrator can also comment on the effects that the manner of speech and its accompanying actions can have on other characters. It seems that the more information is packed into a suspension the more it actually interrupts the flow of speech which in turn also gives prominence to the information in the suspension.

(15) a. "Yes! And lookee here, Mr. Snagsby," resumes Bucket, taking him aside by the arm, *tapping him familiarly on the breast*, and speaking in a confidential tone.

b. "Now, what YOU want," pursues Bucket, *again tapping Mr. Snagsby on the breast* in a comfortable and soothing manner, "is […]"

(Chapter 22)

(16) a. "[…] so you chance to find, you know," Mr. Bucket went on, stooping over him with an air of cheerful raillery which Mr. Smallweed by no means reciprocated, "and so you chance to find, you know, a paper with the signature of Jarndyce to it. Don't you?"

b. "[…] That's the drollery of it," said Mr. Bucket with the *same* lively air of recalling a joke for the enjoyment of Mr. Smallweed, who still had the *same* crest-fallen appearance of not enjoying it at all; "what do you find it to be but a will?"

(Chapter 62)

Compared to example (16), example (11) contains relatively unobtrusive information: the suspension is much shorter and it does not contain narrator's interpretation or comment. Instead of focusing on the interruption that a suspension entails to the flow of speech, in the case of example (11) the suspension seems to suggest a simultaneousness of Bucket's body language with his speech. He has just entered the room and greeted all the adults before he now addresses the children and gives them a hug.

When a suspension contains explicit character information, as in example (13) above, or refers to character traits that occur repeatedly, such as Bucket's use of his forefinger, it appears straightforward to see them as textual cues for characterization. For examples such as (12), however, it is not immediately obvious whether Bucket's seriousness is part of his character or whether it results from the kind of situation he is faced with. This question is not specific to examples in suspensions but holds for all potential textual cues of character information. Culpeper (2001) draws on attribution theory to assess the relevance of textual cues. However, it seems that the analysis of the concordance in Figure 1 also gives some pointers as to how individual instances fit into a bigger picture. We find examples that present Bucket as pleasant or cheerful: line 1 "with an engaging appearance", line 18 "looking pleasantly at the blaze", line 25 "asserts with cheerfulness". But there are also examples showing him more serious and composed: line 19 "glancing gravely at Sir Leicester, line 26 "in a cool determined manner, line 30 "with the greatest composure. At the same time, the concordance also contains information that helps explain such variety in behaviour. Line 34 refers to an instance of Bucket "instantaneously altering his manner", or line 43 shows him "dismissing his agreeable manner all at once and becoming strictly business-like". He is able to adjust his behaviour and uses this ability strategically. We can see his versatility as a characteristic feature. Throughout the novel Bucket appears very friendly and cheerful, but also very serious and business-like. This feature is very apparent in Chapter 49 when he arrests his friend George. He does what he sees as his duty as an officer investigating a murder case, but he also wants to "make things as pleasant as is consistent with [his] duty" and offers George the option of more comfortable handcuffs. With the detail that the suspensions provide on Bucket, they appear as useful places to look for information on this character. It is important, however, to stress that the investigation of suspensions, as all corpus stylistics methods, is not a replacement for reading the novel. It is a method to complement the 'manual' analysis of the novel. For instance, one of the aspects that the suspension information links up with is Bucket's way of suggesting that his presence is incidental. Similar to adjusting his manner to serve his investigation, he also tries to make his presence appear natural. When he arrests George he appears to be joining in the celebration of Mrs Bagnet's birthday (cf. Chapter 49), or when he recounts how he saw Lady Dedlock in the garden at night he claims to have been on his way to visit his aunt (cf. Chapter 53).

By highlighting Bucket's variation in manner and attempts of being calculating and appearing controlled the opposite effect is created. He is not portrayed as a subtle person, but has a very strong presence, much like his active forefinger. Limits to his attempts at controlled behaviour are illustrated in examples (17a) and (17b) below (corresponding to concordance lines 15 and 13): Bucket finds it hard to avoid being overly friendly which is not only made clear through the narrator's comment but also through Bucket's reddening – body language that he cannot control.

(17) a. "Why you see, miss," returns Mr. Bucket, bringing the finger into persuasive action – and such is his natural gallantry that he had almost said "my dear" – "it ain't easy to […]"
b. "[…] society, miss," says Mr. Bucket, quite reddening at another narrow escape from "my dear."
(Chapter 53)

Also his business-like manner appears not to fit the business he is in, as shown by example (18), corresponding to concordance line 6:

(18) "Now, George," continues Mr. Bucket, putting his hat upon the table with an air of business rather in the upholstery way than otherwise, "my […]"
(Chapter 49)

In contrast to inspector Bucket, the lawyer Tulkinghorn is portrayed as more reserved and calculating. The concordance in Figure 2 contains the occurrences of *Tulkinghorn* and *lawyer* in suspensions. Only those suspensions are listed that refer to Tulkinghorn's speech. I added *lawyer* to the search to obtain more examples. In line 1 Tulkinghorn is described as "a cautious man", line 7 refers to "his methodical, subdued, uninterested way", line 10 to "his jog- trot style", line 17 to "his dry passionless manner". The possessive *his* highlights these references to his manner as permanent features, thus examples such as line 11 "returns methodically" and 16 "with undisturbed calmness" fit into the picture of permanent features.

It is ironic that although Tulkinghorn appears to be cautious and systematic, he ends up being killed by Hortense, a minor character whom he thinks he can easily threaten. While Bucket in contrast appears less professional with his exaggerated gallantry or his business approach that resembles that of an upholsterer, he is successful in solving a murder case. Tulkinghorn's passionless manner not only relates to him being methodical, it also is a sign of him being aloof. Concordance lines 19 and 20 are given below in examples (19). Here Tulkinghorn threatens that he will have Hortense arrested if she comes to see him uninvited again. Although he apologizes for being "unpolite", his aim is to threaten her and he takes no note of her reactions. The two suspensions highlight that he continues "without minding her".

(19) "In a word, mistress," says Mr. Tulkinghorn, "I am sorry to be unpolite, but if you ever present yourself uninvited here – or there – again, I will give you over to the police. Their gallantry is great, but they carry troublesome people through the streets in an ignominious manner, strapped down on a board, my good wench."

"I will prove you," whispers mademoiselle, stretching out her hand, "I will try if you dare to do it!"

"And if," *pursues the lawyer without minding her*, "I place you in that good condition of being locked up in jail, it will be some time before you find yourself at liberty again."

"I will prove you," repeats mademoiselle in her former whisper.

"And now," *proceeds the lawyer, still without minding her*, "you had better go. Think twice before you come here again."

(Chapter 42)

1	oceedings in a cause--cautious man Mr.	Tulkinghorn,	taking no more responsibility than neces
2	you say?" "I say I am afraid," says Mr.	Tulkinghorn,	who had risen hastily, "that Lady Dedloc
3	did." "There was one of them," says Mr.	Tulkinghorn,	carelessly feeling-- tight, unopenable o
4	it." "Hadn't you better see," says Mr.	Tulkinghorn	to Krook, "whether he had any papers tha
5	, my dear." "I supposed, sergeant," Mr.	Tulkinghorn	resumes as he leans on one side of his c
6	u can go. So you are the man," says Mr.	Tulkinghorn,	opening his door with the key, "in whose
7	es the air. "The question is," says Mr.	Tulkinghorn	in his methodical, subdued, uninterested
8	n--Mob. "It's the place, you know," Mr.	Tulkinghorn	goes on to say in the fast-increasing da
9	y. "And he was much assisted," says Mr.	Tulkinghorn	as a wind-up, "by his son." "By his son,
10	arable." "Go on!" "Therefore," says Mr.	Tulkinghorn,	pursuing his case in his jog- trot style
11	g more to be said to-night?" "Why," Mr.	Tulkinghorn	returns methodically as he softly rubs h
12	wide open. "Now, let us see," says Mr.	Tulkinghorn,	tapping his chin with the key and lookin
13	dismissed by your lady, you know," Mr.	Tulkinghorn	observes, following her out upon the sta
14	r." "She seems after all," observes Mr.	Tulkinghorn,	loitering a little forward with his hand
15	concentrated. "This woman," thinks Mr.	Tulkinghorn,	standing on the hearth, again a dark obj
16	lly-- I was about to say," resumes the	lawyer	with undisturbed calmness, "that whether
17	have got it here, sir." "Sergeant," the	lawyer	proceeds in his dry passionless manner,
18	matters this much, mistress," says the	lawyer,	deliberately putting away his handkerchi
19	u dare to do it!" "And if," pursues the	lawyer	without minding her, "I place you in tha
20	former whisper. "And now," proceeds the	lawyer,	still without minding her, "you had bett
21	nt, sir?" "Why, Lady Dedlock," says the	lawyer,	taking a chair at a little distance from

Figure 2. Concordance of *Tulkinghorn* in suspensions

While Tulkinghorn only threatens Hortense, it is in fact Bucket who arrests her. Bucket talks to Hortense "in a cool determined way" (cf. line 26 in Figure 1), but he still stresses that he wants to be polite if possible and he insists that she sits down on the sofa and makes herself comfortable.

The character information that is revealed through the study of suspensions complements the information revealed by body language clusters. While Bucket appears as more engaged, communicative and hands-on in the literal sense of the word, Tulkinghorn is portrayed as distanced and passionless. Buckets gets closer to people and the movements of his forefinger accompany his speech and actions. Tulkinghorn, in contrast, is shown to have his hands in his pockets or behind him, which in the given contexts can be interpreted as showing distance.

4. Challenges for corpus stylistics

Clusters resemble lexical bundles in that they are repeated sequences of words. However, the term 'lexical bundle' in the sense of Biber et al. (1999) is clearly defined through criteria of frequency and distribution. Biber et al. (1999: 993) want to exclude idiosyncracies of individual speakers or writers and therefore focus on bundles that appear across at least five different texts. Thus clusters such as *not to put too fine* that are part of Mr Snagsby's favourite phrase and only occur in one text in Dickens and nowhere in 19C would be excluded. The cluster *his hands in his pockets* occurs in eight texts in 19C so meets the minimum requirement for distribution. For five-word lexical bundles Biber et al. (1999: 993) use a cut-off of five per million, which *his hands in his pockets* meets when we look at its frequency in a corpus made up of both the Dickens corpus and 19C. When we only consider the frequency of this cluster in a corpus consisting of 19C and *Bleak House* the cluster only just misses the five per million threshold. Put differently, *his hands in his pockets* is significantly more frequent (or a 'key cluster') in the Dickens corpus compared to 19C (cf. also Mahlberg 2007a).

The definition of lexical bundles uses cut-offs so that characteristics of a register or "general building blocks used frequently by many different speakers/writers within a register" (Biber 2006: 174, endnote 4) can be found. By collecting clusters based on the requirement that a cluster has to occur a minimum of five times in one text, clusters are found that might be lexical bundles, but they do not have to be; the clusters might be key clusters, but do not have to be. Also finding a cluster in a text does not automatically mean that the cluster is necessarily associated with one character. We have seen that of the five occurrences of *his hands in his pockets* only two refer to Tulkinghorn, but those two still add to the picture that is created of the character Tulkinghorn. Thus, I initially want to see the relevance of clusters in the following way: clusters are building blocks of fictional worlds in the sense that they reflect aspects of the fictional world – mainly through the description of characters, comments by the narrator and references to place and time. Clusters are different from lexical bundles reflecting discourse functions of a given register, because they may be less frequent or less general. However, the areas of meanings that the clusters refer to – reflected not by individual clusters but by cluster groups – are general aspects of the fictional world. While individual clusters in the group may not be frequent, a group such as 'body language' clusters refers to general aspects of the novel.

To quantitatively assess the significance of the findings, however, is not straightforward. Already the notion of normalization to compare the number of occurrences of body language expressions across different texts causes some questions. Novels will normally contain different numbers of characters, individual characters differ in the space they take up in a novel, and the descriptions of characters may vary with regard to the level of detail that can be found. Some characters may speak more, while others are presented more through description. It is easy to see how this list could be continued. However, related to the quantitative information that corpus methods can provide is the fact that already the organization and display of textual patterns can contribute to discovering information that may be less clearly visible when simply reading a text. By looking at character names in suspensions, prominent places for character information are grouped together and thus highlight the information provided in these places.

Body language in literature seems to be an area where the study of clusters (and then more flexible patterns) and suspensions can make an important contribution. While Korte's (1997) study provides a very comprehensive overview of different types of body language in literature, surprisingly little research seems to have been done to study the forms and patterns in which body language is expressed in literary texts. If we want to follow Culpeper's (2001) approach, the impressions that readers form about body language are affected by the cues in the text. At the same time, they are affected by the readers' knowledge of people in the real world. In the real world, we typically perceive body language by looking at people, while in literary texts we encounter descriptions of body language. When readers relate the character information in the text to their knowledge of people, their views on what is 'normal' body language for a person, may be different from what is 'normal' body language for a specific character simply because of the linguistic forms in which the body language is presented. Also, the description of body language has different functions in literary texts than in non-literary texts. So non-literary texts may not be very useful to find out how 'normal' body language is typically described. A search for the cluster *his hands in his pocket* in the BNC returns only one hit and the occurrence is from a classroom discourse where the discussion seems to refer to *Oliver Twist*.

Findings about body language in literature can also reveal information about the body language of the time and links to other sources of information on body language might be useful, e.g. etiquette books or guides for actors. While this option is not available for 19th century data, linking findings in literature with the study of multi-modal corpora additionally suggests ways of investigating the relationship between the body language of real people and descriptions of body language. However, methods for the analysis of multi-modal corpora might contribute to studying links between novels and their screen adaptations to find out to what extent body language in the film corresponds to what is described in the book. Such approaches will need consideration in the further development of corpus stylistics.

Another promising link to be followed is between corpus stylistics and psycholinguistics. Corpus studies can reveal patterns and highlight places in the literary text that appear to be relevant for providing cues about body language and ultimately characters. However, to what extent readers are aware of such patterns cannot be determined by looking at corpus data alone. It is often pointed out as one of the key achievements of corpus linguistics that corpus findings can reveal information about the language that language users are not aware of. In particular, language users do not seem to be very good at making frequency judgements. Further investigations as to how readers perceive repetitions of patterns may add to our understanding of why some body language of characters is perceived as habitual while other body language may go unnoticed but still contributes to the overall impression of a character.

Particular questions that seem to call for participant testing also relate to suspensions. Lambert (1981) claims that suspensions that are five or more words long appear to be "intrusive". He admits that he does not have firm evidence as to why five is a crucial number here, but his hunch might be related to the observation in psychology that sequences of about five words is what most people will be able to store in their short term memory. Additionally, it is not only the length of the interruption but also the kind of information that affects the readers' perception. In example (11) above, the suspension contains information that contextualizes Bucket's speech. In Korte's (1997) terminology, "opening his arms" is an illustrator, i.e. body language that functions to support the verbal information. Example (12), in contrast, contains a comment by the narrator that does not refer to body language at all, but gives an evaluation of Bucket's behaviour. A question to investigate further is to what extent readers notice the difference between body language that is presented as such, or comments by the narrator that suggest underlying body language.

The examples discussed here are based on observations in Dickens and the study of other authors can contribute further questions. Overall, however, crucial challenges for corpus stylistics refer to the fact that quantitative data in literary texts might have to be treated differently to quantitative data in large corpora. While large amounts of data enable the testing of statistical significance, corpus stylistics emphasizes the need for detailed qualitative interpretation. In this process the investigation of clusters and suspensions provides a starting-point for identifying textual functions and links to literary criticism. As the fictional worlds created in literary texts depend on the way in which readers process textual cues, corpus stylistics faces a major challenge in relating textual patterns to cognitive processes. Patterns identified by corpus methods and the development of descriptive concepts in corpus stylistics can inform further psycholinguistic research. The developments that corpus stylistics will be able to make with regard to linking textual cues to the description of cognitive processes as well as the wider context of criticism will determine whether the fiction we are dealing with is in the text or in the approach.

Notes

1 I would like to thank Catherine Smith for the XML mark-up of the texts and her help with providing a concordance tool to search the XML texts.

References

Biber, D. (2006), *University Language: A Corpus-based Study of Spoken and Written Registers*. Amsterdam: John Benjamins.

Biber, D., S. Johansson, G. Leech, S. Conrad and E. Finegan (1999), *Longman Grammar of Spoken and Written English*. Harlow: Longman.

Busse, B. (2010), 'Recent trends in new historical stylistics', in: D. McIntyre and B. Busse (eds.), *Language and Style*. Basingstoke: Palgrave Macmillan. 32-54.

Carter, R. (2004), *Language and Creativity: The Art of Common Talk*. London: Routledge.

Carter, R. (2010), 'Methodologies for stylistic analysis: Practices and pedagogies', in: D. McIntyre and B. Busse (eds.), *Language and Style*. Basingstoke: Palgrave Macmillan. 55-68.

Chapelle, C.A. (2011), *The Encyclopedia of Applied Linguistics*. Oxford: Wiley-Blackwell.

Culpeper, J. (2001), *Language and Characterisation: People in Plays and Other Texts*. Harlow: Pearson Education.

Jeffries, L. and D. McIntyre (2010), *Stylistics*. Cambridge: Cambridge University Press.

John, J. (2001), *Dickens's Villains: Melodrama, Character, Popular Culture*. Oxford: Oxford University Press.

Korte, B. (1997), *Body Language in Literature*. Toronto: University of Toronto Press.

Kucich, J. (1994), 'Dickens', in: J. Richetti (ed.), *The Columbia History of the British Novel*. New York, NY: Columbia University Press. 381-406.

Lambert, M. (1981), *Dickens and the Suspended Quotation*. New Haven, CT: Yale University Press.

Leech, G. and M. Short (2007), *Style in Fiction: A Linguistic Introduction to English Fictional Prose*. 2nd edition. London: Pearson Education.

Lindquist, H. (2009), *Corpus Linguistics and the Description of English*. Edinburgh: Edinburgh University Press.

Mahlberg, M. (2007a), 'Clusters, key clusters and local textual functions in Dickens', *Corpora*, 2: 1-31.

Mahlberg, M. (2007b), 'Corpus stylistics: Bridging the gap between linguistic and literary studies', in: M. Hoey, M. Mahlberg, M. Stubbs and W. Teubert (eds.), *Text, Discourse and Corpora: Theory and Analysis*. London: Continuum. 219-246.

Mahlberg, M. (2007c), 'A corpus stylistic perspective on Dickens' *Great Expectations*', in: M. Lambrou and P. Stockwell (eds.), *Contemporary Stylistics*. London: Continuum. 19-31.

Mahlberg, M. (2009), 'Corpus stylistics and the Pickwickian watering-pot', in: P. Baker (ed.), *Contemporary Corpus Linguistics*. London: Continuum. 47-63.

Mahlberg, M. and C. Smith (2010), 'Corpus approaches to prose fiction: Civility and body language in *Pride and Prejudice*', in: D. McIntyre and B. Busse (eds.), *Language and Style*. Basingstoke: Palgrave Macmillan. 449-467.
McIntyre, D. (2010), 'Dialogue and characterization in Quentin Tarantino's *Reservoir Dogs:* A corpus stylistic analysis', in: D. McIntyre and B. Busse (eds.), *Language and Style*. Basingstoke: Palgrave Macmillan. 162-182.
McIntyre, D. and B. Busse (eds.) (2010), *Language and Style*. Basingstoke: Palgrave Macmillan.
O'Keeffe, A. and M. McCarthy (eds.) (2010), *The Routledge Handbook of Corpus Linguistics*. Abingdon: Routledge.

How can Joseph Wright's *English Dialect Dictionary* be used as a corpus?

Manfred Markus

University of Innsbruck

Abstract

The paper will first provide a short introduction to EDD Online, and then illustrate the potential of its interface by topicalising interjections as a word class and compounding as a productive type of word formation in dialect. In Section 3 the theoretical question of a dictionary used as a corpus will be tackled. Section 4 is dedicated to the contents and structure of Wright's sources, Section 5 to what he calls "citations". Quantitatively speaking, probably more than half of Wright's English Dialect Dictionary *(EDD), now available in a beta version from the Innsbruck project EDD Online, consists of citations, i.e. text passages from dialect literature, glossaries or other sources. While these citation passages are meant to illustrate particular lexical points, they are often fairly extensive, so that the idea may occur to isolate them from the rest of the entries to create an autonomous dialect corpus. My paper will investigate the feasibility of this idea, mainly analysing in close-up Wright's citations and the sources attributed to them. Further aspects to consider will be the dates of sources, as well as the correlation of the sources with dialectal areas and formal features of word formation including compounds, derivations, and phrases. The study will give evidence that the EDD provides not just some kind of a corpus of dialect texts, but a very structured one, with time, place and source being the main parameters.*

1. Introduction to Wright's *English Dialect Dictionary*

There have been several general introductions to Joseph Wright's *English Dialect Dictionary* (EDD) and to EDD Online, mainly published by members of the Innsbruck project SPEED (*Spoken English in Early Dialects*). The present introduction can, therefore, be short, focussing on the main facts concerning Wright and the data and figures that demonstrate the comprehensive quality of the EDD. Moreover, a basic overview of EDD Online will be given, demonstrating the enormous potential for queries and research opportunities that the electronic version of the dictionary offers.

The official publishing years of the EDD are 1898 to 1905, but the nearly 5,000-page dictionary required a far more substantial investment of time, both by Wright and his many helpers. Wright started working on the dictionary in the early 1880s and relied on over 1,000 sources, and more than 12,000 questionnaires. With his team he gathered 1.5 million "slips" (EDD Pref. 1898-1905: I,iv), the pieces of paper on which lemmas were collected. While the number of lemmas included in the EDD only amounts to some 65,000, the many compounds, word "combinations", derivations and phrases add to that figure considerably, so that the number of dialect "words" in the dictionary can be estimated to be twice or thrice as high as that of the lemmatised words.

The EDD is imposing not only in quantitative terms, but also qualitatively – by its historical dimension and excellent philological quality. In terms of historical dialectology, the six volumes cover the time from 1700 to 1900, but many of the sources take us back to the Early Modern English period and, in fact, to Middle English (for a detailed description of the sources see Markus 2009). As a scholar and person, Wright was the ideal director of the EDD project. Due to his experience as a child worker he had a strong sense of solidarity with the people whose language he seems to have known better than most other dialectologists. His object of study was motivated by his background as a Yorkshire dialect speaker. Moreover, he spent 6 1/2 years studying and doing research with renowned scholars in Heidelberg and Leipzig, who equipped him with a remarkable competence in German and historical linguistics. As a result of this neogrammarian schooling, he later wrote grammars and/or primers of German, Gothic and various historical phases of both English and German, partly with his wife Elizabeth Mary Wright. She shared his linguistic interests, was very much fascinated by dialects and cultural studies (to use the modern term) and was one of the most committed amongst the 600 helpers who supported the EDD project.[1]

In other words, Wright was the ideal figure to be the compiler of the EDD; moreover, he lived at a time when (rural) dialect was still in full swing. This coincidence of positive and supportive factors may hold a certain caveat for all those researchers who are now planning to compile an English dialect corpus but do not share Wright's home advantages. They may care to have a look at the complexity of EDD entries, e.g. in view of common-and-garden words such as *go*. Such words are, of course, not interesting as such, but rather with respect to their variant forms, their specific dialectal meanings and usages. Figure 1 shows that the verb/noun *go* occurs in 24 present tense forms. Underneath these forms, dialect sources ('Cum.1' for a special glossary of Cumberland dialect as identified in Wright's reference list), dialect areas ('Cum.') and quotations ("He gaas net to kirk...") are listed, correlated to the grammatical forms of the first paragraph by the numbers in parentheses.

The search filters in Figure 1 – in addition to various query options outside its frame of reference – help users to retrieve entry sections according to dialect area, but also according to seven other criteria which may be of philological interest, from parts of speech to time span and etymology. I have given evidence of the complexity of the EDD and, accordingly, of the EDD Online interface in a recent paper (Markus, forthcoming).

To simplify matters for this introduction, we may schematically attribute the large number of entry sections to either of two informative purposes, the 'what' of the material, and the 'where (and when)' of its attribution. The former comprises grammatical forms, variants, meanings of lemmas as well as compounds, combinations and phrases, and their respective meanings. The 'where (and when)' of the attribution mainly includes sources (and their dates), dialect markers and citations.

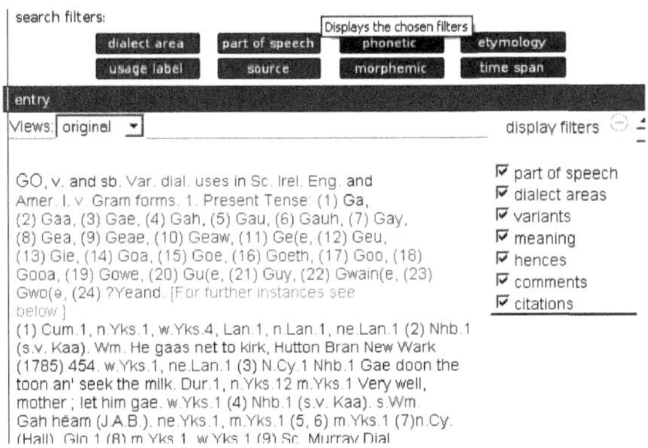

Figure 1. Screen shot with search results for GO

2. Two examples of innovative results: Interjections and compounding

As the proof of the pudding is in its eating, I suggest looking at EDD Online 'in action' by discussing two topics that can claim some innovative value, at least in view of English dialect. The first is the – highly neglected – role of interjections. To summarise the results of another paper, which focusses on this "Cinderella" of word classes (Markus, forthcoming): interjections are an important dimension of spoken language and, therefore, of dialects. They contribute to the strategy of solidarity that has been identified as the central function of dialect use (Soukup 2009). They are not "the negation of language" (Jespersen 1923: 415), but – in line with everyday needs – a most flexible instrument of language. As simple (= monomorphemic) interjections they tend to be iconic, short survivals from the past and products of allegro effects. As complex interjections they are often non-transparent in word formation and function, at least at first sight. A query for interjections in EDD Online, triggered by the part-of-speech filter 'interjection', provided 738 hits in total.

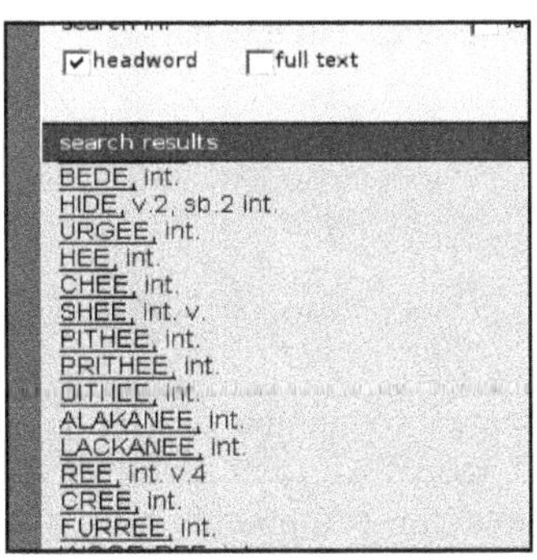

Figure 2. Extract of list of interjections arranged in the reverse mode

Figure 2 shows an extract of the list of these hits after the activation of the reverse sorting mode so that suffixes and final syllable structures of words may more easily be studied. We can learn from this extract that in some of the *-ee* words the assumed 'suffix' stands for a distorted *ye* ('you'), as in *urgee* and *prithee.* On the other hand, *lackanee* now appears as an obvious clipping of *alackanee. Alackanee* derives from *Alas on yee* (as Wright convincingly explains), but *lackanee*, which basically means the same thing as *alackanee,* is left unexplained. In other words: without the advantage of the reverse arrangement, i.e. corpus linguistics, even Wright was not in a position to see the connection between the two words.

Another interesting and innovative aspect of interjections is their pragmatics, particularly in view of the implied addressee of a word. 153 interjections in the EDD are used for addressing animals – the high figure does not come as a surprise since animals, especially in their functional form as helpers to man, played clearly a more important role in rural life up to the 19th century than today. In Markus (forthcoming) I have given a "ranking list" of animals as addressees of interjections in the EDD, with horses, pigs, dogs and cattle ranking highest. The terms addressed to horses alone, mostly commands, would be worth a detailed discussion. But, in fact, the whole fauna plays a role in the EDD according to its relevance to man and as a productive contributor to metaphors (for some of the details cf. Markus, forthcoming).

Another topic where EDD Online may be used fruitfully as a corpus is the productivity of compounding. Everyday language use (at least in English and German) suggests that native speakers are fairly productive in coining new compounds. *Milkman* may be classified as a lexicalised compound, but if a man brings or produces or takes care of yoghurt or cream or whatever, we readily refer to him *ad hoc* as 'the yoghurt man', 'the cream man', etc. This creative language use may be subject to individual and language specificity, but is – like colloquialisms and slang – mainly a feature of spoken language. It can, therefore, be expected in dialect, in particular with (easily memorable) words of obvious high frequency. Table 1 provides a survey of the high productivity of such words in the EDD in forming dialectal compounds.

Table 1. Readiness of words to be determinata of compounds (EDD Online)

-man	192	-foot	60
-house	142	-horse	47
-head	136	-dog	32
-hand	65	-woman	31
-way	65		

Table 1 only lists a random collection of hyphenated compound determinata. Given that separate spellings without a hyphen, and, moreover, joint spellings are two other options for compounds, the real figures for compounds with the determinata listed in Table 1 are much higher. ~ *man*, for example, occurs 7,559 times, ~*man* more than 16,000 times.[2] Admittedly these figures include findings of either a compound or a syntactic group. What is worse, they include strings (like in *manner*) that have nothing to do with the lexeme *man*. While they are quantitatively unreliable, going through the result list reveals at first sight that productive and *ad hoc* compounding seems to have been one of the 'joys' of using dialect.

To demonstrate how this *ad hoc* compounding works, the following list provides five random examples of compounds with *-man*, *-house* and *-head*.

fortune-man: 'a prophet, a diviner'
beggar-man: 'a beggar'
hot-house: 'the stove in which salt is dried in saltmaking'
air-head in mining: 'a passage for ventilation'
*besom-head**: 'the joint in an apple-tree trunk where the branches separate'

The meanings of these words are partly self-evident, as with *beggar-man*, but generally they are very specific, based on everyday matters, as in the case of *hot-house*, with its rather different meaning from the present standard use of the word. On looking at the long list of occurrences, one has the impression that the meanings are often metaphorical or metonymical, as in the cases of *air-head* and *besom-head*. A high frequency of compounds would then testify to the fondness of popular/dialect language for visual vividness.

3. Wright's EDD as a corpus?

Interjections and compounding, the two topical examples used here to illustrate the innovative research potential of EDD Online, can only provide valid results on condition that the basis of our analysis, the EDD itself, is acceptable as a corpus. But is it? Is not a corpus a corpus, and a dictionary a dictionary?

The impact of corpora on dictionaries has been both theoretically claimed (e.g. by Hanks 2009) and widely applied, e.g. by the *Collins Cobuild Advanced Dictionary*. However, the opposite direction of influence, to my knowledge, has only rarely been suggested. While the EDD is not as comprehensive as the OED, it contains a sufficient amount of material to be representative of English dialect. Representativity is one of the defining criteria of a corpus according to Gries and Stefanowitsch (2006: 3). Others are: "naturally occurring language" and machine-readability (ibid.: 4). And a corpus-linguistic method claims a "systematic and exhaustive" analysis and a statistical interpretation "on the basis of frequency lists (of words, morphemes, grammatical patterns, etc.)" (ibid.). As to statistical relevance, Gries has demonstrated on various occasions how misleading corpus linguistics can be if different "levels of granularity" are matched (e.g. in Gries 2011).

EDD Online clearly fulfills these criteria, except for statistical relevance and granularity, which we will discuss shortly. The EDD is representative of British dialects from 1700 to 1900 (less so of the overseas dialects that are included); and EDD Online is machine-readable. Moreover, it allows systematic and exhaustive analyses of linguistic features as long as these can be kept apart within the mixed structure of the EDD's entries. The question of representativity, therefore, depends on whether the important sections of the dictionary can be isolated.

The entries have eight potential constituents or sections: headword, word class, usage label, spelling variant, phonetic transcription, "meaning" (subdivided into "grammatical form" and "dialect use") and citations (mainly subdivided into dialect attributes, dialect sources and quotations proper). In principle, each of these sections, taking all entries of the dictionary combined, can be defined as a corpus. Thus, the relative relevance of word classes could be studied, given that some of them, such as interjections, may be more frequent than in Standard English. Within the headwords, morphemes or syllables could be analysed (as I have recently done for diminutive morphemes, see Markus 2010). The main constituent suitable for use as a corpus, however, is the section of citations. As subsections it includes dialect markers, source markers and the quotations proper. The dialect markers and their representativity have recently been studied (Praxmarer 2010). But the marking of sources and the quotations have, to my knowledge, not yet been investigated closely. They deserve our special attention, since the sources, partly those published even before 1700, were – in addition to Wright's own competence in dialect – his main supplier of information. And the quotations are, to a great extent, primary dialect texts so that they naturally offer themselves to be used as a corpus.

4. Wright's sources

The sources Wright used are of interest from various perspectives, including their types, their dates and their dialectal attribution.[3] Typologically, the main sources are the 91 glossaries published by the *English Dialect Society* before the compilation of the EDD. However, as many as 2,103 authors of written sources, i.e. manuscripts and published books, are listed in the dictionary's bibliography, with many authors named repeatedly for several book titles. Moreover, the bibliography gives evidence of 291 books of general reference (incl. literary works, such as by Chaucer and Shakespeare). Finally, the EDD draws on information gained from unprinted collections and information contributed by 750 correspondents. They are generally referred to by three-letter initials.

The second interesting aspect of the sources concerns their dates. While it is theoretically difficult to pinpoint time for dialect use, the dates attributed by Wright to his sources are at least *termini ad quem* – the word at issue was known at the time given, say 1850, minus x (where x stands for a fuzzy number of years). The immanent fuzziness is somewhat compensated by cumulative evidence. Wright's EDD usually refers to several sources per headword, as in the case of the entry on *Holland*.[4] The use of this proper name is testified in word combinations by sources published between 1865 and 1895 – this span of time will be produced automatically by our interface. While the dates do not explicitly exclude earlier or later use of *Holland* terms, they suggest that the 30 years mentioned constitute the peak time of their being fashionable. This is no high-density granularity, but since Wright used so many sources, absence of sources in a given case (as with *Holland* combinations) can be trusted to imply that there was no evidence for such sources outside the given time frame of reference.

It should, however, be added that a fully convincing analysis of the sources has to be based on statistics indicating how many sources were used by Wright per decade or century. The distribution of dates is clearly uneven, since there were far more sources available to Wright from the 19th century (in particular, its second half) than from the 18th, not to mention earlier centuries. The EDD Online interface, however, is not quite ready for a statistical analysis of this kind. I hope that a "systematic and exhaustive" analysis (to use Gries's terms) of the EDD sources will soon be possible.

The third aspect of the sources is their interpretability as to dialect. As Wright used abbreviations such as *Chs.1* and *Shr.1* for his glossary sources, they automatically include the markers for dialect areas, in this case Cheshire and Shropshire. This dialect information has to be added to the explicit dialect markers, i.e. the three-letter abbreviations without the raised index numbers standing for books in the reference list. In many entries these two types of dialect marking co-occur.

5. Citations in EDD Online

"Citations" is Wright's term for the entry constituent that contains the quotations to illustrate a point. As just mentioned, these segments also include source and dialect abbreviations. Beyond this information of contents, which already disturbs the picture of the homogeneity of these sections, the citations have an interpretable and informative structure. As Figure 3, taken from the entry CESS, shows, they are correlated with the section of "meanings" by numerus currens.

2. Comp. (1) **Cess-collector**, (2) **Cess-gatherer**, a tax-collector; (3) **Cess-money**, money paid in rates or taxes; (4) **Cess-payer**, ratepayer.

(1) w.Som.1 Saes· kulaktur. (2) n.Yks.12, ne.Yks.1, e.Yks.1 n.Lin.1 John Lockwood, th' cess-getherer's been for th' coort o' sewers raate. (3) Sc. Contrived to keep this blackmail a secret from him, and passed it in his account for cess-money, Scott Waverley (1814) xv. (4) Ir. There'd have bin a heavy claim agin the cess-payers of the barony, too, M°Nulty Misther O'Ryan (1894) xxi.

Figure 3 Correlation of "meanings" with "citations" in entry CESS

The first paragraph in Figure 3 lists four compounds as examples of the compound "meaning" of the word CESS, the second is the block of citations illustrating them. The example is a fairly simple one; many entries are far more complex. Meanings and citations are often correlated on three different levels, simple numbers, letters and numbers in parentheses. This is shown schematically in the right half of Figure 4.

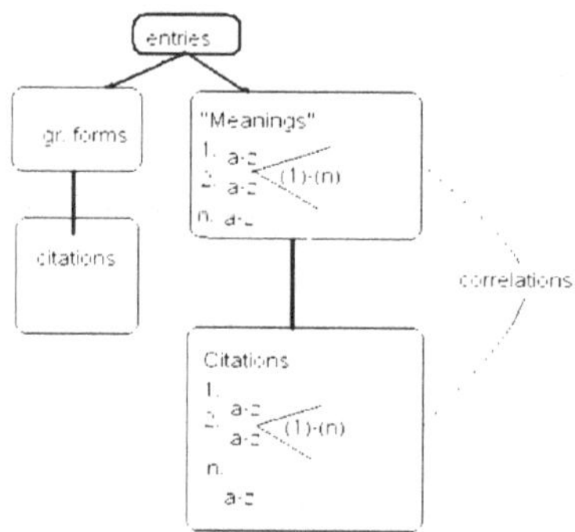

Figure 4. Correlation within EDD entries

Categories of word formation are counted in simple Arabic numbers, letters are used to distinguish sub-categories, and the numbers in parentheses stand for individual lexemes. The same branching is applied for grammatical forms (left-hand side of Figure 4). This notation using numbers and figures indicates that a given citation does not illustrate the entry as a whole, but rather a particular 'grammatical form' or a particular 'meaning' of it. In view of this complexity, we may have a second look at Figure 4. It reveals that the section of "Meanings" does not only contain the correlational numbers and meanings proper, but also compound samples and their transcription into Standard English (their "meanings"). The sections of citations are not homogeneous either, but contain – in addition to the quotations proper and the correlational numbers – sources and dialect markers, as well as the dates of the sources. In order to include all possible options, we need a fairly complicated structural mapping, as shown in Figure 5. Ignoring the left half of Figure 5 (i.e. the formal aspects) to focus now on "Use" (which is frequently identical with the semantic explanation of a word), we can interpret Figure 5 by pointing out that quotations proper (on the second level from the bottom) are subject in the EDD to a certain notational system making clear what they are meant to illustrate, and that they are, moreover, correlated to the features in the other boxes on their level, i.e. to a certain expression (e.g. one of the compounds in Figure 3), to the definition of this expression and to the three features "dialect", "source" and "date".

The difficulties of disentangling this complexity of information are obvious. But given that our Interface keeps the bits and pieces of the EDD apart, it should yield not only a useful corpus of dialect texts, but a conglomerate of several sub-corpora of dialect language: monemes, compounds, derivations, phrases, dialect sources, publication dates relevant to dialects, dialect areas, or etymological background – to mention only the close-at-hand options.

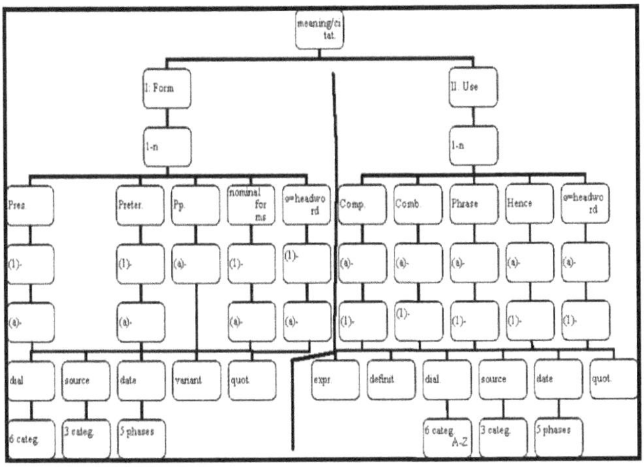

Figure 5. Structural complexity of EDD entries as to "meaning" and "citations"

In addition, for those interested in the spokenness of dialect, EDD Online lends itself to being interpreted in regard to variant spelling and phonetic transcriptions. While Wright did not transcribe all headwords of the dictionary, but only those with a less well-known pronunciation, such cases seem still frequent enough to be viewed as a corpus, in particular if we complement information gained that way by conclusions to be drawn from the spelling of variants, which Wright listed in abundance. Thus, the lemma ABOON ('overhead') is also written *abun*, *aboun*, *abune*, *abeun*, *beun*, *abeune*, *abeyun*, *abyun*, *byun*, *abuon*, *oboon*, *abou*, *aboo* and *abew*. And the two pronunciations [əbū·n, əbū·.] are added as a kind of standardised pronunciation of all those spellings.

Such observations, however, relate to the heads of the entries, i.e. single-word spellings and pronunciations given directly after the headwords. Now concerned with the "citations" section, we may focus on the frequent pseudo-phonetic spellings of the quotations there. If we wish to go *ad fontes*, we will have to filter out the quotations from the dictionary. This is something EDD Online can already do, at least entry-specifically. If we, in the case of ABOON, filter out all entry sections except "citations", we get the source texts containing some spellings of *aboon* in isolation (only 'disturbed' by source, date and dialect marker abbreviations). The entry ABOON, for its first of five functions, provides the quotations presented in Figure 6 (excerpt). This is spelling practice in action, mostly but not completely congruent with the list of variant spelling listed by Wright at the beginning of the entry. These lists of variants and phonetic transcriptions are, of course, the output of Wright's interpretative achievement.

What we see in Figure 6 is about a third of the mini-corpus of ABOON citations. It is true, in the EDD Online interface there is no routine of producing a corpus of all the citations in the EDD – such a corpus would be a mixed bag anyway, and a very big one at that. However, EDD Online always allows citations to be singled out as the focus of a query. In other words, the total of the citations is virtually available for searches, but practically accessible only lemma-specifically or in bits and pieces in line with some sensible question raised by the user.

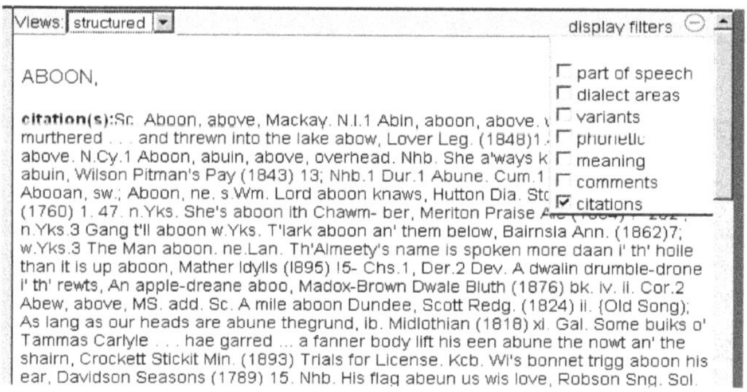

Figure 6. Excerpt of first citations passage in the entry of ABOON (EDD Online, with filter application)

Such sensible questions raised in combined queries may, for example, refer to dialect specification (e.g. Berkshire: 31 matches). However, the more interesting aspect of source texts is probably their investigation in the context of full utterances, with elision and many other features of natural language suggested by spelling. Pseudo-phonetic spellings were a very common practice both in literature and in non-fictional texts before the establishment of a transcription system by the *International Phonetic Association* (in 1897) and even thereafter. In an edition of working-class stories of the 1890s (Keating 1971), one can easily be convinced of the ubiquity of this practice.[5] In the context of fiction, dialect colouring has, in addition to local attribution of protagonists, various functions such as characterisation or expression of attitude. In linguistic terms, researchers may investigate phonotactics, tendencies of word formation and other aspects of language structure, but also the sociolinguistic, psycholinguistic and pragmatic implications of dialect use.[6]

6. Conclusion

After an introduction to Wright as a scholar and lexicographer and to EDD Online, the paper has tried to demonstrate the enormous potential of the EDD with two examples: the role of interjections in English dialects, and the importance and function of compounding. It then goes on to discuss the question of the quality of the EDD as a corpus. While the dictionary entries contain eight main constituents and dozens of sub-features and can thus be seen as a mixed raw corpus, the interface of EDD Online, even in its present beta version, allows searching for, and consideration of, isolated features, though they are structurally embedded in a complex way.

To show that the pre-processing of the raw corpus by parsing and its accessibility by our interface allows for many research issues, I have focussed on the sources Wright used and on the quotations which are cited in the EDD to illustrate both grammatical forms and dialectal use (= "meanings"). The sources have been viewed in terms of their attributes (their types, dialect areas and dates). The reason they may be seen as a 'corpus' also lies in their quantity – the EDD is based on more dialect sources, written and spoken ones, than present-day corpus compilers of English dialect texts could possibly have the energy to analyse. The texts taken from these sources are, thanks to their frequent pseudo-phonetic spellings, which were quite popular until the 19th century, a treasure-trove of the variation of dialect words in their natural contexts. While many of the texts used are literary and thus not authentic, the cumulative evidence provided by suggestive 'mis-spellings' allows for a large number of conclusions on the levels of pragmatics, psycho- and sociolinguistics. This paper is not meant as an in-depth study of one particular aspect of the dictionary, but an invitation to analyse this architecturally designed corpus. It provides representative results and a granularity of a much higher resolution than has been common in English dialectology and word geography to date.

Notes

1 Cf. her book *Rustic Speech and Folklore* (1914).

2 I used *WordSmith* 4 to identify these figures since the EDD Online interface does not yet provide a concordance mode; this is one of the features planned for the future. 16,000 is the maximum frequency *WordSmith* can track.

3 For these and the following facts, and for a more detailed discussion of Wright's sources, see Markus (2009).

4 I have used this example before on the occasion of presenting a paper in Leiden/Holland (see Markus 2009).

5 See, in particular, the story "The Inevitable Thing" by Edwin Pugh, in Keating (1971: 100-123).

6 In recent sociolinguistic theory on dialect, the interactional strategy of dialect use has been brought into play (Soukup 2009). This strategy includes diverse interactional activities from irony to empathy, and from peer-group solidarity to disparagement and arrogance.

References

Gries, S.T. and A. Stefanowitsch (2006), *Corpora and Cognitive Linguistics: Corpus-based Approaches to Syntax and Lexis*. Berlin: de Gruyter.

Gries, S.T. (2011), 'Corpus data in usage-based linguistics: What's the right degree of granularity for the analysis of argument structure constructions?', in: M. Brdar, S.T. Gries and M. Žic Fuchs (eds.), *Cognitive Linguistics: Convergence and Expansion*. Amsterdam: John Benjamins. 237-256.

Hanks, P. (2009), 'The impact of corpora on dictionaries', in: P. Baker (ed.), *Contemporary Corpus Linguistics*. London: Continuum. 214-237.

Jespersen, O. (1923), *Language: Its Nature, Development, and Origin*. London: Allen & Unwin.

Keating, P.J. (ed.) (1971), *Working-Class Stories of the 1890s*. London: Routledge & Kegan Paul.

Markus, M. (2009), 'Joseph Wright's *English Dialect Dictionary* and its sources', in: I. Tieken-Boon van Ostade and W. van der Wurff (eds.), *Current Issues in Late Modern English*. Bern: Peter Lang. 263-282.

Markus, M. (2010), 'Diminutives in English standard and dialects: A survey based on Wright's *English Dialect Dictionary*', in: M. Markus, C. Upton and R. Heuberger (eds.), *Joseph Wright's* English Dialect Dictionary *and Beyond*. Frankfurt am Main: Peter Lang. 111-129.

Markus, M. (forthcoming), 'Interjections as spoken features in English dialect (based on the electronic version of Joseph Wright's *English Dialect Dictionary*)', in: I. Moskovich-Spiegel Fandiño and B. Crespo (eds.), *Encoding the Past, Decoding the Future: Corpora in the 21st Century*. Newcastle upon Tyne: Cambridge Scholars Publishing.

Praxmarer, C. (2010), 'Joseph Wright's *EDD* and the geographical distribution of dialects: A visual apporach', in: M. Markus, C. Upton and R. Heuberger (eds.), *Joseph Wright's* English Dialect Dictionary *and beyond*. Frankfurt am Main: Peter Lang. 61-73.

Soukup, B. (2009), *Dialect Use as Interaction Strategy. A Sociolinguistic Study of Contextualization, Speech Perception, and Language Attitudes in Austria*. Wien: Braumüller.

Wright, E.M. (1914), *Rustic Speech and Folk-Lore*. Oxford: Oxford University Press.

Wright, J. (ed.) (1898-1905), *The English Dialect Dictionary*. 6 volumes. London: Henry Frowde.

Uncovering hidden constraints in micro-corpora of contact Englishes

Miriam Meyerhoff

University of Auckland

Abstract

This paper explores the effect of language contact on English and considers the subtle effects of variable input from one or more languages on contact varieties of English. It uses corpus data to assist in this and takes a sociolinguistic approach to variation. It considers how contact between English and indigenous languages in Vanuatu (SW Pacific) has shaped properties of current day Bislama, focusing on the fact that variable input often results in variable output. It proposes some general principles of contact-induced replication of variation, and identifies parallels between the creole data and migrants' acquisition of English in the UK. [1]

1. Introduction

The history of English is a history of language contact and there is a rich tradition of research documenting this history of contact. In this paper, I explore some of the issues that arise when we look at the putative impact of language contact on English focussing on those areas where the effects of contact are subtle, and non-categorical. I will consider the use of corpus data to assist in exploring language contact issues, particularly issues associated with the challenges speakers face in processing variable input and variable targets. I will do this by working within the general framework of variationist sociolinguistics, so I will first outline aspects of the methods variationist sociolinguists use when analysing data in corpora – often smaller corpora than are typical for modern corpus linguists. I will then review some data using these methods and evaluate the extent to which they provide evidence of variation being a target for replication in contexts of contact, and I will conclude by proposing some general principles associated with the replication of non-categorical input in contact English.

In the main case study, I will focus on data from Bislama, an English-lexified creole spoken in the SW Pacific. Drawing on micro-corpora of both Bislama and a local vernacular language in Vanuatu, I will ask questions about how much impact variable input from substrate languages might have had on the variation attested in spoken Bislama today. Corpus-based work on lesser-known varieties of English can be challenging for researchers since it depends on an investment of time and expertise in manually collecting, transcribing and marking up a language variety that may not be supported by a balanced ICE corpus. These problems are often compounded further when we consider substrate influences, because corpora in such languages may be even less extensive.

This paper will not spend time establishing the obvious – namely that English can be moderately or radically affected by language or dialect contact – since that would be otiose. Instead, in the next section we will introduce some of the general terminology, principles and methods behind sociolinguists' studies of variation. The next section will move directly on to explain the sociolinguistic context of Bislama and to outline the nature of the corpora I am drawing on. I'll show that the methods of corpus linguistics work adequately even with quite modest corpora, and that micro-corpora of this nature can provide a basis for exploring some of the contact issues that are of interest for an established creole variety of English.

In the last section, the general principles for transfer of variation that are proposed will be contextualised further by drawing parallels with ongoing work where we are studying the acquisition of variation among Polish migrants to the United Kingdom.

2. Sociolinguistic approach to variation

The study of variation in sociolinguistics operates with a small set of guiding principles:

1. Variation is a necessary, but not sufficient, condition for language change.
2. Variation is often, but not always, structured in non-deterministic ways.
3. Variation is part of our linguistic competence.

Principle 1 connects the study of synchronic variation with the field of historical linguistics. Principle 2 holds that there is *structured heterogeneity* in the system. That is, what had in the past been considered *free variation* is, in fact, not always free, there are consistencies across individuals and across groups of individuals in how the variation is distributed. These constraints may interact with and be dependent on features of the linguistic system (linguistic structure) or they may interact with aspects of the structure of the speech community (social structure).

To say that this heterogeneity (variation) is not categorical is to distinguish it from categorical variation such as defines allophones of a phoneme or allomorphs of a morpheme. Instead, it is probabilistic, that is, a particular variant is more or less likely to surface under given (linguistic or social) conditions than any other variant. So generalisations about the distribution of such variation must be in terms of their relative (not absolute) frequency.

A question that arises from this is whether speakers pay attention to the variation if it is not categorical. Principle 3 distinguishes the sociolinguist from formal linguists, who position non-deterministic variation in the domain of performance. Sociolinguists consider what we know about variation – its social and linguistic constraints – to be part of our linguistic competence.

This is supported by empirical evidence. Studies show that children – and adults – pay attention to the relative frequency of different forms. This has been demonstrated experimentally for children's ability to segment the relative frequencies of sound combinations into syllables and words (Saffran et al. 1996), and it appears that this skill does not disappear entirely in adults (Saffran et al. 1999). There is also an increasing body of evidence that variation in natural speech is used strategically by caregivers and that children are sensitive to the linguistic and social constraints on this variation from an early age (Roberts 1997; Smith et al. 2007).

In short, it seems very reasonable to treat the relationship between abstract *variables* and their realisation by different *variants* as analogous to the relationship between the abstract phoneme or morpheme and its realisation by allophones and allomorphs. What differs crucially is that environments in which an allophone occurs can be categorically defined; the environments in which a sociolinguistic variant occurs are probabilistically defined.

Having established the approach of variationist sociolinguistics to data, the next section outlines the source of the data for the principal case study we will examine in this paper. I outline the nature of the variation that will be investigated and the nature of the corpora used to explore the question of whether variation in a language like Bislama, that has clearly arisen from contact between speakers of English and numerous substrate languages, can be traced back to variation in the input, or whether it seems more likely that the variation might have arisen independently, through internal change. I then turn from this historical context of language contact to some data from a situation of more recent language contact. It is always difficult to make firm claims about the effects of language contact when we are reconstructing contact situations that have decades or hundreds of years of history (as is the case between Bislama and the local languages in Vanuatu). However, I will suggest that some of the inferences I draw about the ways in which contact has manifested itself in ongoing linguistic variation in Vanuatu are supported by data from an ongoing situation of contact, namely the patterns of variation found in migrant teenagers' English in the UK.

3. Overview of Vanuatu and Bislama

Varieties of creole Englishes are spoken throughout Melanesia today. The origin of the varieties spoken in the Solomon Islands (known as Solomon Islands Pijin) and Vanuatu (where it is known as Bislama) were the Queensland canefields of the late 19th century (the origin of Tok Pisin, spoken in Papua New Guinea is open to more debate, plantations in both Queensland and Samoa appear to have had input). Melanesian indentured labourers who went to Queensland to work on the plantations, subsequently took the vehicular forms of English spoken there back with them to the islands when their contracts expired.

In Vanuatu (or the New Hebrides, as it was called at the time), this introduced a new language into what was already a highly multilingual context. Bislama, as the now creolised form of English spoken in Vanuatu is called, is now spoken alongside about 100 vernacular languages that all belong to the larger Oceanic language family.

My own corpora of Bislama are taken from spoken and written texts collected on six fieldtrips made to the islands since 1994. I outline the composition of the spoken corpus that I will be using for analysis here shortly. Here, I explain the regional context of my data.

In 1994-95 I spent ten months living in Santo township, a.k.a. Luganville, the administrative centre for the northern half of Vanuatu. It had a population of (at that time) c. 8-9,000 people. I spent about a third of my time on Malo, an island of approximately 134 km^2, offshore from Santo which is largely dependent on subsistence agriculture and small entrepreneurial businesses and whose population at that time was c. 2,000. The area where I was based, West Malo, is comparatively densely populated. This area has been inhabited for several thousand years: archaeologists have found Lapita pots dating to more than 3,000 years BP from West Malo (Galipaud 1998). Many of the Bislama speakers in my corpus were L1 speakers of Tamambo, the language spoken on Malo.

4. Research question and variables

The variable that I will focus on is the presence or absence of overt arguments in subject and object position in Bislama. This is clearly not an option that Bislama acquired from English (while English allows for some arguments to be omitted, the conditions for this are very restricted). It is, however, a very likely candidate for substrate transfer. Most of the vernacular languages in Vanuatu that I am familiar with allow for the option of a full NP/pronoun or its absence (often indexed with some form of clitic or agreement marker on the verb).

In this section I will outline the facts for both Bislama and Tamambo, the substrate language spoken as an L1 by a number of the speakers in my Bislama corpus. I will compare spoken data only to control for possible register effects. We will see that there are sufficient parallels between Bislama and Tamambo to suggest that substrate languages might be the source of this variability in Bislama. We will use the available corpora to go one step further though and ask how similar the patterns of variation are underlying in Bislama and Tamambo. How similar are the constraints on this variable in both languages? Based on that, how likely is it that the Bislama pattern is an internal, independent development? Is there instead a plausible contact-based explanation?

This work stems from research I have previously done looking at Bislama data alone (Meyerhoff 2000, 2003). However, I became concerned about the *ad hoc* nature of some of my explanations about the source of these features. It became clear that what was needed was a similar investigation of these variables in an appropriate local language.

4.1 Bislama null arguments

Let us look first at argument deletion in Bislama. Example (1) shows that a full NP may alternate with a pronoun and an empty subject slot.

(1) Ale boe ya i ... karem wan masket redi i stap.
Ale hem i fasem ... ae blong hem wetem tawel,
ale Ø i putum ... maot blong masket ya insaed long maot blong hem,
ale Ø i prestem masket wetem to blong hem.
(M-95-10, Lolan [edited])

'So the boy ... had got a gun ready.
Then he tied up ... his eyes with a towel,
then (he) put ... the mouth of the gun in his mouth,
then (he) fired his gun with his toe.'

There is a similar possibility with objects. Example (2) shows direct object deletion in a family conversation between Mesek, the father, Saemon, his son, and Alis, Saemon's aunty. In theory, objects, too, alternate between full NPs, pronouns and phonetically null arguments. But in (2), the reference to 'turtles' as direct objects goes directly from full NPs (*sam bigbigwan* 'some really big ones') in Mesek's and Saemon's turns, to null variants in Alis's turn.

(2) Mesek: I gat sam bigbigwan.
Saemon: Mifala i luk wan bigbigwan.
Alis: Hem i se bae i mas luk Ø. I se i go longwe,
Janette i soem Ø nao. Afta hem i stap askem nao se 'Be yufala i gat Ø?'
(M-95-19)

Mesek: There are some really big ones (turtles).
Saemon: We saw a really big one.
Alis: She said she wants to see (some). She said she went up there, and Janette showed her (some). So now she's asking "So, do you have (any)?"

Both of these variables are found quite often in ordinary Bislama conversation. About 45% of all subjects are non-overt and about 25% of all direct objects – clearly a pattern that is more Oceanic than English. I now provide examples of parallels with Bislama's argument deletion in Tamambo, spoken on Malo.

4.2 Tamambo null arguments

Tamambo is an Eastern Oceanic language spoken on Malo island by c. 2,000 people. It has been documented in Jauncey (1997, 2002). The example in (3) shows that, like Bislama, Tamambo subjects alternate between a full NP (*suina* 'his bones') and a non-overt option (*Ø na-waladalihahi* '(they) go all around'). In principle, an independent pronoun could also fill this slot instead of the full NP. All examples of Tamambo in this paper are from Jauncey (1997) or from Dorothy Jauncey (personal communication). I explain the corpus in more detail shortly.

(3) Suina na-vano na-rasirasitaka ana hurina.
bone 3p-go 3p-poke.out 3s.poss skin

Ø na-waladalihahi na embena
Ø 3p-go.round 3s.poss body

'His bones poked out of his skin. (They) went all around his body.' (Manji atolu, l.10-11)

Likewise, it is possible to realise Tamambo direct objects with full NPs or with a phonetically reduced form analogous to a null option as shown in (4).

(4) Ku-mai ku-mbo-lai na wembe
1s-come 1s-FUT-get DET wembe.bird
matan ku-vinei-a mo-iso.
because 1s-arrow.shoot-3s 3s-finish

'I'll get the wembe bird because I have shot it with my arrow.' (*Tarikoko*, l.12-13)

Tamambo and Bislama differ somewhat in this respect because the most phonetically reduced variant in Tamambo is an argument clitic (*-a* 'it'), not absence of the direct object. However, since these options are more alike than either one is like the English full NP~overt pronoun alternation, I will treat them as suitable bases for exploring the question about how alike the constraints are on reduced argument forms in Bislama and a substrate language.

4.3 Constraints on variable realisation of arguments in Bislama

Meyerhoff (2000) discusses constraints on the form of subject arguments in Bislama. In the conversational corpus used for that investigation (which includes speakers with a variety of different first languages), it was found that third person subjects are more likely to be non-overt than first and second subjects are: c. 80% of 's/he/it' and 'they' subjects are not realised phonetically, while c. 20% of 'I', 'we' and 'you' subjects are phonetically unrealised. While there are other languages where different persons and numbers favour being overt or unrealised, generally such split systems retain a quasi-functional bias. First and second person arguments are more likely to be unrealised than third person subjects. So the direction of the split system in Bislama is typologically odd. This means that on the face of it, it is less likely to be the result of independent, language-internal innovation. Its typological oddity makes it a good candidate for exploring possible substrate influence.

Meyerhoff (2003) explores constraints on the realisation of objects in Bislama (again with a corpus that includes speakers with a range of different L1s). A surprising, but statistically significant effect was found in that study for the semantics of the direct object referent.

Objects that would be considered inalienable possessions (e.g. 'your child', 'her foot') were found to be more likely to be overt than they were to be phonetically null (alienable possessions such as 'our car', 'your spouse' had no significant tendency either way).

This semantic distinction is not one that is marked particularly strongly in English. There are very subtle alienable/inalienable distinctions, thus, *he had an accident and busted* (*his*/**the*) *arm* versus *he had an accident and busted* (*his*/*the*) *side mirror* show that inalienable nouns are treated a little bit differently in English to alienable possessions. However, the distinction between alienable and inalienable possession is marked obligatorily on all possessive NPs in the substrate languages of Vanuatu. For example, (5) shows the distinction in Tamambo:

(5) *no-na* *itevi*
CLASS-3SG broom
'her/his broom'
tina-na
mother-3SG
'her/his mother'

Again, this is a typologically unusual feature (Haspelmath et al. 2005) so it is also a good candidate for exploring the possibility of contact-induced transfer from local languages to Bislama.

5. Methods

In order to test the possibility of contact-induced transfer of variation and to explore the extent of this transfer, comparable corpora were required. As noted earlier, research on lesser-known languages like Bislama and Tamambo is seldom able to draw on large and well-balanced corpora. Typically, what corpora we have are collected by an individual researcher, who has to transcribe and gloss the recordings by hand. Corpora gathered under these circumstances tend to be organised to suit the needs of individual researchers (so they may not systematically mark phonetically null constituents, for example) and they are not always in the public domain (This is beginning to change with the *Digital Endangered Languages and Music Archives Network* – DELAMAN, <http://www.delaman.org> – see for example Barwick and Thieberger 2005.).

Researchers working on such languages tend to be grateful for whatever data they can get, and have learnt to exploit as fully as possible corpora much smaller than the mega-corpora that researchers working on major languages, such as English, typically can avail themselves of. There are no automatic parsers for Bislama or Tamambo, and there is no army of Ni-Vanuatu linguistics students that can be recruited to do the transcription of the recordings. So the work has to be done by hand, by the researcher. Naturally, there are limitations on what we can infer from such small corpora, but I will try and show that there is still a useful place for micro-corpora like these in exploring linguistic questions about variation in situations of language contact.

5.1 Outline of two micro-corpora

The Bislama corpus consists of narratives and conversation recorded in 1994-95 in Santo and Malo island with a total of 43 speakers. In total, the conversational corpus is more than 30,000 words, but only a sub-set is appropriate for exploring subject and object deletion. Approximately 4,600 finite clauses are available for analysis of argument realisation and the average number of clauses per speaker is 109.

The Tamambo corpus consists of *tandono* ('custom' or traditional stories) recorded by Dorothy Jauncey on West Malo in 1994-95. This is a much smaller corpus (272 clauses) than the conversational Bislama one, and it consists of fewer speakers. Jauncey kindly agreed to share this unpublished corpus consisting of texts and translations with me for the purposes of this exercise. Although my Tamambo is by no means fluent, it was good enough to allow me to use her texts and translations as a basis for the comparison I wanted to do.

There is no overlap of speakers in the two corpora which rules out the possibility that any similarities between them might be due to idiosyncratic tendencies of individual speakers.

5.2 Variationist tools to address a variation problem

Since the problem here is intimately involved with patterns of variation in two languages, I will draw on the tools of variationist sociolinguistics to evaluate the patterns of subject/object deletion in Tamambo, the substrate language, and then compare these patterns with the patterns associated with the same variable in Bislama.

5.3 Sampling and coding

In order to make the comparison meaningful, we extract only the Bislama from Malo speakers in the Bislama corpus. Every instance of a subject and a direct object in both corpora is coded in the following manner:

- form – full NP, pronoun, phonetically reduced variant (the dependent variable)
- person and number of the referent – 1s, 2s, 3s, 1p, 2p, 3p
- status of the referent in the previous clause – null/overt subject, null/overt direct object, null/overt other argument, not present in previous clause
- animacy of the referent – human, other animate, inanimate
- alienability – alienable or inalienable possession.

In other words, one dependent variable and four independent factor groups, with two or more factors in each group.

This approach has its roots in work by Rickford and McNair-Knox (1994) and has been expanded considerably in recent years (e.g. Poplack and Tagliamonte 2001; Tagliamonte 2002; Walker and Meyerhoff 2006; Blondeau and Nagy 2008).

Where convergent patterns of variation are found in two languages that we know have been in contact, this body of work considers this to support a claim that transfer has occurred – assuming the feature is not so widely distributed cross-linguistically that it might be a universal. Note though that this is a one-tailed hypothesis – divergent patterns are not so telling. They could be absence of evidence, or they could be evidence of absence.

5.4 Seeking evidence of transfer

My approach is to undertake a multivariate analysis of the data in both languages using *Goldvarb* (Sankoff et al. 2005), a regression software package widely-used in sociolinguistics. The outputs are rather different from regression analyses in more familiar packages such as SPSS, but the approach is congruent.

The outputs of *Goldvarb* are an overall likelihood of subject deletion (and an overall rate for direct objects, *mutatis mutandis*). This is accompanied by probability weightings for the independent factors (whether linguistic or non-linguistic) also under investigation. These weightings express the extent to which a given factor favours or disfavours the application of the overall rule. A weighting of greater than 0.50 indicates that that factor favours the application of the rule (increases the probability of a subject or object being deleted), while weightings of less than 0.50 indicates that the factor disfavours the application of the rule (decreases the overall probability of the subject or object being deleted). A factor weight of 0.50 indicates no predictive effect for that factor.

I will then use the outputs of the *Goldvarb* analysis as the basis of comparison. Where the same factor groups are significant in both languages (e.g. in both languages there is some significant effect for animacy of the referent), we will call this *weak transfer*.

Where the same factor groups are significant in both languages, and they occur in the same order of importance (e.g. person and number is the most significant factor group in both languages, and animacy is the next most significant factor group), we will call this *strong transfer*.

Where the ranking of factor groups and the factors within groups is the same in both languages (e.g. in both languages person and number of the referent is the most significant factor group and third person favours deletion most in both languages), we will call this *calquing* (by analogy with the use of the term in studies of morphosyntactic transfer).

In short, the approach is one that looks for similarities of kind and quantity.

6. Results

First, we consider the results for deletion of subject arguments in Bislama and Tamambo. Then we look at the constraints on direct object deletion.

6.1 Constraints on null subjects

Table 1 shows that the principal constraint on null subjects in both Tamambo and Bislama is the discourse status of the referent. This is the only constraint that is significant in both languages. If the referent was already a null subject in the preceding clause (an indicator of high discourse salience), then it is highly likely to be null in the current clause in both languages.

Animacy of the referent, and person and number of the subject were significant constraints in one language or the other but not in both. Animacy was significant for Tamambo (where there is a split between human and non-human referents) but it was not a significant constraint on the form of subjects in Bislama. The trend in the Bislama data from Malo is, if anything, towards a different semantic distinction, namely a split between discourse participants (first and second person) and non-participants (third). This is consistent with the significant effect found for person and number in the larger Bislama sample in Meyerhoff (2000). Person and number of the subject was not significant in Tamambo – an interesting finding since the subject-verb agreement in Tamambo is more informative than it is in Bislama so we might expect speakers to use the person and number clitics on verbs to uniquely identify the referent of a null subject. Instead, as Table 1 shows, the multivariate analysis found a significant effect for animacy of the referent. Animacy is, in a sense, a subset of the person and number of the subject, but the statistical analysis found no significant effect when first, second and third person were separated out as singular and plural; instead a better fit to the data was achieved by distinguishing different semantic types of subject in third person.

Table 1. Linguistic constraints on the form of a subject in Tamambo (spoken on Malo island) and Bislama (as spoken on Malo): % = percent phonetically null subject in this condition; factor weights > 0.50 favour a phoneticcally null subject; factor weights < 0.50 disfavour null subject (i.e. favour use of pronoun or NP). Note apparent animacy (human versus non-human) distinction in Tamambo.

	Tamambo			**Bislama**		
	Weighting	%	N	Weighting	%	N
Referent's role in prior clause:						
Subject (null)	0.74	92	148	0.91	85	116
Other argument (null)	0.69	88	16	0.73	47	19
Subject (overt)	0.34	63	19	0.64	30	786
Other argument (overt)	0.26	53	15	0.50	32	133
Not present	0.13	41	74	0.29	18	781
	Range: 61			*Range: 62*		
Animacy:						
1st/2nd person	0.57	80	26	[0.21]	[05]	823
3rd human	0.60	82	147	[0.76]	[52]	787
3rd animate (other)	0.37	65	74	[0.70]	[57]	14
3rd inanimate	0.20	44	25	[0.71]	[33]	213
	Range: 40					

6.2 Constraints on null objects

The principal constraint on null objects is also discourse status, as shown in Table 2. Alienable/inalienable possession is also significant in both Tamambo and Bislama. That means that whether an object would be considered an inalienable possession (the leaf or branch of a tree; the child of a parent; the bones of a fish) has a significant effect on the overall probability of a direct object being phonetically null. But notice the reversal of values for alienability in the two languages. This can be seen in the factor group headed "Possession type": the factor that disfavours use of a reduced form in Tamambo is indirect possessions (weighting = 0.42); in Bislama, direct possessions disfavour a reduced form (weighting = 0.35). In Tamambo, direct objects that would be considered alienable possessions favour being realised as overt NPs; in Bislama, direct objects that would be considered *in*alienable possessions have a higher probability of being realised as a full NP.

Table 2. Linguistic constraints on the form of direct objects in Tamambo (spoken on Malo island) and Bislama (as spoken on Malo): % = percent phoneticcally null subject in this condition; factor weights > 0.50 favour a reduced object (clitic in Tamambo; null in Bislama); factor weights < 0.50 disfavour reduced object (i.e. favour use of pronoun or NP). Note reversal of weightings in Tamambo and Bislama for possession type.

	Tamambo			**Bislama**		
	Weighting	%	N	Weighting	%	N
Referent's role in prior clause:						
Subject	0.89	77	22	0.82	37	93
Direct object	0.87	81	37	0.90	62	217
Other argument	0.35	30	10	0.70	28	195
Not present	0.20	17	78	0.11	02	364
	Range: 69			*Range: 79*		
Possession type:						
Direct	0.71	54	39	0.35	21	134
Indirect	0.42	38	106	0.53	27	735
	Range: 30			*Range: 18*		

6.3 Weak versus strong transfer

Evidently, there are similarities in the patterns underlying the variation in form of subjects and objects in Bislama and Tamambo. However, are these good candidates for a transfer analysis?

We saw that discourse salience of the referent was a significant constraint on subjects, but note that the areas of convergence are constraints shared by many languages. There is a strong effect for givenness and/or grammatical role perseverance in constraining argument deletion in a wide variety of languages. So it would be premature to assume that we are seeing the result of transfer when we see this variable emerge as significant in Bislama and Tamambo. Bislama speakers might just as easily be reproducing universal, cognitive preferences for the organisation of information as taking their lead from the substrate. The typologically unusual pattern of subject deletion in Bislama (a split system with 3rd person favouring null) was not found in Tamambo. In sum, with respect to subject deletion, it seems hard to argue that there is clear evidence of contact-induced transfer.

In the case of objects, we find similar constraints on the variable in Bislama and Tamambo. Here, the constraint is a semantic feature that is rather unusual typologically, and not one we would expect to find marked in two languages chosen at random. Contact, therefore, seems a more likely factor. But we noted a reversal of the direction in which the (in)alienable possession factor pushes objects in the two languages. So if transfer has occurred, it has not occurred in a simple or straightforward way. Instead, it seems helpful to distinguish between different kinds, or levels, of transfer in the manner outlined above.

I earlier proposed a distinction between *weak* and *strong transfer*. The data on direct object deletion can be applied to this distinction. I proposed that the term weak transfer might be used in cases where the same factor groups are significant in the source language (Tamambo) and in the replicating language (Bislama). This is satisfied for both the status of the referent in the previous clause and the alienable/inalienable possession factor groups. In both languages, these general factor groups are a significant constraint on the form of the direct object.

I proposed that the term *strong transfer* might be used in cases where the same factor groups are significant in the source and replicating languages *and* in addition, those factors are ranked in the same order. In this case, for both Tamambo and Bislama, the factor group that has the strongest effect on the realisation of direct objects is the status of the referent in the previous clause. In both Tamambo and Bislama, the factor group that has the second strongest effect is the alienable/inalienable distinction. Hence the example of variable realisation of direct objects seems to be evidence of strong transfer.

However, the patterns of direct object deletion do not satisfy the proposed definition of calquing, because as we saw the ranking of the constraints within the alienable/inalienable factor group are not the same in the two languages. In Tamambo, alienable NPs had a higher probability of being realised overtly; in Bislama, inalienable NPs had a higher probability of being realised overtly.

In the next section, I would like to look a little more closely at this reversal of constraints and explore its significance. Specifically, I want to consider data from ongoing language contact in order to explore the extent to which these kinds of transfer effects might be taken as a more general outcome of language contact.

7. Transformation under transfer?

In previous work (Meyerhoff 2003, 2009), I have suggested that variationists might focus more explicitly on the apparent transformations that occur when constraints on variation are replicated. Such rerankings of constraints within significant factor groups have been observed in several studies looking at language or dialect contact (Blondeau and Nagy 2008 (Table 10); Meyerhoff 2009; Buchstaller and D'Arcy 2009), but as yet our case studies are too limited for us to know (a) how widespread this phenomenon is, and (b) what gives rise to it.

The first question is particularly important, because the data I provided in Section 6 involved inferences about how contact between Bislama and the vernacular languages in Vanuatu might have affected Bislama over time. Bislama has been in contact with languages like Tamambo since plantation workers returned to the islands from periods of indentured labour in Queensland in the late 19th century. Hence, we are in a situation where we are using synchronic variation to infer things about processes of language contact that are diachronic in nature. Perhaps the kinds of rerankings I have noted for constraints on subject and object deletion are a function of the levelling that occurs when a multiplicity of languages are in contact, as they have been over the history of Bislama in Vanuatu? Perhaps these kinds of rerankings only emerge when new languages (like Bislama) emerge? In other words, I have suggested that a reranking of constraints is a general process of language contact, but the evidence I have provided might be particular to the typological or sociohistorical ecology of Bislama in Vanuatu.

In the following section, I will build on the work cited above and suggest that this kind of reranking is more common than we might think in cases of language contact, and offer some highly speculative comments about what gives rise to it. I will again use a corpus of spoken English to illustrate my claim that transformation of constraint rankings is a general phenomenon that is neither linked to long-term, diachronic situations of contact, nor to situations of intense multilingualism such as characterise Vanuatu. In doing so, I will show that reranking of constraints not only affects linguistic factors, but may involve non-linguistic factors, too. I will do this by introducing data from a corpus of speech we have collected from teenagers in London and Edinburgh in the UK.

7.1 Sociolinguistics and immigration project

In recent work with Erik Schleef (University of Manchester), we have been looking at how migrant teenagers to the UK have (or have not) acquired patterns of variation similar to their locally-born peers (Schleef et al. 2011). In this work, we have observed a similar tendency for constraints to be reranked within factor groups. Our data looks at Polish teenagers who migrated to Edinburgh and London with their families following the expansion of the EU in 2004. We recorded 16 Polish-born teenagers and 21 locally-born teenagers in Edinburgh, and in London, we recorded 21 Polish-born and 24 locally-born London teens. The teenagers recorded some sentences in reading aloud mode and we also recorded conversations that they had in pairs talking to a locally-born woman in each city. The resulting 200,000 word corpus is transcribed in time-aligned files using *ELAN* (<http://www.lat-mpi.eu/tools/elan/>, freeware developed and distributed by the Max-Planck Institut in Leipzig). In our analysis of the first variable we have looked at in this corpus, we have found evidence of transformations (rerankings) of native speaker constraints in the English of the Polish migrants.

The variable we have looked at is (*ing*) – the alternation between an apical and velar nasal in unstressed <*ing*> syllables in English. This is a well-studied variable in native speaker Englishes and the typical constraints on (*ing*) have been documented in varieties globally. The main constraint that recurs in studies of native speakers' use of (*ing*) is a strong effect for word class: verbs favour [ɪn] while nouns favour [ŋ]. In Edinburgh, we found a local interpretation of this constraint among the Edinburgh-born teenagers, and partial replication and partial transformation of this ranking among the Polish teens.

7.2 Grammatical category constraints on (*ing*)

Figures 1 and 2 show the results for the Edinburgh teenagers. In Edinburgh (as in most of Scotland), the default pronunciation of this variable is the apical nasal, so we are interested in when speakers instead use a velar. Figures 1 and 2 show the log odds from the regression analysis for each grammatical factor within the grammatical category constraint: bars above the x-axis indicate that this grammatical category favours the velar realisation of (*ing*) and bars below the x-axis indicate that these grammatical categories disfavour the velar realisation (the length of the bar is proportional to the strength or weight of that grammatical category).

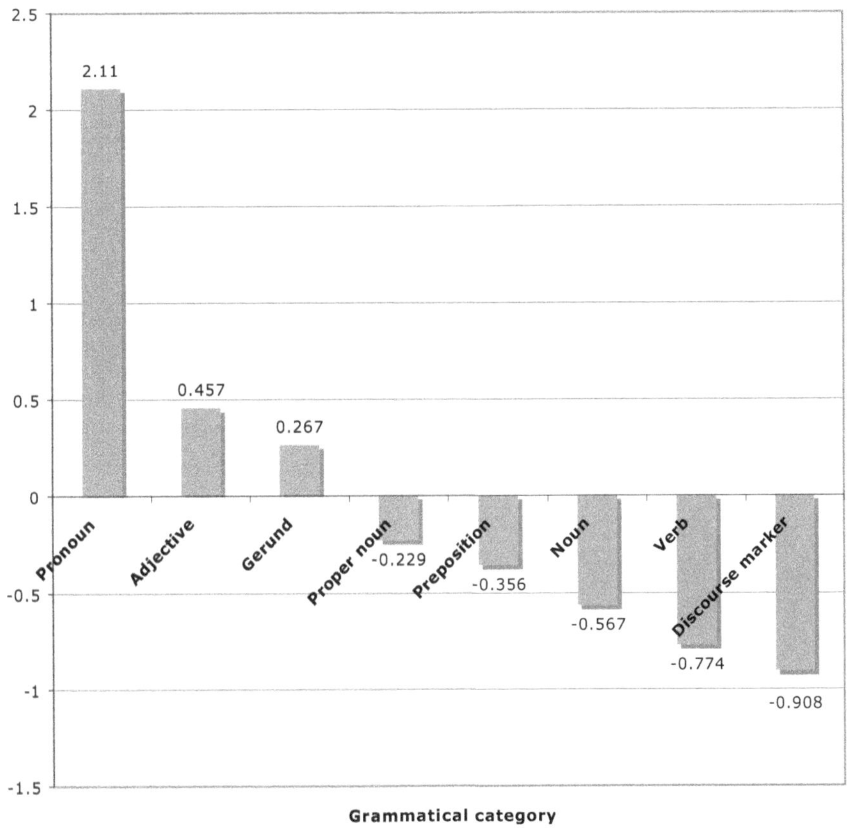

Figure 1. Log odds effect of grammatical category on use of velar nasal in (*ing*), Edinburgh-born teenagers showing absence of typical noun-verb split. Note very different behaviour of words like *anything*, *nothing*, *something* when used as pronouns (bar on the far left) and when used as discourse markers (bar on the far right).

Figure 1 shows how the grammatical category constraint patterns for Edinburgh-born adolescents. There is no evidence of the typical nominal-verbal continuum which generally is the strongest constraint on (*ing*). Nouns and verbs behave no differently. But in Edinburgh we find instead a split between the way that the -*thing* compounds behave (e.g. *something, nothing, anything, everything*). A -*thing* compound behaving as a pronoun (e.g. *I've not heard anything about it)* favours the velar (as shown by a log odds = 2.11, on the far left of the figure), while a -*thing* compound behaving as a discourse particle (e.g. *I've not heard about it or anything*) favours the apical nasal (as shown by a log odds = -0.908, on the far right of the figure).

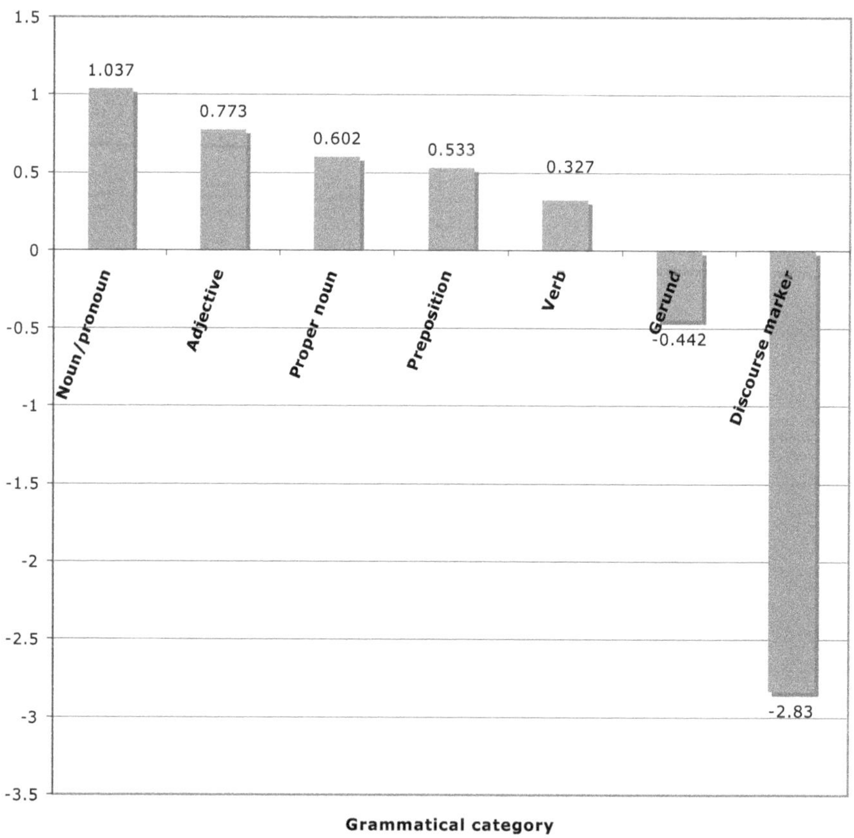

Figure 2. Log odds effect of grammatical category on use of velar nasal in (*ing*), Polish-born Edinburgh teenagers. Note replication of locally-born teenagers' distinction between pronoun and discourse marker uses of *anything, nothing, something*, but what appears to be emerging distinction between nouns and verbs (like other varieties of English).

In sum, it appears that, with respect to the grammatical category constraint, the migrant teenagers are replicating both a local and supra-local pattern of variation, but in neither case are the constraints replicated faithfully to the model in L1 speakers' speech. There seems to be some form of transformation of the constraints as they are replicated. It therefore seems that reranking of linguistic constraints (such as we saw when comparing constraints on Tamambo and Bislama subject and object deletion) can be observed in synchronic data that is recording ongoing language contact. It is not particular to diachronic or historical perspectives on contact and variation. Moreover, it seems that such rerankings can occur when only two language varieties are involved, that is, it does not occur only in the context of intense multilingualism (cf. Buchstaller and D'Arcy 2009).

7.3 (Non-)Transfer of style effects

I turn now to some data relating to what we can call style effects. I introduce this data in order to demonstrate that the reranking of constraints not only affects linguistic and cognitive variables, but may also affect variables that index social (i.e. non-linguistic) meaning. As noted, the teenagers all read aloud a series of sentences as well as conversing in a more naturalistic way with the researcher and a friend. When we compare the distribution of variants of (*ing*) in the reading styles and the conversation we find a typical pattern for the Edinburgh- and London-born teens. They all use [ŋ] more when reading and use [n] more in conversation. This is true even for the Edinburgh-born teens whose default is the apical [n]. This is a very typical result for (*ing*) in English worldwide and it reflects the perceived 'standardness' of the velar.

The situation is different for the Polish-born teenagers. In both cities, they do not show any systematic effect for style comparable to the native speaker patterns. However, this does not mean that they fail to show any social (non-linguistic) constraints on (*ing*). The Polish teenagers in London show a significant effect for gender (though intriguingly, the Polish girls favour [n], not the boys, as other studies of (*ing*) in native speaker communities usually show). In Edinburgh, the Polish teenagers show a significant effect for friendship network, that is, teenage migrants with more local-born friends use [n] more than those who have more Polish-born friends.

7.4 Replication of linguistic and cognitive constraints

In general, the only local constraints that the Polish teenagers replicated perfectly are linguistic or cognitive constraints, for instance the assimilation/dissimilation effects that may be caused by following and preceding segments, a priming effect of the form of the immediately preceding token of (*ing*). However, as with the discourse constraints on argument deletion in Bislama, I would not like to claim that these are strong arguments for contact-induced transfer. Dissimilation effects within words can be attributed to very general phonological principles (e.g. the

Obligatory Contour Principle) and assimilation effects with an immediately following segment are widely observed for nasals cross-linguistically, whether at word boundaries, as in the case of (*ing*), or within words, as in the nasal grade consonants widely observed in Oceanic languages (Lynch et al. 2002). Likewise, priming effects have been observed at all levels of linguistic structure, and seem to reflect much more general cognitive tendencies towards convergent accommodation (the preceding token of (*ing*) might have been produced by the same speaker or a different speaker in our corpus).

7.5 Summary of (*ing*) findings

In short, we have seen evidence of the same fundamental linguistic and cognitive constraints being reproduced in the Polish teenagers' use of (*ing*), partial transfer of the grammatical category constraint, but no evidence of any replication of the native speakers' main non-linguistic constraint on (*ing*). The Polish migrants fail to pick up (or replicate) a systematic distinction between the frequency of the main variants in reading aloud and conversational speech.

However, we noted that this doesn't constitute complete failure in the non-linguistic domain. There seems to be some evidence that the migrant teenagers have understood that variation between [n] and [ŋ] does social work in the larger speech community, however, they have reinvented this social significance, and transformed (*ing*) into a marker of social factors which (we must infer) are salient for them. In Edinburgh, (*ing*) is a significant indicator of more or less local friendship networks. In London, it marks gender – boys use more velar [ŋ] than girls (a reranking of the gender effect found in other studies of native speaker use of (*ing*)). Since gender is not a significant variable among the London-born teenagers, there is no reason why the Polish-born boys might not strongly favour the velar variant, thereby transforming the values of (*ing*) variants.

8. Some larger questions and directions for future research

Having reviewed several examples of what I have suggested is a more general process of transformation under transfer, this raises the question of why speakers transform constraints. This seems to me to be a profitable avenue for further research by variationists and contact linguists, and it is certain that computational analyses of small and large corpora will play a crucial role, complementing more qualitative observations, in answering this question.

The best account I can offer at present is a descriptive one: it seems plausible that the process of contact itself is what motivates the transformation of constraints. The task of replicating variation is cognitively complex consider what steps are involved:

(1) First, it requires identifying forms that constitute variants, and attending to their absolute frequency.
(2) Second, it requires identifying which variants are linguistically and socially meaningful.
(3) Third, it requires identifying what linguistic and non-linguistic constraints are used by native speakers as a basis for organising the relative frequencies of the variants.
(4) Fourth, it requires mapping variants onto the same social and linguistic constraints.
(5) And fifth, it requires doing so with the same relative frequency as in the L1 population.

Given this, I believe that it is very likely that a transformation or reranking of factors is unavoidable 'noise' that naturally arises somewhere in Steps 3 and 4 from the complexities of the different steps required.

Another question that I have not addressed in this paper is whether all variables are equally open to transformation. The Bislama case showed transformation of a variable with purely linguistic constraints. The Polish teenagers in Edinburgh and London showed transformation of social constraints. I suggested in Section 7.3 that the instances of reranking of non-linguistic constraints in the Polish teenagers' data supported the generality of the process of transformation under transfer. And I do believe that there is no reason why linguistic and non-linguistic constraints might behave fundamentally differently in respect of this.

Conversely, I strongly suspect that not all social and linguistic variables are equally open to these kinds of transformation – indeed, a number of socio-linguists suggest that not all variables are the same. I will give just one example to illustrate this. If, as people like Ochs (1992), Silverstein (2003) and Eckert (2008) have argued, a social index such as gender is always derived from other more substantive indexical relationships such as a speaker's stance towards their utterance or interlocutor or the speaker's engagement in particular activities (such as reading aloud), then transformation might be more likely to occur with derived social indices than with substantive ones. Perhaps something like direct or inalienable possession is also complex and derived, since it requires the speaker to master not only structural knowledge, but cultural knowledge as well.

Because these patterns emerge subtly and probabilistically through the investigation of corpora, as I have shown, I hope that further corpus-based work exploring what happens to linguistic variables when English has been brought into contact with other languages will help to advance our understanding of these larger questions a good deal further. I am hoping that historical linguists, who bring a longer-term perspective to the study of variation and change in English, having documented its development over centuries of language contact, will lend their voices and expertise to the discussion.

Moreover, there is clearly a need for us to draw on the quantitative sophistication that characterises much of corpus linguistics. I imagine these questions will have to be refined a good deal more in order to obtain enlightening answers. If so, more refined questions may well require more refined exploratory tools. So, future collaborations between people working on the sociolinguistics of contact and corpus linguistics will be essential.

Where should we start with this enterprise? The perfect place to start such discussions and such collaborations must surely be publications such as this, where established scholars and those beginning their careers share insights garnered from their intimate knowledge of corpora that document and describe language variation and change.

Note

1 This paper is based on data collected in Vanuatu in 1994-1995 with the support of the *Wenner-Gren Foundation for Anthropological Research* and data collected in Edinburgh and London in 2009 with the support of the UK's *Economic and Social Research Council* (ESRC, RES 000-22-3244, Co-I Dr. Erik Schleef). I thank James Stanford, Dennis Preston, Erik Schleef, Joybrato Mukherjee and Magnus Huber for encouraging me to press this data into further service here. Thanks also to the audience at ICAME 31 (Giessen), Erik Schleef and James Kirby for constructive comments on earlier versions of the paper. Errors and infelicities are all my own.

References

Barwick, L. and N. Thieberger (2005), 'Cybraries in paradise: New technologies and ethnographic repositories', in: C. Kapitzke and B.C. Bruce (eds.), *New Libraries and Knowledge Spaces: Critical Perspectives on Information and Education*. Mahwah, NJ: Lawrence Erlbaum Associates. 133-150.

Blondeau, H. and N. Nagy (2008), 'Subordinate clause marking in Montreal Anglophone French and English', in: M. Meyerhoff and N. Nagy (eds.), *Social Lives in Language: Sociolinguistics and Multilingual Speech Communities*. Amsterdam: John Benjamins. 273-313.

Buchstaller, I. and A. D'Arcy (2009), 'Localized globalization: A multi-local, multivariate investigation of quotative *be like*', *Journal of Sociolinguistics*, 13: 291-331.

Eckert, P. (2008), 'Variation and the indexical field', *Journal of Sociolinguistics*, 12: 453-476.

Galipaud, J.-C. (1998), 'The Lapita site of Atanoasao, Malo, Vanuatu', Port Vila: ORSTOM BP 76, Report No. 8.

Haspelmath, M., M.S. Dryer, D. Gil and B. Comrie (2005), *The World Atlas of Language Structures*. Oxford: Oxford University Press.

Jauncey, D. (1997), *A Grammar of Tamambo*. Unpublished Ph.D. dissertation, The Australian National University.

Jauncey, D. (2002), 'Tamabo', in: J. Lynch, M. Ross and T. Crowley (eds.), *The Oceanic Languages*. Richmond, Surrey: Curzon. 608-625.

Lynch, J., M. Ross and T. Crowley (eds.) (2002), *The Oceanic Languages*. Richmond, Surrey: Curzon.

Meyerhoff, M. (2000), 'The emergence of creole subject-verb agreement and the licensing of null subjects', *Language Variation and Change*, 12: 203-230.

Meyerhoff, M. (2003), 'Formal and cultural constraints on optional objects in Bislama', *Language Variation and Change*, 14: 323-346.

Meyerhoff, M. (2009), 'Replication, transfer and calquing: Using variation as a tool in the study of language contact', *Language Variation and Change*, 21: 1-21.

Ochs, E. (1992), 'Indexing gender', in: A. Duranti and C. Goodwin (eds.), *Rethinking Context: Language as an Interactive Phenomenon*. Cambridge: Cambridge University Press. 335-358.

Poplack, S. and S.A. Tagliamonte (2001), *African American English in the Diaspora*. Oxford: Blackwell.

Rickford, J.R. and F. McNair-Knox (1994), 'Addressee- and topic-influenced style shift', in: D. Biber and E. Finegan (eds.), *Sociolinguistic Perspectives on Register*. Oxford: Oxford University Press. 235-276.

Roberts, J. (1997), 'Hitting a moving target: Acquisition of sound change in progress by Philadelphia children', *Language Variation and Change*, 9: 249-266.

Saffran, J.R., R.N. Aslin and E.L. Newport (1996), 'Statistical learning by 8-month-olds', *Science*, 274: 1926-1928.

Saffran, J.R., E.K. Johnson, R.N. Aslin and E.L. Newport (1999), 'Statistical learning of tonal sequences by human infants and adults', *Cognition*, 70: 27-52.

Sankoff, D., S.A. Tagliamonte and E. Smith (2005), *Goldvarb X: A Variable Rule Application for Macintosh and Windows*. Department of Linguistics, University of Toronto and Department of Mathematics, University of Ottawa. <http://individual.utoronto.ca/tagliamonte/goldvarb.htm> (15.09. 2011).

Schleef, E., M. Meyerhoff and L. Clark (2011), 'Teenagers' acquisition of variation: A comparison of locally-born and migrant teens' realisation of English (*ing*) in Edinburgh and London', *English World-Wide*, 32: 206-236.

Silverstein, M. (2003), 'Indexical order and the dialectics of sociolinguistic life', *Language and Communication*, 23: 193-229.

Smith, J., M. Durham and L. Fortune (2007), '"Mam, my trousers is fa'in doon!": Community, caregiver, and child in the acquisition of variation in a Scottish dialect', *Language Variation and Change*, 19: 63-99.

Tagliamonte, S.A. (2002), 'Comparative sociolinguistics', in: J.K. Chambers, P. Trudgill and N. Schilling-Estes (eds.), *The Handbook of Language Variation and Change*. Oxford: Blackwell. 729-763.

Walker, J.A. and M. Meyerhoff (2006), 'Zero copula in the Caribbean: Evidence from Bequia', *American Speech*, 81: 146-163.

Hidden structures in English corpora

Hagen Peukert

University of Hamburg

Abstract

Why do young children prefer child-directed speech (CDS) to adult language? A possible reason for this phenomenon could be attributed to the specific arrangement of phoneme chain distributions in CDS. If so, a quantitative linguistic analysis would contribute acutely to understanding one of the mysteries of first language acquisition, that is, word segmentation. The present study undertakes such an attempt. A computer program transcribed 190 texts containing CDS and adult language to IPA, removed all whitespaces and randomly extracted a defined number of n-*grams from all texts. To these phoneme chains, a logistic regression model was applied. The model makes meaningful predictions on the distribution of phoneme chains. English CDS reveals a remarkable different distribution from adult language, which gives an additional cue to why babies prefer CDS.*

1. Introduction

Computational approaches to linguistics become more and more important in the study of language. This is especially true for quantitative investigations of corpora and suggestions for models that can be better understood when huge amounts of data are processed. Within a quantitative framework, traditional linguistic methods are often inappropriate for a more detailed inquiry. Therefore, linguists also have to work on formal descriptions of probabilistic language phenomena and their methodological specifications. Once linguistic patterns can be described formally, machines can be programmed to do the work. The following study on phonemic distributions in child-directed speech is a case in point for such a circumstance. It pays tribute to automated language processing and in doing so gives rise to new questions in the study of early first language acquisition.

When studying phonemic clusters in text corpora, it is important to know how the distribution of phoneme combinations differs among text registers. While the literature in quantitative corpora analyses mainly focuses on the distribution of words, word classes, syntactic and morphemic constructions as well as on discourse analyses, little attention has been paid to the relative occurrences of phoneme chains (see Baroni 2009; Best 2003; in general Köhler et al. 2005). However, knowledge about the distribution of phonemic clusters is important for a wide range of applications such as word boundary detection, morpheme analysis or context-independent analyses of texts (Jurafsky and Martin 2000). In addition, these distributions play a major role in research in first language acquisition. More specifically, phonemic distributions could explain why six- to eight-month-olds favor some word segmentation strategies to others (Thiessen and Saffran 2003) and why child-directed speech (CDS), if present, is preferred (Dominey and Dodane 2004; Thiessen et al. 2005).

In what follows, a possible model is suggested that makes meaningful predictions on the distribution of phoneme clusters within different text registers. This is especially interesting when looking at the difference between English CDS and adult language, since it could give an additional hint as to why babies prefer CDS (Fernald 1985; Jusczyk 1997; Kemler-Nelson et al. 1989). It is argued here that English CDS should provide a substantially different distribution of phoneme chains as compared to adult English language usage across other registers. Hence, we pursue the following hypothesis. The distribution of phonemes in English child-directed speech differs significantly from English adult language usage. This means one can predict the register of motherese on the basis of its distribution of phoneme clusters and, at the same time, this prediction is not possible among other registers of adult speech. Thus, it is argued that the distribution of phoneme clusters has the potential to impact the initial acquisition process.

The hypothesis implies a quantitative approach, which is necessary for two reasons. First, it is a prerequisite for distributions in general and for representative sets of data in particular. Second, no study so far systematically investigates the distribution of phoneme clusters for representative corpora of English CDS (Foulkes et al. 2005: 200). There are, indeed, frequency lists and co-occurrence patterns of words, word phrases, and entire sentences (Mintz 2003). The focus of phonological analyses, however, has not really departed from qualitative investigations. The qualitative differences of prosodic, lexical, and syntactic constructions seem more promising for describing the very nature of CDS (Cameron-Faulkner et al. 2003). Thus, an all-embracing quantitative approach to English motherese is still missing.

2. Method and procedure

The methodological problem in measuring the distribution of phoneme chains is threefold. First, handling the immense amount of data when processing representative samples is a main challenge. Extracting all chains, two and three phonemes long, from about 200 texts containing approximately 10,000 signs each results in a list of about 2,400 non-idiosyncratic items. Hence, a computer program has to be designed and the statistical analysis has to be automated as well.

Second, there is no statistical method that processes several thousand independent variables in a meaningful manner for the problem at hand. In addition, it seems without prospect to construct a new method from scratch. It is unlikely that the latter could promptly be discovered. Therefore, an appropriate method, to which the number of independent variables is adjusted, has to be chosen, that is, the number of phoneme chains has to be decreased without losing relevant information. Consequently, one must work with representative samples from the total population of phoneme chains. The issue here is to find the right trade-off between a method that best maps the premises of the hypothesis, and one that accepts a high number of independent variables (predictors).

Third, ensuring the independence of these variables is tricky, for superset and subset relations as well as intersections of phoneme clusters have to be excluded as variables. To illustrate, a sequence of sounds such as */ɪshaʊ/* could be a possible phoneme cluster in English occurring with a certain probability in either CDS or adult speech. Choosing */ɪshaʊ/* as an independent variable predicting the register CDS or adult speech (dependent variable) would become problematic when the phoneme chain */sha/* is also selected in the model. Since */sha/* is a subset of */ɪshaʊ/*, */sha/* will be at least as frequent as */ɪshaʊ/*.[1] So both variables are highly dependent and correlate; thus they would distort the prediction of the correct register. In addition, intersections show up if at least two different phoneme clusters are part of one word or a group of words that frequently occur together (e.g. idioms or article-noun combinations). */mɒ/* and */mi/* are likely to be interdependent because they both occur in */mɒmi/*, a high-frequency word in CDS. More delicately, */kʌm/* and */ɒn/* are independent high-frequency words and, even more, the construction */kʌmɒn/* is also very frequent.

The procedure starts with defining a set of texts to be used in the investigation. The original language sample was designed to consist of a hundred texts for each of the two categories – CDS and adult language usage. For CDS, *CHILDES* (MacWhinney 1995) was used to randomly select one hundred files. From these files, irrelevant information was deleted so that only the care taker's utterances remained as data. For all *non-CDS-files*, texts from different registers were selected to control for effects between the registers of typical adult language usage and different time spans. These files consisted of a *SCOSE*-sample (SCoSE 2010) and collections from the *Gutenberg Digital Library* (GDL 2010). All files were normalized to a length of 10,000 signs. Four CDS-files and six non-CDS-files were excluded because they contained substantially less than 10,000 signs. No two of the excluded files belonged to the same register of adult language usage. Hence, the set of text files comprised 96 files of CDS and 94 files of typical adult language usage.

Coding the following algorithm in *Java* solved the first problem. From the given set of 190 text files, a first text is input and transferred to Arpabet using the *CMU-Pronouncing Dictionary* (CSLI 2010). From this transcription all white spaces are deleted and all bigrams and trigrams are extracted. These *n*-grams are saved in an ordered list together with the information of its file name, register, and frequency. As a next step the algorithm starts from the beginning by opening a new text file from the specified set of 190 texts. The list is updated in the following way: adding new *n*-grams, incrementing the frequency for existing *n*-grams, and inserting the respective file name and, if applicable, a new register.

The second problem outlined above required a subtle appreciation of a model's premises and the research hypothesis. To test the hypothesis, a model is needed that maps a set of data points with a certain probability to one of two categories. From a first superficial survey, three methods could portray the potential to fulfill this requirement: factor analyses, cluster analyses, and binary logistic regression. Behind cluster analyses and factor analyses many different variants have to be considered. Neither can we elaborate on the assumptions of each variant, nor would we exclude these methods as possible alternatives. It would be enlightening to see how well a model works with a specification of any of these methods. We decide at this point for a binary logistic regression model since, on the one hand, the interpretation of a cluster analysis based on several dimensions can be cumbersome. On the other hand, the factor analysis would help to narrow down the variables, but would merely reveal possible correlations without distinguishing between independent and dependent variables. The simpler way for the given problem here is to group the independent variables directly to their dependent counterparts. In either case, the amount of independent variables will be adjusted (Schendera 2010: 12, 185), which will be done for the binary logistic regression as well. A binary logistic regression model has the advantage of a fairly easy calculation and interpretation. There is really only the power of the Euler number, *e*, shaping the slope of the function by adding factors for each of the independent variables and a constant. These can be calculated numerically by a simple automation or statistics software.

Still, a binary logistic regression model requires the number of cases and variables in due proportion of up to 1:10. If too many variables are fitted to only a few cases, the regression function cannot be well defined in the middle. In the given 190 cases, more than 20 variables would distort the function. If one finds a representative set of about 15 to 19 independent variables, the binary logistic regression will be a good choice for testing the research hypothesis. Clearly, it will be insufficient to select the predictors randomly from the text, because the probability is high that idiosyncratic phoneme chains – the correspondent to *hapax legomena* in word distributions – will be selected. The sum of phoneme chains that appear only once is by far the highest; frequencies of equal *n*-grams are moderate. Each specific *n*-gram occurs on average only 39 times in some of the 190 texts together. To circumvent the problem of idiosyncrasies, which only predict a very specific text but not the typicality of the text register, from all the variables occurring at least 10 times in at least one third of the 190 texts, a random sample of 17 predictors is drawn. On this set alone a binary logistic regression is carried out. In other words, the two dependent variables are CDS and adult language usage. The independent variables are 17 phoneme chains representing typical phoneme combinations of both dependent variables. The initial stage of the model is assumed to be CDS.

For the third problem, the methodological proceeding is already well established (Field 2005: 258ff.). In addition to the standard Pearson and significance table, the independent variables will be checked further for collinearity using both the *Variance Inflation Factor* (VIF) and the *condition index*. Although these indices are usually employed in linear regression models, for the particular case at hand, they manifest a complementary and meaningful tool to test for multicollinearity of the independent variables. While the VIF measures how much the variance of the regression coefficients raises dependent on their collinearity with each other, the condition index is not based on the *coefficients of determination* and, therefore, gives a more complete picture of possible correlations. The index reveals how small changes in one of the variables largely affect the end result. Thus, they also show how accurate the model is. The *eigenvalues* of the matrix of all independent variables multiplied by their inverses are put into a certain relation, that is, a square rooted relation of the largest (or smallest) *eigenvalue* of the matrix and the *eigenvalue* of interest.

3. Results

The tests for the variables' dependencies are processed first. The Pearson correlation and significance table turns out to be unproblematic. In the 21 cases, in which the twofold significance is below 0.05, the Pearson correlation is not even close to 0.8. The highest value that the Pearson achieves in the entire table at all is 0.396. Hence, the Pearson correlations are never violated.

The values for the VIF and tolerance, however, are in four cases close to 5 or 0.2 respectively. So there is at least a tendency towards multicollinearity for some variables that one should further follow up on using the condition index. Table 1 depicts the values of the condition index calculated for each additional dimension (variable). In each case, it is substantially below 30 and increases slightly in each new dimension so that the critical tolerance and VIF values can be disregarded. In summary, the independent variables do not occur jointly in frequent constructions unless they also appear significantly more frequently in other diverse phonemic environments to the extent that the joint occurrence would be insignificant.

Table 1. Condition index

Dimension	Condition Index	Dimension	Condition Index	Dimension	Condition Index
1	1.000	7	5.350	13	8.210
2	2.887	8	5.572	14	8.447
3	4.154	9	5.900	15	8.698
4	4.702	10	6.652	16	8.939
5	5.148	11	6.805	17	9.409
6	5.315	12	7.401	18	10.032

Having assured the independence of the model predictors, the exact form of the S-curved logistic function can be determined. According to the definition of the logistic function each regression coefficient is multiplied by the frequency of its predictor. The sum (logit) of these products and a constant (intercept) are taken as the negative power to the reciprocal Euler's number (*e*) plus one. This means that positive coefficients increase the probability of the respective variable to be CDS, whereas negative coefficients decrease it. Still, from these numbers it is hard to see how the overall function is exactly shaped, that is, how much the gradient in each point impacts the slope and inflection of the curve (see 3rd column in Table 2).

The effect coefficients, Exp(B), are the inversed natural logarithm of the logit. It provides an easier understanding of the effect of the variable in terms of the odds. Since a chance of 50:50 corresponds to the odds of 1, the Exp(B) should be interpreted along the same lines. An effect coefficient smaller than one means a negative impact, i.e. the slope of the logistic function approximates one half. The opposite is true for Exp(B)-values greater than one. They positively impact the CDS probability. The slope becomes steeper. The interpretation of the effect coefficients relative to one allows us to evaluate the strength of each variable. For example, the positive effect of the phoneme chain /*ʌb*/ is much stronger than the negative effect of the /*ʌf*/-chain (Table 2).

Table 2. Significance and model coefficients

Independent variable		**Regression coefficient**	**Standard deviation**	**Wald**	**df**	**Sig.**	**Exp(B)**
Arpabet	**IPA**	**B**					
AHF	*ʌf*	-.723	.266	7.370	1	.007	.485
AHB	*ʌb*	.723	.233	9.636	1	.002	2.060
EHN	*in*	-.365	.118	9.560	1	.002	.695
DIH	*dɪ*	-.624	.252	6.141	1	.013	.536
IHZ	*ɪz*	.234	.126	3.453	1	**.063**	1.264
TDH	*tð*	.290	.221	1.724	1	**.189**	1.337
RI	*ri*	-.319	.159	4.017	1	.045	.727
DAH	*dʌ*	-.619	.247	6.304	1	.012	.538
LI	*li*	-.245	.114	4.647	1	.031	.783
SAH	*sʌ*	-.622	.230	7.318	1	.007	.537
AHM	*ʌm*	.409	.170	5.758	1	.016	1.505
AHP	*ʌp*	.298	.146	4.182	1	.041	1.347
DHAET	*ðət*	.519	.190	7.461	1	.006	1.680
AHL	*ʌl*	-.230	.120	3.651	1	**.056**	.795
IHT	*ɪt*	.441	.167	6.991	1	.008	1.555
TS	*ts*	.230	.101	5.194	1	.023	1.259
TUW	*tu*	-.139	.104	1.777	1	**.183**	.870
constant		.698	.410	2.899	1	.089	2.010

This is hard to see from the regression coefficients alone, which read -0.723 and 0.723 respectively. Four of the seventeen variables turned out to be insignificant. Taking their standard deviation into account, they do not affect the model in either way, as the significance values above 0.05 illustrate. The regression coefficients and the inflation of the standard error are fairly low so that the Wald statistic gives a valid complementary idea of the individual contribution of the predictors. /ɪz/, /tð/, /ʌl/, and /tu/ can be taken out of the model. Their effects for CDS or the other adult language registers equal out and have no influence on the shape of the logistic function.

The initial assumption is that all 190 texts are CDS. After 11 iterations the coefficients have been numerically adjusted by a statistics software. These are now the optimal values for the model. Given these values, the result (Table 3) shows that the distribution of sound clusters is significantly different among the chosen sample of CDS. 95 out of 96 CDS-samples were correctly predicted as CDS. Only eight samples from the other adult registers were wrongly classified as CDS, which averages above 95 percent.

Table 3. Model classification

	Predicted		
Observed	Adult	CDS	% correct
Adult	86	8	91.5
CDS	1	95	99.0
Total Percentage			95.3

The χ^2-value for all 17 degrees of freedom (predictors) amounts to about 210 (sig. 0.000). This number is fairly large. Compared to the negative 2 log-likelihood, the χ^2-value reveals how much the model performance would improve if only the constant were included as a logit (null hypothesis), i.e. all other regression coefficients are assumed to be zero. Normalizing the χ^2-value by adding the negative 2 log-likelihood to it in the denominator results in a R^2 of 0.8. Hence, the model accounts for 80 percent of the variance of phoneme chains. The goodness of fit of the model can be elaborated if the Nagelkerke and Cox & Snell indices are considered (Table 4).

Table 4. Fit of the model after 11 iterations

-2 Log-Likelihood	**Cox & Snell's R-Square**	**Nagelkerke's R-Square**
53.184	.669	.892

They take into account the specific biases of non-linear functions and can be interpreted along the same lines as other determination coefficients. The indices are defined between zero and one, more specifically Nageklerke will never reach one and Cox & Snell cannot become zero. Both numbers support a good fit of the model. Taking all results together, we can preliminarily claim that, on average, CDS is highly predictable on the basis of typical phoneme clusters.

4. Discussion

The results of the model are overall very convincing and fully support the initial motivation. The distribution of phonemic clusters is significantly different between CDS and other adult language registers. Nonetheless, we should critically discuss the assumptions of the model.

First, the pre-selection of the model predictors could be raised as an issue. Why would a phoneme cluster have to occur at least ten times in at least one third of the 190 cases? From a psycholinguistic perspective, one could argue that the child has to hear a phonemic cluster at least some times (e.g. 10 times) before it can memorize or further process the sequence at all. The frequency effect of words is well founded in experimental settings (e.g. high-amplitude-sucking-procedure or head-turn-preference-procedure). For six- to eight-month-old infants, who have usually not mastered the segmentation problem yet, the word is probably nothing else but a sequence of sounds. There is no reason why the priming effect should be different for other phoneme sequences. The only difference is that phoneme clusters might cross word boundaries. Since a child of that age has not figured out where the word boundaries are, the argument that there is a difference between words and phoneme clusters, does not hold.

It is possible to also suggest a second objection regarding the necessity of a random sample. Indeed, it is feasible and totally in agreement with the requirements of the method to pick out phoneme clusters selectively from both registers as long as their representativeness for the group is ensured. A random sample is not a necessary prerequisite and a model based on such a procedure would just as well prove the difference between CDS and the other adult language registers. One would likely get even better results and build a perfect fit and prediction of the model. Still, the random sample is advantageous, because it is the easiest way to account for the representativeness. Here, each phoneme cluster has the same chance to be part of the sample and, thus, on average the chosen predictors will always give a similar result.

The random sample has another advantage, which can be used to argue against possible objections. It is still unclear whether sound models could be built around other registers involving subsets of CDS. As an illustration, it is possible to categorize the well studied difference between spoken and written language or texts from different time spans. Its feasibility remains an open question as long as a formal proof is still lacking. From all attempts carried out so far, we found no indicator that another classification based on a general phonemic clustering is possible. On a theoretic level we could dismiss relevant alternative classifications by exclusion. The decisive point is that every phoneme cluster has the same chance to enter the sample – all those that potentially represent different classifications of CDS and adult language usage would also be present in the sample. If so, these representatives must be mirrored in the results. At least they would not allow the present shape of the logistic function and the unexplained variance would be larger than 20 percent. Yet, one could assume sub-classifications among the adult language registers. Their effect can only be minor. Otherwise the CDS classification could not be so clear. All in all, we cannot give direct proof for the existence of other classifications. Indirectly, we can exclude them or claim that their effects are only minor. The predominant classification consists of CDS and other adult language registers.

Finally, one could ask why bigrams and trigrams are used. Simply put, they provide the largest number of independent variables. A unigram gives only the distribution of single phonemes. It seems relatively implausible to predict a language register from the frequency distribution of single phonemes (see Lehfeldt 2005). These distributions are supposedly by far the most alike among all registers. Moreover, infants are unlikely to process only single phonemes. They may in part do so, but especially for consonantal clusters infants are likely to process diphones, triphones, or syllabic constructions (Bertoncini and Mehler 1981; Bijeljac-Babic et al. 1993; Gerken and Aslin 2005; Goldinger and Azuma 2003; Hillenbrand 1983; Houston 2005; Jusczyk 1997). Therefore, bigrams and trigrams are chosen as the typical representatives for the processing units. Technically, 4-grams could also be included, though for two reasons we decided to exclude them. First, the number of all 4-grams is very low and so they would not add substantial information. Second, 4-grams are more likely to co-occur with words and be supersets of the included 3-grams. This would result in a correlated dependence, which would have to be adjusted later on when tested for multicollinearity. The interrelations between bigrams and trigrams are negligible because the number of non-idiosyncratic bigrams is so much larger than those of trigrams that they wash out with a large enough sample.

5. Summary

The present study sheds some more light on the nature of English CDS. It looks at the distribution of typical phoneme chains and shows how these clusters can be used to predict a corresponding register. The basic motivation is to show the difference between CDS and other registers of English adult language usage based on the phonemic organization.

First, we showed the existence of sound chains that are predominant in CDS, but in none of the other registers of English. As a second step, we demonstrated that this is not true for other registers of English adult language usage. While the first step is coercive because it directly provides reliable data from the model, the second step grants only indirect evidence because no data is presented. However, from the results of the model we can make a valid conclusion *modus ponens* that strongly supports the claim. Since a random sample is drawn, all phonemic clusters have the same chance to represent any of the registers involved in the sample. The clear result of above 95 percent of correct classifications and only 20 percent unexplained variance suggests that there is little room for an equally successful model for any other register provided that the raw data remains unchanged. So we may reasonably reject these alternatives by exclusion.

The investigation at hand suggests that English CDS and adult language usage differ in the distribution of their phonemic clusters. This finding gives some more evidence why babies prefer CDS. Thus, the study bridges corpus linguistics and cognitive linguistics using a computational framework to arrive at a more profound understanding of the underlying linguistic principles of child-directed speech.

Notes

1 */sha/* will probably occur more frequently because it is not only a subset of the common superset e.g. 'this house', but also of 'this half' and others.

References

Baroni, M. (2009), 'Distributions in text', in: A. Lüdeling and M. Kytö (eds.), *Corpus Linguistics: An International Handbook*. Berlin: de Gruyter. 803-821.

Bertoncini, J. and J. Mehler (1981), 'Syllables as units in infant speech perception', *Infant Behavior and Development*, 4: 247-260.

Best, K.-H. (2003), *Quantitative Linguistik*. Göttingen: Peust und Gutschmidt.

Bijeljac-Babic, R., J. Bertoncini and J. Mehler (1993), 'How do 4-day-old infants categorize multisyllabic utterances?', *Developmental Psychology*, 29: 711-721.

Cameron-Faulkner, T., E.V.M. Lieven and M. Tomasello (2003), 'A construction based analysis of child directed speech', *Cognitive Science*, 27: 843-873.

CSLI 'CMU Pronouncing Dictionary', <http://www.speech.cs.cmu.edu/cgi-bin /cmudict> (15.09.2011).

Dominey, P.F. and C. Dodane (2004), 'Indeterminacy in language acquisition', *Journal of Neurolinguistics*, 17: 121-145.

Fernald, A. (1985), '4-month-old infants prefer to listen to motherese', *Infant Behavior and Development*, 8: 181-195.

Field, A.P. (2005), *Discovering Statistics Using SPSS: And Sex, Drugs and Rock'n'roll*. 2nd edn. London: Sage.

Foulkes, P., G. Docherty and D. Watt (2005), 'Phonological variation in child directed speech', *Language*, 81: 177-206.

Gerken, L. and R.N. Aslin (2005), 'Thirty years of research on infant speech perception', *Language Learning and Development*, 1: 5-21.

Goldinger, S.D. and T. Azuma (2003), 'Puzzle-solving science: The quixotic quest for units in speech perception', *Journal of Phonetics*, 31: 305-320.

Gutenberg Digital Library 'Project Gutenberg'. <http://www.gutenberg.org/wiki/ Main_Page> (15.09.2011). [GDL]

Hillenbrand, J.M. (1983), 'Perceptual organization of speech sounds by infants', *Journal of Speech and Hearing Research*, 26: 268-282.

Houston, D.M. (2005), 'Speech perception in infants', in: D. Pisoni and R. Remez (eds.), *The Handbook of Speech Perception*. Malden, MA: Wiley-Blackwell. 417-448.

Jurafsky, D. and J.H. Martin (2000), *Speech and Language Processing*. Upper Saddle River, NJ: Prentice Hall.

Jusczyk, P.W. (1997), *The Discovery of Spoken Language*. Cambridge, MA: MIT Press.

Kemler-Nelson, D.G., K. Hirsh-Pasek, P.W. Jusczyk and K.W. Cassidy (1989), 'How the prosodic cues in motherese might assist language learning', *Journal of Child Language*, 16: 55-68.

Köhler, R., G. Altmann and R.G. Piotrowski (eds.) (2005), *Quantitative Linguistik – Quantitative Linguistics: Ein internationales Handbuch – An International Handbook*. Berlin: de Gruyter.

Lehfeldt, W. (2005), 'Phonemdistribution', in: R. Köhler, G. Altmann and R.G. Piotrowski (eds.), *Quantitative Linguistik – Quantitative Linguistics: Ein internationales Handbuch – An International Handbook*. Berlin: de Gruyter. 181-190.

MacWhinney, B. (1995), *The CHILDES project*. 2nd edition. Hillsdale, NJ: Erlbaum.

Mintz, T.H. (2003), 'Frequent frames as a cue for grammatical categories in child directed speech', *Cognition*, 90: 91-117.

Schendera, C.F.G. (2010), *Clusteranalyse mit SPSS*. München: Oldenbourg.

SCoSE – *Saarbrücken Corpus of Spoken English*. <http://www.uni-saarland.de/fak4/norrick/scose.html >, (15.11.2011).

Thiessen, E.D. and J.R. Saffran (2003), 'When cues collide: Use of stress and statistical cues to word boundaries by 7- to 9-month-old infants', *Developmental Psychology*, 39: 706-716.

Thiessen, E.D., E.A. Hill and J.R. Saffran (2005), 'Infant-directed speech facilitates word segmentation', *Infancy*, 7: 53-71.

Automatically exploring lexical tendencies in English

Thomas Proisl

Friedrich-Alexander-Universität Erlangen-Nürnberg

Abstract

The present article will introduce the Pareidoscope, a new web-based research tool for exploring the lexis-grammar interface. Its user interface allows the user to explore the interactions between word forms and syntactic structures in an interactive, network-like fashion. Sample analyses will highlight some of the abilities of the Pareidoscope to find associations between structures (which can be partially filled with word forms) and word forms or between the different word forms in a structure.[1]

1. Introduction

With the advent of corpus-based approaches to language study, phenomena on the lexis-grammar interface have increasingly come into focus and reshaped the way we think about language. Sinclair (1991: 110), one of the pioneers of corpus linguistics, formulated this new perspective on language in his idiom principle, stating "that a language user has available to him or her a large number of semi-preconstructed phrases that constitute single choices, even though they might appear to be analysable into segments". These "semi-preconstructed phrases" have been observed in various subdisciplines and have been given different names – the most prominent facet probably being collocations.

Among the numerous approaches to describing at least part of the wealth of phenomena on the lexis-grammar interface there are quite a few that try to capture them in the form of patterns or constructions. Hunston and Francis (2000: 37), for example, try to identify "[t]he patterns of a word" and by "patterns" mean "all the words and structures which are regularly associated with the word and which contribute to its meaning". In the *Valency Dictionary of English* (Herbst et al. 2004), the term pattern is interpreted differently. Valency theory makes a distinction between complements and adjuncts. Valency patterns only include complements (cf. Herbst et al. 2004: xxiv); adjuncts, no matter how strong their (statistical) association with the valency carrier is, are not part of valency patterns.[2] Construction grammar,[3] a theory that has its origins in what has been called the "periphery" of language by generative grammarians (cf. Chomsky 1986: 147), represents all grammatical knowledge uniformly as constructions. Constructions are form-meaning pairings covering everything from morphemes to word forms to idioms to argument structure constructions. Herbst and Schüller (2008: 139) draw from argument structure constructions in construction grammar (cf. Goldberg 2006), extend the notion of valency patterns by specifying the participant roles of the complements, and call these representations valency constructions.

The focus of the present article lies on formal patterns that can be observed in linguistically annotated corpora. The article will introduce the Pareidoscope, a novel tool for exploring the various patterns of lexicogrammatical interaction. As its methodology is inspired by collostructional analysis, we will give a short overview of collostructional analysis first.

2. Collostructional analysis

2.1 Methodology

Collostructional analysis is an extension to collocational analysis introduced by Stefanowitsch and Gries (2003). Its origins lie in the theory of construction grammar (especially the Goldberg version) and it has been designed to analyse the association between constructions and word forms. There are three flavours of collostructional analysis (cf. Stefanowitsch and Gries 2009: 941f.):

- collexeme analysis is used to find out which particular word forms occur in a particular slot of a construction, e.g. which verbs occur in the caused motion construction (for a detailed discussion of the caused motion construction cf. Goldberg 1995: 152-179);
- distinctive collexeme analysis is used to determine the association between a word form and the members of a set of constructions, e.g. between *advise* in V NP PP[*about*] vs. V NP PP[*on*] (i.e. verb followed by a noun phrase, followed by a prepositional phrase headed by *about* or *on*);
- covarying collexeme analysis is used to determine the association between two word forms in different slots of the same construction, e.g. between the verb and the direct object in the caused motion construction.

All three flavours make use of the usual 2×2 contingency table from classical statistical hypothesis testing to calculate association strength (cf. Table 1, explained below). Such tables are of course also used in traditional collocational analysis.

Table 1. 2×2 contingency table

	B	¬B	
A	O_{11}	O_{12}	R_1
¬A	O_{21}	O_{22}	R_2
	C_1	C_2	N

The difference between the three types of analysis lies in their assignment of values to A, ¬A, B, and ¬B (cf. Stefanowitsch and Gries 2009: 942; the notation makes use of the negation operator '¬' from classical logic):

- in collexeme analysis, A corresponds to a particular construction, ¬A to all other constructions in the corpus, B to a particular word form occurring in a particular slot of A or ¬A, ¬B to all other word forms in the corpus;
- in distinctive collexeme analysis, A corresponds to the first of a pair of constructions, ¬A to the second, B to a particular word form occurring in a particular slot of A or ¬A, ¬B to all other word forms in these slots;
- in covarying collexeme analysis, A corresponds to a particular word form in slot 1 of a particular construction, ¬A to all other word forms occurring in this slot, B to a particular word form in slot 2 of the construction, ¬B to all other word forms occurring in this slot.

Association strength can be determined by calculating a statistical association measure on the basis of the contingency table. Because of the highly skewed distributions that can be observed in natural language data, Stefanowitsch and Gries (2003: 217ff.) argue for the use of the Fisher exact test, although "nothing hinges theoretically on the choice of association measure" (Stefanowitsch and Gries 2009: 942).

2.2 Problems

A practical problem that one encounters while filling in the contingency table for a collostructional analysis is determining the size of N. For collexeme analysis, determining R_1, i.e. the frequency of a given construction, is fairly easy with standard corpus query tools (depending of course on the particular construction and the annotation of the corpus). Also, determining O_{11} and O_{12} is easy, as one only needs to count the words occurring in a particular slot of the construction. The difficult part is R_2. Assuming, as construction grammar does, that everything is a construction, it is extremely difficult to determine in how many constructions a single word occurs, let alone how many constructions there are in a corpus. In practice, the analysis will focus on a particular kind of construction, e.g. some argument structure construction, and the total number of relevant constructions, in this case the number of all argument structure constructions in the corpus, will have to be estimated by some heuristic, e.g. the assumption that the number of argument structure constructions roughly equals the number of (lexical) verbs in the corpus.[4]

To some extent, this difficulty is caused by the definition of a construction as form-meaning pairing. While computers excel at finding repetitions, regularities, patterns, etc., they are still not on par with humans regarding the identification of meaning. Thus, applying a meaning-based definition of construction hinders the automated extraction of meaningful constructions and construction candidates at least to some extent.

3. The Pareidoscope

3.1 Characteristics

The Pareidoscope (<http://www.lexi.uni-erlangen.de/pareidoscope>) is a research tool for investigating patterns of lexicogrammatical interaction that aims to avoid some of the practical difficulties of collostructional analysis by focussing on (mainly) formal patterns. Therefore, the term 'construction' is avoided – especially the meaning part – and we talk about syntactic 'structures'. By 'patterns of lexicogrammatical interaction' we mean the observable statistical associations between word forms and syntactic structures, e.g. between the noun *feeling* and the syntactic structure 'noun governing a preposition with a nominal prepositional complement (pc)' or between the partly lexicalized structure '*feeling* governing a preposition with a nominal pc' and the various prepositions or the heads of the nominal pc.

Of course, one of the prerequisites for examining the interaction between word forms and syntactic structures is access to the correct syntactic structures – and providing the correct syntactic analyses for huge collections of authentic language data is not a trivial task. Manual analysis for huge corpora is far too expensive and time-consuming, and while parsing programs are getting better and better in parsing the *Wall Street Journal* sections of the Penn Treebank, performance on less homogeneous material, such as samples drawn from the *British National Corpus* (BNC), is even worse (cf. Foster and von Genabith 2008). Additionally, parsing a corpus the size of the BNC is a challenging task, requiring special hardware or a lot of patience.[5] Therefore, the Pareidoscope tries to approximate 'syntactic structure' on three different levels.

The first, most basic abstraction is to not look at sequences of word forms but to look at sequences of part-of-speech tags (POS tag *n*-grams) instead. Part-of-speech tagging can be done reasonably fast even on modest machines and already offers an interesting abstraction layer for syntactic structures. We can, for example, find out that the noun *friendship* is strongly associated with the tag sequence VVD–AT0–AJ0–NN1[*friendship*].[6] We can then find out that the past tense verb slot of this *n*-gram is associated with verb forms such as *formed, developed, began* and that the adjective slot is associated with words like *close, lifelong, lasting*. A more sophisticated approximation can be obtained by performing a partial or flat syntactic analysis and then looking at sequences of chunks (cf. Abney 1991). That way, chunk-internal variation can be abstracted away and different tag *n*-grams can be subsumed under one chunk sequence. The tag *n*-grams VVD[*gave*]–PNP–AT0–NN1, VVD[*gave*]–PNP–AT0–AJ0–NN1, and VVD[*gave*]–AT0–NN1–CRD–NN2, for example, can all be subsumed under the chunk sequence VC[*gave*]–NC–NC, i.e. a verbal chunk followed by two nominal chunks. The third level makes use of an automatically derived full syntactic analysis in the form of dependency graphs.[7] Dependency graphs can be used to overcome the limitations of linear sequences of tags or chunks. We can, for example, analyse the grammatical relation between verb and subject regardless of their order or any intervening tags or chunks. However, we should keep in mind that using more sophisticated techniques introduces new sources of error. Currently, the Pareidoscope implements only the first approximation: linear sequences of part-of-speech tags, so called part-of-speech *n*-grams, with $1 \leq n \leq 9$ (see Figure 1 for a screenshot of the Pareidoscope in action).

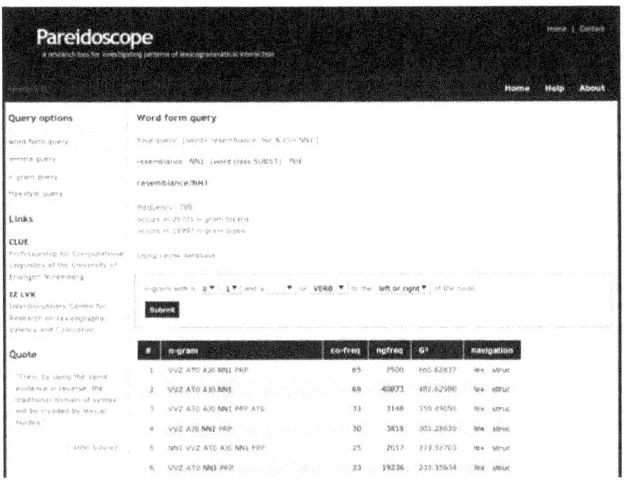

Figure 1. Screenshot of the Pareidoscope showing some query results

3.2 Structural and lexical queries

The Pareidoscope provides two styles of queries: structural queries (struc) and lexical queries (lex). Structural queries take a word form, a structure, or a (partly) lexicalized structure as the starting point and find out which structures are associated with it. With a structural query, we could, for example, find out which tag *n*-grams are associated with a given word or we could find out which larger tag *n*-grams are associated with a given tag *n*-gram. Lexical queries take a structure or a (partly) lexicalized structure as the starting point and find out which word forms are associated with its particular slots. If we want to know which word forms occur in the slots of a given tag *n*-gram or how the word forms in a given *n*-gram interact with each other, we use lexical queries. Figure 2 shows how structural and lexical queries are connected. As can be seen, the Pareidoscope can be used to explore the phenomena of lexicogrammatical interaction in a network-like fashion by combining structural and lexical queries.

Considering that the Pareidoscope is intended to be used with large corpora and that there are tens or even hundreds of thousands of tag *n*-gram types co-occurring with most of the more frequent word forms in a corpus the size of the BNC, the choice of the statistical measures to be used has a certain impact on the speed with which queries can be processed. The Pareidoscope currently uses the log-likelihood test which is a very good approximation to the computationally much more expensive Fisher exact test (cf. Evert 2004: 114).

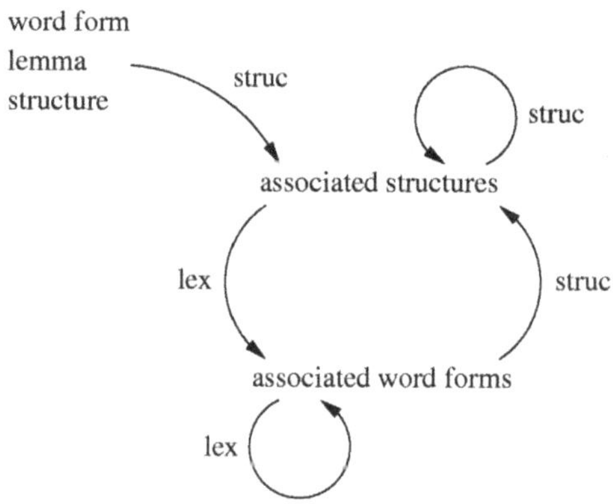

Figure 2. The Pareidoscope as a network

4. Case studies

4.1 The data

The following analyses were all conducted using the freely available web interface of the Pareidoscope with its current default corpus, a small sample of the English Wikipedia XML dump from 2010/03/12.[8] This sample corpus contains 222,642,217 tokens corresponding to 3,104,672 types in 14,368,722 sentences. There are 1,550,975,762 part-of-speech n-gram tokens with $1 \leq n \leq 9$ in the corpus. They correspond to 183,724,952 part-of-speech n-gram types. The corpus has been tagged with C5 part-of-speech tags (Leech and Smith 2000) using HunPos (Halácsy et al. 2007). The tagger has been trained on the BNC Sampler, a two-million-word subset of the BNC.

4.2 Case study 1: NN1[*feeling*]

Our first example focuses on the noun *feeling*. The first step in our analysis is to perform a structural query on the word form *feeling* tagged as a noun. *Feeling* occurs 2,894 times as a noun in the corpus, all occurrences tagged as NN1. It occurs in 104,610 n-gram tokens which correspond to 70,309 n-gram types. Table 2 shows the ten tag n-grams which are most strongly associated with *feeling* tagged as a singular noun.

The tag n-grams in Table 2 are ordered by their log-likelihood values. The part-of-speech tag in italics (NN1) marks the position of *feeling* in the n-gram.

The third column indicates the frequency of co-occurrence of the tag *n*-gram and the noun *feeling*, the fourth column indicates the overall frequency of the tag *n*-gram. The sequence VHB–AT0–NN1–CJT, for example, occurs 1,146 times in the corpus and in 143 instances the NN1 slot is filled with the word form *feeling*. Of course, the Pareidoscope enables us to take a look at the concordances by clicking on the corresponding frequency numbers.

Table 2. The ten tag *n*-grams most strongly associated with NN1[*feeling*]

rank	*n*-gram	co-freq	ngfreq	log-likelihood
1	*NN1* CJT	577	313,726	2,707.07
2	PNP VHB AT0 *NN1*	309	22,026	2,688.78
3	VHB AT0 *NN1*	326	34,684	2,575.65
4	AT0 *NN1* CJT	399	155,124	2,130.97
5	VHB AT0 *NN1* CJT	143	1,146	1,884.54
6	PNP VHB AT0 *NN1* CJT	134	900	1,816.79
7	*NN1* VBZ CJT	190	18,951	1,525.38
8	DPS *NN1* VBZ CJT	138	3,221	1,511.89
9	PNP VHB AT0 *NN1* PNP	75	285	1,112.19
10	VHB AT0 *NN1* PNP	75	315	1,094.92

Now let us have a look at the tag *n*-grams. One of the first things that looks interesting is that the unigram NN1 does not occur in the top ten. In fact, it has rank 62 (2,894; 30,345,112; 317.46), meaning that 61 tag *n*-grams with $n > 1$ are more strongly associated with *feeling* than its own part-of-speech unigram. Here we will concentrate on the top ten of those *n*-grams.

As we can see, there is a considerable amount of overlap between the *n*-grams. There are some smaller *n*-grams like NN1[*feeling*]–CJT or VHB–AT0–NN1[*feeling*] that are part of some of the larger *n*-grams and there are *n*-grams that only seem to be shifted one word to the left or to the right. All in all, it seems that we can identify three larger structures and some fragments that fit into these structures. The first is PNP–VHB–AT0–NN1[*feeling*]–CJT (ranked 6th). In this case, the word forms that fill the slots of the tag *n*-gram are quite predictable as the PNP and AT0 slots are the only ones that allow for different word forms – and there are not that many personal pronouns or articles in English. Performing a lexical query reveals that the most strongly associated pronoun is *I* and that the most strongly associated article is *a*. The result is a commonly used chunk that could well occur in an advanced learner's dictionary (and in fact does): PNP[*I*]–VHB[*have*]–AT0[*a*]–NN1[*feeling*]–CJT[*that*]. Now we can look at the fragments that make up the structure by inserting opening and closing parentheses for the beginnings and endings of the fragments: $(_1(_2$PNP $(_3(_4$VHB $(_5$AT0 $(_6$NN1[*feeling*]$)_1)_3$ CJT$)_2)_4)_5)_6$. There seems to be a rather sharp break after CJT, indicating that there is a considerable amount of variation after the subordinating conjunction *that*. So *that* appears to be a good delimiter of the structure. To the left of *feeling*, we can see the beginnings of a range of *n*-grams. The only place inside the structure where two tag *n*-grams start is between PNP and VHB. That seems to make sense as we could of course also have non-pronominal subjects of *have*. Nevertheless, the whole sequence seems to be fixed enough for it still being strongly associated with the noun *feeling*. The second sequence is DPS–NN1[*feeling*]–VBZ–CJT. Here, only the DPS slot can show some variation. It is most strongly associated with the word form *my*, yielding the following chunk: DPS[*My*]–NN1[*feeling*]–VBZ[*is*]–CJT[*that*]. As there are only two *n*-grams in the top ten that fit into this structure, looking at the fragments is less interesting: $(_1$DPS $(_2$NN$_1$[*feeling*] VBZ CJT$)_1)_2$. We see a trigram that is extended by a possessive determiner-pronoun to the left. The right delimiter is again the subordinating conjunction *that*. The last structure is PNP–VHB–AT0–NN1 [*feeling*]–PNP. There are two pronoun slots and one article slot where lexical variation can occur. A lexical query shows that the PNP slots are most strongly associated with *I* and *it* and that the AT0 slots seem to prefer *a*. The resulting chunk is PNP[*I*]–VHB[*have*]–AT0[*a*]–NN1[*feeling*]–PNP[*it*/*I*]. The structure contains four tag *n*-grams: $(_1(_2$PNP $(_3(_4$VHB AT0 NN1[*feeling*]$)_1)_3$ PNP$)_2)_4$. At the core we see a trigram which is extended to the left and to the right by personal pronouns. Interestingly, that structure is almost identical to the first one (PNP–VHB–AT0–NN1[*feeling*]–CJT), with the exception of the last element. Both seem to have a common 'core', VHB–AT0–NN1[*feeling*], which is preceded by a personal pronoun. In the first structure that 'core' is followed by *that*, in the third structure by a personal pronoun. We could put forward the hypothesis that the first and the third structure are really one structure that contains the subordinator *that* as an optional element (which would be in accordance with our intuition), however, we would have to take a closer look at the data in order to support this hypothesis.

We have lots of possibilities to continue our investigations. For example, if we wanted to focus only on *n*-grams containing *feeling* followed by CJT, we could use a filter to limit the results to *n*-grams that have a CJT somewhere to the right of *feeling*. Or if we were interested in all *n*-grams with CJT directly following *feeling*, we could perform a structural query on NN1[*feeling*]–CJT for a list of all *n*-grams that are associated with *feeling that*.

4.3 Case study 2: VVI–DPS–NN2[*feelings*]

In our second example, we will make use of the Pareidoscope to investigate how the word forms in a given structure interact with each other. The structure we are looking at is VVI–DPS–NN2[*feelings*]. The trigram VVI–DPS–NN2 occurs 44,731 times in our corpus, 162 times with *feelings* in the plural noun slot. Table 3 gives an overview of the word forms most strongly associated with the structure.[9]

Table 3 itself is already quite interesting as it shows us which verbs are typically used to talk about someone's feelings. However, it does not tell us whether the possessive determiner-pronouns interact in some way with the infinitives, i.e. whether different verbs are commonly used with different pronouns. The Pareidoscope can perform a lexical query on a partially filled structure, for example VVI–DPS[*her*]–NN2[*feelings*], and thus reveal the influence of *her* on the VVI slot. We can do this for all word forms in the DPS slot and considering only infinitives that co-occur more than twice, we get the following picture: *express her feelings*, *hurt your feelings*, *express/confess/show his feelings*, *hurt my feelings*, *express/respect/resolve their feelings*. Apparently, the VVI and the DPS slots do interact and it seems to make a difference if we are involved in direct dialogue or if we talk about a third party. When referring to oneself or directly addressing somebody, there seems to be a tendency to talk about hurt feelings. When talking about a third party, the third party appears to be commonly reported as expressing her feelings.

Table 3. Word forms associated with VVI–DPS–NN2[*feelings*]

VVI			**DPS**			**NN2**		
hurt	32	297.32	her	31	103.00	feelings	162	2,144.56
express	21	102.77	your	40	69.37			
confess	6	49.78	his	32	23.12			
spare	3	23.23	my	28	12.03			
respect	4	18.01	our	3	5.55			
contain	2	16.98	my	1	3.54			
control	4	15.57	his/her	1	1.76			
project	2	14.17	their	26	0.03			
hide	3	12.17						
conceal	2	11.42						

5. Conclusion and future work

The Pareidoscope is a research tool for investigating patterns of lexico-grammatical interaction. It is work in progress and currently approximates syntactic structure with part-of-speech tag *n*-grams. Therefore, at the moment, investigations are limited to phenomena that can be observed in the form of linear sequences. Two major enhancements are in preparation. Future versions will include the possibility to approximate syntactic structure by means of chunks, thus allowing researchers to ignore chunk-internal variation of part-of-speech tags. Additionally, future versions will make use of full syntactic analyses in the form of dependency relations, thus overcoming the limitations of linear tag or chunk sequences. The Pareidoscope is available online with a Wikipedia-based corpus of roughly 220 million word forms.

Notes

1 I would like to thank Peter Uhrig, Besim Kabashi, and Susanne Lipp for their valuable comments and suggestions.

2 However, the distinction between complements and adjuncts is not always easy to apply. The two categories are thus seen as prototypes and with regard to user friendliness "the category complement has been interpreted rather generously" (Herbst et al. 2004: xxxiv) in the dictionary.

3 Construction grammar is used as a general term here, not meant to give preference to one of the various versions of construction grammar, such as Construction Grammar (Kay and Fillmore 1999), the construction grammar of Lakoff (1987) and Goldberg (1995), Cognitive Grammar (Langacker 1987, 1991) or Radical Construction Grammar (Croft 2001).

4 Stefanowitsch and Gries (2003: 218), for example, analyse "a clause-level construction" (*N waiting to happen*) and approximate the total number of constructions by the number of verbs in the corpus.

5 Parsing experiments for the Erlangen Treebank.info project (Uhrig and Proisl 2011a, 2011b; http://treebank.info) showed that parsing all of the BNC with the Stanford Parser (Klein and Manning 2003) on a single desktop PC would take more than four weeks. Using the university's high performance computing facilities, however, parsing could be done in less than two days.

6 All examples use the C5 tagset (Leech and Smith 2000). Here is a key to the tag symbols that occur in the present article: AJ0: adjective (general or positive); AT0: article; CJT: subordinating conjunction *that*; CRD: cardinal number; DPS: possessive determiner-pronoun; NN1: singular common noun; NN2: plural common noun; PNP: personal pronoun; VBZ: -s form of the verb *be*; VHB: finite base form of the verb *have*; VVD: past tense form of lexical verbs.

7 Strictly speaking, the third level is not an approximation of syntactic structure as it uses the 'real thing'. Given the automated nature of the analysis, it may however still be regarded as a kind of approximation of the 'true' syntactic structure.

8 Wikimedia database dumps for all languages are available online at <http://download.wikimedia.org/backup-index.html>.

9 Note that not all of the word forms listed in Table 3 are significantly associated with the structure. P values of 0.05, 0.01 and 0.001 correspond to log-likelihood values of 3.84, 6.63 and 10.83.

References

Abney, S. (1991), 'Parsing by chunks', in: R. Berwick, S. Abney and C. Tenny (eds.), *Principle-Based Parsing.* Dordrecht: Kluwer Academic. 257-278.

Chomsky, N. (1986), *Knowledge of Language: Its Nature, Origin, and Use.* New York, NY: Praeger.

Croft, W. (2001), *Radical Construction Grammar: Syntactic Theory in Typological Perspective*. Oxford: Oxford University Press.

Evert, S. (2004), *The Statistics of Word Cooccurrences: Word Pairs and Collocations*. Ph.D. dissertation, University of Stuttgart, published 2005. <http://elib.uni-stuttgart.de/opus/volltexte/2005/2371/> (15.09.2011)

Foster, J. and J. van Genabith (2008), 'Parser evaluation and the BNC: Evaluating 4 constituency parsers with 3 metrics', in: N. Calzolari, K. Choukri, B. Maegaard, J. Mariani, J. Odjik, S. Piperidis and D. Tapias (eds.), *Proceedings of the Sixth International Language Resources and Evaluation Conference (LREC'08)*. Marrakech: ELRA. 3047-3051.

Goldberg, A. (1995), *Constructions: A Construction Grammar Approach to Argument Structure*. Chicago, IL: University of Chicago Press.

Goldberg, A. (2006), *Constructions at Work: The Nature of Generalization in Language*. Oxford: Oxford University Press.

Halácsy, P., A. Kornai and C. Oravecz (2007), 'Hunpos – an open source trigram tagger', in: *ACL '07: Proceedings of the 45th Annual Meeting of the ACL*. Morristown, NJ: ACL. 209-212.

Herbst, Th., D. Heath, I.F. Roe and D. Götz (2004), *A Valency Dictionary of English*. Berlin: de Gruyter.

Herbst, Th. and S. Schüller (2008), *Introduction to Syntactic Analysis: A Valency Approach*. Tübingen: Narr.

Hunston, S. and G. Francis (2000), *Pattern Grammar: A Corpus-driven Approach to the Lexical Grammar of English*. Amsterdam: John Benjamins.

Kay, P. and Ch. Fillmore (1999), 'Grammatical constructions and linguistic generalizations: The what's X doing Y? construction', *Language*, 75: 1-33.

Klein, D. and C.D. Manning (2003), 'Accurate unlexicalized parsing', in: *ACL '03: Proceedings of the 41st Annual Meeting of the ACL*. Morristown, NJ: ACL. 423-430.

Lakoff, G. (1987), *Women, Fire, and Dangerous Things: What Categories Reveal About the Mind*. Chicago, IL: University of Chicago Press.

Langacker, R. (1987), *Foundations of Cognitive Grammar, Volume 1: Theoretical Prerequisites*. Stanford, CA: Stanford University Press.

Langacker, R. (1991), *Foundations of Cognitive Grammar, Volume 2: Descriptive Application*. Stanford, CA: Stanford University Press.

Leech, G. and N. Smith (2000), *Manual to Accompany the British National Corpus (Version 2) with Improved Word-class Tagging*. <http://www.natcorp.ox.ac.uk/docs/bnc2postag_manual.htm> (15.09.2011).

Sinclair, J. (1991), *Corpus, Concordance, Collocation*. Oxford: Oxford University Press.

Stefanowitsch, A. and S.T. Gries (2003), 'Collostructions: Investigating the interaction of words and constructions', *International Journal of Corpus Linguistics*, 8: 209-243.

Stefanowitsch, A. and S.T. Gries (2009), 'Corpora and grammar', in: A. Lüdeling and M. Kytö (eds.), *Corpus Linguistics: An International Handbook*. Berlin: de Gruyter. 933-952.

Uhrig, P. and T. Proisl (2011a), 'The Treebank.info project'. Paper presented at ICAME 32, Oslo, 4 June 2011.

Uhrig, P. and T. Proisl (2011b): 'A fast and user-friendly interface for large treebanks'. Paper presented at Corpus Linguistics 2011, Birmingham, 20 July 2011.

Exemplifying constructions with *for example* and *for instance* as markers: A historical account

Paula Rodríguez-Abruñeiras

University of Santiago de Compostela

Abstract

Exemplification entails explaining something through the citing of an example. Prototypical exemplifying constructions consist of two units: the first unit is a general description of the phenomenon in question, and the second a specific example of it. The present paper explores the origin and development of for example *and* for instance *as markers used to link these two typical units in exemplification. Several British English corpora will be used as sources of data. The acquisition of the exemplifying function has led to the fossilization of* for+instance/example *as invariable prepositional phrases, which may suggest that they have undergone a process of grammaticalization (cf. Heine et al. 1991; Hopper and Traugott 2003; Fischer et al. 2004). Material from the corpora will be analysed as a means of discovering whether the form and function of these two phrases has been stable over time, or if they have shown variations at some point in the history of the language, such as the use of prepositions other than* for *or the insertion of a determiner between the preposition and the substantive. Cases of exemplification in which the first unit is omitted will also be considered.*

1. Introduction

According to Quirk et al. (1985) and Meyer (1992), exemplification conveys a relation of inclusion between two units: the referent of the second unit (which I will call the *exemplifying element* or *EE*) is more concrete, and is included within the referent of the first unit (henceforth, *general element* or *GE*). There are a few words and phrases frequently used to link these units, known as *exemplifying markers* (EM). Quirk et al. (1985) and Meyer (1992) list the following EMs in present-day English (PDE): *including, included, like, say, e.g., such as, for example* and *for instance*. The present paper focuses on two of these markers, *for example* and *for instance*, as in (1) and (2) below:

(1) The aim, however, is not to give one parent or the other a general 'right' to make decisions about a particular aspect of the child's upbringing, *for example* his education or medical treatment (...). (FLOB, H13: 150)

(2) I'm tellin' you, there's different asylums; *for instance*, a deaf an' dumb asylum! (ARCHER, 1955, ocsy.d8b)

In example (1), *the child's upbringing* is the GE, whereas *his education or medical treatment* is the EE which provides an example of the GE; *for example* is the EM which joins both units. In (2), *different asylums* and *a deaf an' dumb asylum* are the GE and EE respectively, and the EM is *for instance*. However, the division into two units is not always so simple. On occasion, the GE and the EE are complex units, even whole sentences, as in example (3) below. In this example, *an insufficient and declining number choose to study S&T* is the GE, whereas everything after the EM is the EE. Conversely, there are cases where the GE is not overtly manifested at all, cf. example (4). Here, it is omitted because it is presupposed and can be easily deduced from the context; its presence would therefore be redundant. Thus, the whole exemplifying construction in (4) below would be something like: 'say *many things*, for instance, "I am going to ring you up shortly to say something very serious to you"'. However, such a construction does not sound very natural, and for that reason the GE is omitted.

(3) But too few pupils stay in education after the age of 16 and of those who do, an insufficient and declining number choose to study S&T. *For example* the numbers taking 'A' level physics declined from 44,871 in 1989 to 42,564 in 1990. (FLOB, H12. 177)

(4) One trick of his is to ring up a man and say, *for instance*, "I am going to ring you up shortly to say something very serious to you". (ARCHER, 1920clar.j7b)

2. (*For*) *example* and (*for*) *instance* in the OED

One of the main consequences of the contact between English and French in the Middle Ages is the Romanization of the English lexicon. Many words were borrowed from French at that time, among them the nouns *example* and *instance*, which are the ultimate source of the markers under analysis. In the following sections, I will first comment on the origin of *for example* and *for instance* using the online version of the *Oxford English Dictionary* (OED, cf. Simpson and Weiner 2011) as a source of theoretical background. I will then consider this information in light of the current corpus data. For historical material I have used *The Helsinki Corpus of English Texts: Diachronic and Dialectal* and *A Representative Corpus of Historical English Registers* (ARCHER, cf. Biber 2006); present-day English (PDE) analysis is based on the *Lancaster-Oslo/Bergen Corpus of British English* (LOB, cf. Leech et al. 1961) and *Freiburg-LOB Corpus of British English* (FLOB, cf. Mair 1991).

2.1 *For example*

The first occurrences of the noun *example* mentioned in the OED date back to the year 1382. In these early cases, the meaning of *example* is that of a person functioning as a role model, either a good (OED s.v. *example*, n. 3) or a bad role model (OED s.v. *example*, n. 6). However, we have to wait until 1447 to find the meaning of *example* from which our marker (namely, *for example*) ultimately derives (cf. (5) below). In this instance, the meaning of *example* is that of 'a typical instance' (OED s.v. *example* n. 1). The first occurrence of the EM *for example* was recorded more than one century later according to the OED, namely in the year 1585 (cf. example (6) below).

(5) And to thys manyfold of nature *Exaimplys*, acordyth weel scrypture. (OED, 1447, *Lyvys of seyntys*)

(6) As *for exempill* ȝe man not say Then feir nocht Nor heir ocht. (OED, 1585, *The essayes of a prentise, in the divine art of poesie*)

2.2 *For instance*

The OED dates the first use of the noun *instance* with the meaning of 'example' as 1586 (OED s.v. *instance* n. III.6.a), see example (7) below. The earliest occurrence of the EM *for instance* is in the year 1657, as in example (8):

(7) I will but give you an *instance* of the same. (OED, 1586, *The English secretorie*)

(8) The proof of this I found by looking on the Stars..., *for instance*, there is a little Star call'd Auriga [etc.]. (OED, 1657, *A true and exact history of the island of Barbados*)

3. (*For*) *example* and (*for*) *instance* in the corpora

3.1 First manifestations and development

Roughly speaking, the dates of the first occurrences of (*for*) *example* and (*for*) *instance* found in the corpora are similar to those in the OED. However, my data provides instances of *example* and *for example* even earlier than those given in the OED, although with *instance* and *for instance* the first recorded cases are in this dictionary.

As far as *example* is concerned, it was first used in my corpora at some point between 1250 and 1350, as illustrated in example (9) below.[1] In this early instance the meaning is that of 'model'. In turn, *for example* was used as an EM for the first time in the Early Modern English period (EModE), in the time span running from 1500 to 1570 (cf. example (10) below). In this case, our marker appears in combination with another EM, namely *as* (see Section 3.5 below).

(9) [A]nd ye muee wel understonde be þo speche of þe godspelle þet me sal to dai mor makie offrinke þan an oþren dai. And þer of us yeft *ensample* þo þrie kinges of heþenesse. þet comen fram verrene londes ure louerd to seche. (Helsinki, 1130-1250, cmkentse)

(10) In a matter of lesse weight than Trial of Life and Lande, a Man may by the Law take Exceptions to suche as be impaneld, to trie the Controuersies

betwixt the Parties: *as for example*, a Man may chalenge that the Sheriffe is hys Enemie, and therefore hathe made a parciall Returne. (Helsinki, 1500-1570, cetri1)

As regards *instance*, the corpora provide no example of this noun before 1384-1425 (see (11) below), and the EM *for instance* was not used until the year 1665, as we can see in (12). As was the case with *for example*, *for instance* also combines with the EM *as* in its first occurrence as a marker of exemplification.

(11) [A]nd to ordeyne at oure prayere resonable and intierie remedie in this partie for (goddes) loue and for seynt charite after the (forme) that sueth ȝif it be lykynge to ȝow: That is to seyn that he wole at ȝoure *instance* and prayer in sauynge of his owne right and in fortherynge of (his) trewe lieges (Helsinki, 1384-1425, cmdocu3)

(12) (…) Nor secondly, is this last more difficult to be explicated, then that a Body, *as* Silver *for Instance*, put into a weak (^Menstruum^), as unrectified Aqua fortis should, when it is put in a great heat, be there dissolved by it, and not before. (Helsinki, 1665, cescie3a)

The OED highlights the convergence of meanings of the nouns *example* and *instance*. As a matter of fact, the definition of each of these forms proposed in this dictionary alludes to the definition of the other. While it is true that both nouns are semantically very close, there should have been (at least in earlier stages) some nuance of difference between them. This is indeed the case in example (13) below, where the plural forms *examples* and *instances* appear next to each other:

(13) Now I will set downe *Examples* and *Instances* for the Cure of the said Malady (…). (Helsinki, 1602, cescie2a)

The fact that the two nouns are coordinated by means of the conjunction *and* suggests that their meanings are not real synonyms here. It appears that *examples* might be used with the meaning of 'precedents' (OED s.v. *n.* 5: A precedent appealed to, to justify or authorize any course of action), with *instances* signifying 'proofs' (OED s.v. *n.* 7: Something which proves or indicates; a proof, evidence; a sign, token, mark).

The use of the nouns *example* and *instance*, and the EMs *for example* and *for instance*, increases over time, reaching its highpoint in PDE. Table 1 below illustrates this development. Due to the uneven number of words used for each period, the data are not given in raw numbers but in normalized frequencies (NF) per 100,000 words (full numbers are provided in Table 2).[2] The NFs illustrate the similar level of occurrence of (*for*) *example* and (*for*) *instance* in ME and ModE, and the notably higher occurrence in PDE.

Table 1. Evolution of *(for) example* and *(for) instance* from ME to PDE: Total number of tokens vs. EMs

	ME		**EModE**		**LModE**		**PDE**	
	Tokens	EM	Tokens	EM	Tokens	EM	Tokens	EM
example	11.67	0.66	10.53	1.91	9.19	1.95	29.00	18.34
instance	0.66	0.00	3.97	0.82	9.75	2.51	10.02	7.77
Total	12.32	0.66	14.50	2.74	18.94	4.46	39.02	26.11

3.2 Looking for the EMs: Lexical elements vs. grammatical items

In my data the form *example* (with 897 tokens found in the corpora) is far more frequent than *instance* (339 examples). Table 2 below includes the total number of tokens of *example* and *instance* per period. It also details the raw numbers and percentages of the cases where they function as EMs.[3]

Table 2. *(For) example* and *(for) instance* in the corpora: Total number of tokens (T) vs. EM

	ME		EModE		LModE		PDE		Total	
	T	EM	T	EM	T	EM	T	EM	T	EM
example	71	4 5.6%	77	14 18.2%	66	14 21.2%	683	432 63.3%	897	464 51.7%
instance	4	0	29	6 20.7%	70	18 25.7%	236	183 77.5%	339	207 61.1%
Total	75	4 5.3%	106	20 18.9%	136	32 23.5%	919	615 66.9%	1236	671 54.3%

As Table 2 shows, EMs in ME are scarce. In this period, most of the occurrences of *example* and *instance* correspond to full lexical items. There are no cases of *instance* as an EM in my data, while *example* carries out this function only in 5.6% of its occurrences. However, it should be noticed that in none of these instances does *example* combine with the preposition *for*, but instead occurs in other clusters used as EMs at the time, such as *ensample as thus*, as well as *ensample* on its own (cf. Section 3.4 below). The percentage of *example* and *instance* as EMs increases over time until PDE, at which point most occurrences of *example* appear precisely in the combination *for example* when used as an EM (63.3% cases where *example* is an EM in combination with the preposition *for* vs. 77.5% examples of *for instance* as an EM).

3.3 Bridging context

In order for *example* and *instance* to become EMs when combined with the preposition *for*, there should have been some ambiguous cases where these phrases allowed for an interpretation as both PPs and as EMs. Consider the following example:

(14) Nether mynd I now to speake of that every man thinkes, That wicked conditions being corrected by revenge & brought to the right way by terrour of their prison, to other men may serue *for example* to shun theyr faultes. (Helsinki, 1593, ceboeth2)

In (14), *for example* may be interpreted as a PP which depends on the verb of the sentence, that is, *serue* (<serve>). According to this interpretation, its meaning would be 'wicked conditions (...) may serve as an example/model to other men in order to show their faults'. However, another interpretation is possible. If *for example* is interpreted as an EM, then the meaning of the construction would be closer to: 'wicked conditions (...) to other men may serve, among other things, to show their faults'. Examples like this, where both interpretations are possible, correspond to what Heine (2002: 38-99) calls a *bridging context*. According to Heine, the bridging context is only possible when there is some semantic change in the meaning of the word or construction under analysis. Thus, the *source meaning* (that is, the original meaning of the word or construction) is still possible, but a new interpretation arises. This different interpretation of the meaning of an item is, in Grice's (1967) terminology, an *inference*, *implicature* or *suggestion*. Contexts like these could have contributed to the development of the exemplifying function of these two PPs.

3.4 Early variants of *for example* and *for instance* as EMs

As the OED and *Middle English Dictionary* (MED, cf. McSparran 2001) point out, before the consolidation of *for + example/instance* as EMs, there was a period of variation where other prepositions could be used. In example (15) below, *by* (with its old spelling *be*) is the preposition in this periphrastic marker:

(15) (...) And doctour Palemon, *be exsampyl*, concludyth vpon this tokyn in hys tragedy, the thyrd metyr, vp-on Herculys, qwere he begynnyth (\in aladis oculis\). (Helsinki, 1468, cmmetham)

Although no element can appear between the preposition and the noun in PDE, the insertion of certain forms between both items were, at least in principle, possible in earlier stages. However, these extra elements question the interpretation of these structures as EMs since they have a heavier semantic content. It is probable that the occurrence of such structures characterise the early stages of *for example* and *for instance*, when these phrases were still acquiring their exemplifying function. Thus, in (16) below the preposition is again *by*, and the noun *ensample* is modified by one adjective (*noble*) and two determiners (*many* and *a*). Moreover, the whole construction combines with another EM, namely *as* (see Section 3.4 below).

(16) And the cause is that ther is almost none / that entendeth to the comyn wele but only euery man for his singuler prouffyte / O whan I remembre the noble Romayns / that for the comyn wele of the Cyte of Rome / they spente not only theyr moeuable goodes / but they put theyr bodyes & lyues in Ieopardy & to the deth / *as by many a noble ensample* we may see in thactes of Romayns / as of the two noble scipions Affrican & Asyan / Actilius & many other. (Helsinki, 1420-1500, cmcaxpro)

On some occasions, the marker even occurs without a preposition at all. Such is the case in (17) below, taken from a text about astronomy:

(17) (…) she hath no latitude & whan she passith caput [name of a star] til she be 3 signes (in) distance (\(pro successioneȝ signorum)\) fro caput she is 7trional ascendinge (…) *Ensample* my mone was (…). (Helsinki, 1350-1420, cmeqato)

In these early stages, *example* and *instance* could also combine with other items, and their function was exactly the same as that of our PDE EMs. One of these combinations is shown in (18) below, where we find the cluster *ensample as thus*. According to the MED, n. 1 (c), this cluster was a common EM in ME.

(18) (…) and than wol the point of thi labell sitte in the bordure upon the verrey tyde of the day. *Ensample as thus*: The yeer of oure lord 1391, the 12 day of March, I wolde knowe the tyde of the day. (Helsinki, 1350-1420, cmastro)

However, it is remarkable that *example* combines with elements other than *for* only with older spellings; with its modern spelling it occurs only with the preposition *for*.

3.5 Co-occurrence of *for example* and *for instance* with other EMs

As shown in Sections 3.1 to 3.4 above, *for example* and *for instance* may combine with other EMs. As a matter of fact, in the very first occurrences of these markers in the corpora, they both co-occur with the EM *as* (cf. examples (10) and (12) above). This combination with *as* may indicate that in origin *for example* and *for instance* were not transparent enough to fill the slot of an EM on their own and needed the presence of another marker. In other words, my data suggest that *for example* and *for instance* needed to be reinforced by means of another EM before they were fully consolidated in their exemplifying function. Nevertheless, even if in these early occurrences such combinations seemed to be the norm, in recent stages of the language they are still possible, although they occur far less frequently. Thus, in LOB and FLOB up to 26 examples were found where the markers combined with other EM, combining not only with *as*, but also with *such as* and *like*, as in the following example:

(19) (…) taking such a long time to make even the smallest decision, *like for instance* whether to have lunch at the George, or whether to go instead to the Coach and Horses which you have never cared for. (FLOB, K28: 59)

The fact that such combinations are still possible in PDE may indicate that the two adjoining markers are not completely equivalent; if their meanings were exactly the same, one of them would probably be omitted, given that languages are naturally economical and tend to avoid the redundancy of exact synonyms. The difference between *for example* and *for instance* with these other markers may lie in the fact that *as*, *such as* and *like* have their origin in the comparative domain, something which makes them different from our markers here. However, the co-occurrence of EMs is more problematical to explain, and further research is needed.

4. Conclusion

The EMs *for example* and *for instance* ultimately derive from the French nouns *example* and *instance*, which were borrowed from French in the Middle Ages. The exemplifying function of *for example* was not recorded in English until the ME period, and *for instance* was even later (EModE period). However, their frequency significantly increases over the course of time, both as nouns and as EMs. In PDE, the exemplifying function of *example* and *instance* outweighs their nominal function. *Example* (897 tokens) is much more common than *instance* (339 tokens), and the same applies to the EMs *for example* (464 tokens) and *for instance* (207 tokens).

Earlier stages of the language allowed the interpretation of *for example* and *for instance* as both complements of verbs and as EMs. Such bridging contexts could have contributed to the development of the exemplifying function of these two PPs. But before the consolidation of *for* + *example*/*instance* as EMs there was a period of variation where other forms could be used, such as the marker with no preposition, a preposition other than *for*, a different expression (e.g. *ensample as thus*) or a PP where adjectives or determiners could appear between the preposition and the noun. In the first occurrences of *for example* and *for instance* as EMs, they co-occur with the EM *as*, which may suggest that neither *for example* nor *for instance* were transparent enough to fill in the slot of an EM and needed to be reinforced by means of another EM before they were consolidated in this function. These combinations are still possible in PDE, although they appear less frequently.

Notes

1 On some occasions, an exact date for the creation of a text cannot be given. In these cases, a text is referred to by the date of its subperiod in the Helsinki Corpus.

2 Normalized frequencies are obtained by multiplying the number of examples analyzed by 10, the result then divided by the total number of words used in each period (in this case 100,000).

3 After confirming that no plural forms functioned as EMs in the corpus data, plural forms were excluded from my analysis and for this reason are not considered in this table.

References

Biber, D. (2006), *A Representative Corpus of Historical English Registers 3.1.* University of Northern Arizona. [ARCHER 3.1]

Fischer, O., M. Norde and H. Perridon (eds.) (2004), *Up and Down the Cline: The Nature of Grammaticalization.* Amsterdam: John Benjamins.

Grice, H.P. (1967), 'Logic and conversation', in: P. Cole and J. Morgan (eds.), *Syntax and Semantics 3: Speech Acts.* New York, NY: Academic Press. 41-58.

Heine, B., U. Claudi and F. Hünnemeyer (1991), *Grammaticalization: A Conceptual Framework.* Chicago, IL: Chicago University Press.

Heine, B. (2002), 'On the role of context in grammaticalization', in: I. Wischer and G. Diewald (eds.), *New Reflections on Grammaticalization.* Amsterdam: John Benjamins. 83-101.

Hopper, P.J. and E.C. Traugott (2003), *Grammaticalization.* 2nd edition. Cambridge: Cambridge University Press.

Leech, G., S. Johansson, K. Hofland, R. Garside, E. Atwell, M.-C. Jhar and I. Marshall (1961): *Lancaster-Oslo/Bergen Corpus.* Lancaster University, University of Oslo and University of Bergen. [LOB]

McSparran, F. (ed.) (2001), *Middle English Dictionary.* <http://quod.lib.umich.edu/m/med/> (12.09.2011). [MED]

Mair, C. (1991), *Freiburg-LOB Corpus of British English.* Albert-Ludwigs-Universität Freiburg. [FLOB]

Meyer, C.F. (1992), *Apposition in Contemporary English.* Cambridge: Cambridge University Press.

Quirk, R., S. Greenbaum, G. Leech and J. Svartvik (1985), *A Comprehensive Grammar of the English Language.* London: Longman.

Rissanen, M. (1991), *The Helsinki Corpus of English Texts.* University of Helsinki. [Helsinki]

Simpson, J. and E. Weiner (2011), *The Oxford English Dictionary: OED online.* Oxford: Oxford University Press. (12.09.2011) <http://oed.com> [OED]

Modal *would* as a pragmatic softener in ICE Ireland

Patricia Ronan

Université de Lausanne

Abstract

This paper investigates the attested pragmatic uses of would *in selected spoken and written components of ICE Ireland. Different uses are discerned and the prominence of* would *as a marker of tentativeness, particularly in the spoken genres investigated, is noted. Innovative use of modal categories ties in with the assumption that change in the use of modal verbs happens in spoken genres, and it suggests that the use of* would *as a marker of tentativeness could be a rising use pattern in Irish English. Comparisons of frequency with research on other varieties of English show that some usage patterns differ from patterns so far observed in British English and can be compared to select Outer Circle varieties. These deviant uses in non-past non-hypothetical contexts seem to be due to an extension of tentative marking rather than a lack of distinction between modal* would *and future or volitional* will *marking.*

1. Introduction

It is well known and well documented that tense and aspect systems of international varieties of English may differ considerably from Standard (British) English, and the study of modals in dialects is now also receiving increasing attention (e.g. Collins 2009a, 2009b; Deuber 2010; Deuber et al., forthcoming). For Irish English, the modal *would* is mainly described as a marker of past habituality (Hickey 2009: 263; Ronan 2000). Cross-linguistically, further specific uses of *would* can be observed: Mesthrie and Bhatt (2008: 64) describe it as being used as a declarative softener and politeness marker that is used instead of *will* in some varieties of World Englishes.

In the following, we will first provide a brief contextualisation of the study. Against this background we investigate the uses of modal *would* in our ICE Ireland (ICE-IRL) data sets. These findings will be discussed in comparison with other varieties of English, and we will show that uses as pragmatic markers are also frequent in Irish English.

2. Modal *would* in Irish English and its context

Research on tense and aspect systems in language contact has shown that these categories are likely to be restructured in language contact. Concomitantly we have witnessed an increased amount of study of modals in dialects. For Irish English Filppula (1999), and most recently Hickey (2009) have noted the use of *would* as a marker of past habituality in Irish English. Farr and O'Keeffe have argued that *would* is used as a hedging device in expressions, particularly to decrease the assertiveness of comments by power-holders in some situations, or as a face saving strategy in others (Farr and O'Keeffe 2002: 32, 41).

The current paper addresses the question of what specific pragmatic uses are observable in ICE-IRL, and how frequent these are in relation to other uses in both spoken and written data. The study of Irish English is particularly rewarding as the presence of the English language in Ireland goes back to the 12th century, with a large scale shift to English happening during the 19th century. Hence, Irish English is typically considered to be an 'Inner Circle' variety, following the model of Kachru (2006: 71), i.e. a variety of English as a native language. The 'traditionally' English speaking 'Inner Circle' countries have a different status from 'Outer Circle' varieties, where English is used as an institutionalised second language.

3. Data and method

The present paper investigates the spoken categories of Parliamentary Debates from the ICE-IRL and the written domain of Popular Humanities. It takes into account both the northern and the southern data, consisting of five texts of approximately 2,000 words each, yielding a total of 20,000 words in the categories, and a total sample size of 40,000 words. The investigation has initially been restricted to this relatively small sample size as the close investigation of the examples is very time-intensive. However, it is planned to extend the material of study in the future.

The search method is semi-automatic with the help of *Textwrangler*, and both *would* and *'d* were searched for. The resulting hits were examined and repetitions and incompletes were excluded. Further, those hits in which *'d* represented a shortened form of *had* were also weeded out. The resulting figures show not inconsiderable numbers of attestation.

4. *Would* in ICE-IRL

4.1 Frequencies of *would* in four ICE-IRL data sets

Previous research has identified rather higher counts of *would* in ICE-IRL than in British varieties. Thus, Deuber (2010) has investigated data from ICE Great Britain (ICE-GB), ICE Trinidad & Tobago (ICE-T&T) and ICE-IRL data, based on a search of data sets of 30,000 words each. Her survey shows that the normalized frequencies of the use of *would* are notably higher in the ICE-IRL data, not only than in ICE-GB, but also than in ICE-T&T. This holds particularly in non-scripted data, but not in the more formal news data.

The current investigation of the categories "Parliamentary Debates" and "Popular Humanities (written)" in ICE-IRL has yielded the numbers of *would/'d* attestation as given in Table 1. Normalisation to 30,000 is added to provide better comparability with the data in Deuber (2010) and Deuber et al. (forthcoming).

Table 1. Attestations of *would* in ICE-IRL Parliamentary Debates, spoken genre, and ICE-IRL Popular Humanities, written genre

Provenance	Words	Examples	Per 10,000	Per 30,000
IRL South	10,000	76	76	228
IRL North	10,000	57	57	171
Spoken total	20,000	133	76.5	199.5
IRL South	10,000	16	16	48
IRL North	10,000	20	20	60
Written total	20,000	36	18	54

Table 1 contains two interesting findings. First, as we can see, there is a strong presence of *would* mainly in the spoken genre, less so in the written genre. This may be indicative of a tendency observed in American English by Mair and Leech (2006: 328), namely that spoken language is the driving force of change in the use of modals. The same argument might be used to explain the situation presented in the current data. This suggestion is in need of further, larger scale testing in different textual categories from the ICE-IRL corpora, however, as genre-specific factors may play a role.

Secondly, while the southern spoken data shows considerably higher use of *would* than its northern counterpart, the northern written data leads the southern written in its use of *would*, although counts are quite low. If higher instances of *would* in spoken speech are taken to be a sign of higher innovation, then the low frequencies particularly in the southern written data should indicate that the southern written data is even more conservative than the northern data. In order to investigate this hypothesis further, we will undertake a semantic classification of the corpus data in the following.

4.2 Semantic classification of *would* in the ICE-IRL data sets

In order to provide comparability with the use of the modal *would* in other New Englishes, in this investigation we are broadly following the categories used for the classification of the modals *will* and *would* in Deuber (2010). For the largest part, these categories can be identified in the data sets found in ICE-IRL as well. Differences do, however, emerge. An overview of qualitative results is given below, quantitative findings are presented in Section 5.

4.2.1 Non-past, future, non-hypothetical uses

In this category, we can find examples of *would* being used for prediction and volition (examples (1), (2)), and epistemic *would* (3).

(1) <#> I would <{> <[> expect that the Taoiseach **would** investigate </[> these circumstances with whatever department is involved in that case directly or indirectly <S1B-058$B> (Parliament South)

(2) <#> I **would** accept entirely what the Member has said <#> <S1B-054$B> (Parliament North)

(3) Now the Minister for Finance **would** know <,> that interest rates have started to rise internationally <S1B-060$A> (Parliament South)

The use of *would* for prediction and volition in the corpus data is notable as the use of *will* would be expected in Standard British English. Conversely, in Standard British English we would also expect present habitual *would* to form part of the non-past, non-hypothetical uses, but no examples have been found in the corpus material investigated. This may be due to the fact that Irish English, in its vernacular varieties, uses a system of grammatical marking of habitual aspect by auxiliary *do*, and also by *be(s)* in the present tense (Filppula 1999: 135-139).

4.2.2 Past, hypothetical uses

Under this heading we can subsume past time/backshift uses (4), a category which is well-known from Irish English, namely past habitual uses (5), hypothetical uses (6), and past-hypothetical uses (including perfects) (7).

(4) Bricriu promised the <quote> "hero 's portion" </quote> to the Red Branch knight who **would** prove himself the bravest of the company <W2B-006> (Popular Humanities North)

(5) I 'm sure he must have been quite livid that every morning **he 'd get** up for the past two weeks and read parts of what he was going to do in the budget in the papers <#><S1B-060$A> (Parliament South)

(6) <,> **they 'd** hardly tell you what day tomorrow was if at all they could avoid it <S1B-059$A> (Parliament South)

(7) <,> I **would** 've been here if I had 've stood in North Belfast where I should 've stooden <#><S1B-055$A> (Parliament North)

As illustrated by example (5), Irish English uses *would* as equivalent to StE *used to* (cf. Ronan 2000; Hickey 2009), whereas Quirk et al. (1985: Ch. 4.57) describe it as a more formal variant of *used to* in Standard British English, and note that it is thought to express intentional, often wilfully disturbing behaviour (Quirk et al. 1985: Ch. 4.57, Huddleston and Pullum 2002: 198). The latter seems to be a marginal feature in Irish English past habitual *would*.

Example (7) is illustrative not only in its use of hypothetical marking, but also for the clear dialectal differences it displays. The form *stooden* would be very odd in southern Irish dialects, but is a normal feature of the Scots influenced northern Irish English dialect. This is indeed a reminder that dialectal differences must be allowed for even within one particular country. Here these dialectal differences manifest themselves in distinct morphology, and we should allow for the possibility of further dialectal differences between different dialect areas within a variety under investigation as well.

4.2.3 Tentativeness or politeness markers

Pragmatically specialised uses can be related to the property of past tense verbs in general, and past tense forms of modal verbs in particular, to create a sense of tentativeness and diffidence (Huddleston and Pullum 2002: 200), which can result in speaker dissociation from a statement. This usage is a prominent feature of modal *would* in the ICE-IRL data investigated and may be related to the use of *would* in pragmatically specialised contexts (Quirk et al. 1985: Ch. 4.64 note), where hypothetical *would* is used in contexts with *like*, *love* or *prefer* and expresses tentative desire in polite requests, desires and offers, as in example (8):

(8) <#> Seeing as this is being recorded **I 'd** like to know what I 've done … </&> <S1B-055$D> (Parliament North)

Farr and O'Keeffe (2002) have described uses of *would* as a hedging device in their transcripts of phone-in radio programmes and tutoring sessions from Irish English. The authors see the use of *would* as hedges as due to a socio-cultural reluctance to over-assertiveness, and they observe this type of hedge particularly in the language of speakers who are power-holders in a given situation. They further identify it as a face-saving strategy which serves to down-tone directness in order to avoid potential embarrassment, even where the propositional content of a statement is not in doubt (Farr and O'Keeffe 2002: 37, 43). Down-toning strategies can likewise be observed in the corpus data in hand. There is, however, no restriction to power-holders, and examples are provided both in political discourse, which may be particularly prone to reducing speaker commitment, and also in the more data driven written discourse from the popular humanities as shown in examples (9), (10) and (11).

(9) I **would** ask the Taoiseach [Head of Government, PR] whom I know would share my concerns in this particular regard <,> to take some action because <S1B-059$A> (Parliament South)

(10) There is also a scribe who **would** have played an important part in Armagh 's history and Dr William Crolly who was foremost in the construction of the Roman Catholic Cathedral around 1840 . <W2B-001> (Popular Humanities North)

(11) Recent opinion polls **would** indicate that the English-speaking Irish may let loose the occasional sigh for the language, <W2B-005> (Popular Humanities North)

The attestations of these resemble the tentativeness expressed in the spoken genres and seem to transfer pragmatic habits of reducing speaker commitment from spoken to written registers.

5. Discussion

Tentative politeness is frequent for future prediction and marking willingness in Irish English data. From the above survey it emerges that its usage is partly distinct from the rules set down by prescriptive Standard British English grammar, and it appears to be similar to uses of *would* as a pragmatic softener in Outer Circle varieties of English like "We hereby wish to inform you that the meeting would take place on Thursday" (Mesthrie and Bhatt 2008: 64). However, in the data investigated here, the cases of future prediction *would* are mainly found in expressions of 1st person involvement or internal motivation, i.e. dynamic modality, rather than external motivation, deontic modality (Huddleston and Pullum 2002: 178). In this respect the Irish examples seem to differ from those Outer Circle varieties, which seemingly apply the pragmatic softeners in contexts of less speaker control of the outcome of an event. The point of origin for the examples of tentative politeness in Irish English may be found in pragmatically specialised uses *I would say* or *I would ask*, which may well have been extended to the contexts under investigation here.

Table 2. Survey of token frequencies in the different genres of ICE-IRL investigated

Tokens/ Category	1	2	3	4	5	6	7	8	9	Tenta-tive	Total
Parliament South 10'	11		5		21	1	14	4	11	9	76
Parliament North 10'	7				10	1	19	2	13	5	57
Humanities South 10'					8		7	1			16
Humanities North 10'						2	12	1	1	4	20
Total for 40,000	18		5		39	4	52	8	25	18	169
Total per 100,000	45		12.5		97.5	10	130	20	62.5	45	423

Table 2 shows the frequencies of different categories of use in the ICE-IRL data. Following Deuber (2010), the labels are: 1. Prediction and volition, 2. Present habitual, 3. Epistemic *would*, 4. Habitual or epistemic *would*, 5. Past time or backshift, 6. Past habitual, 7. Hypothetical *would*, 8. Past hypothetical *would*, 9. Pragmatically specialized uses. Tentative usage is added. The frequencies of attestation in apodosis and prostasis of *if*-clauses are included in the relevant semantic categories 1-7. Table 2 illustrates that hypothetical uses are the most frequent both overall and in each individual category, excepting the spoken southern category, which shows prominence of past time/backshift usage of *would*. Further, markers of tentativeness and politeness are prominent. These figures can now be compared to the results of studies on British English. Deuber

(2010) has carried out an investigation of ICE-GB data from the categories "Conversations", "Class-sessions", "Unscripted Speeches" and "Broadcast News" for the purpose of comparison with her ICE-T&T data. The total frequencies for *would* in her ICE-GB is 371 examples per 100,000 words counts of 366 examples per 100,000 words in the ICE-T&T data. The comparison of the data investigated by Deuber (2010) and the data examined in the present study, although from different categories, suggests higher frequencies in the ICE-IRL data.

As the categories investigated differ, and '*unclear*' is a large category in Deuber's evaluation, significance testing is not meaningful. We can see, however, that both ICE-IRL and ICE-T&T have the highest counts of *would* in hypothetical usage (label 7). *Would* is also used in the Irish data sets to indicate prediction and volition (label 1), which in the ICE-GB data was found to be exclusively indicated by *will*.[1] In the respect of using *would* for future prediction and volition, the Irish data thus resembles categorisations in New Englishes, such as Trinidad, Jamaica, Bahamas, Fiji, India and Singapore (Deuber et al., forthcoming).[2] However, the latter varieties, except for the Jamaican material, also use *would* to mark present habituality. As suggested above, this usage might be blocked by the presence of other present habitual markers in Irish English.

In the Irish English data, on the other hand, a neutralisation of the differences between *will* and *would* is certainly not the reason for the use of *would* in non-past, non-hypothetical contexts in Irish English. Further, unlike *the meeting would take place on Thursday*, the marking of prediction and volition in the ICE-IRL data uses *would* to indicate speaker-involvement. Use of predictive *would* therefore differs from that described for the New Englishes varieties by being restricted to dynamic, i.e. speaker centred, modality. Usage in deontic modality seems to be excluded.

6. Conclusion

The use of *would* as a pragmatic marker is most frequent in southern Irish parliamentary debates, and less so in the debates from the Northern Assembly. The instances are used to reduce speaker commitment, not only in parliamentary debate, but also in written contexts, which, as this category has not yet been observed in earlier varieties of written genres, might be a sign of an increasing extension of the category from the potentially more innovative spoken genres to more regulated written registers.

While the modal *would* is most frequently used to express hypothetical situations and backshifted *will*, it also seems to have taken over at least some of the epistemic functions usually covered by *will* in British Standard English. However, *would* is lacking the status of full politeness and future marker in the New Englishes varieties discussed e.g. by Mesthrie and Bhatt (2008) and Deuber et al. (forthcoming), which also makes it applicable to deontic, i.e. externally controlled, contexts. It is, however, used with considerable frequency in dynamic, i.e. speaker driven conditions, to mark tentativeness in Irish English. The Irish

English uses of *would* in these contexts seem to have developed from an extension of politeness or tentativeness concepts, and not from a loss of differentiation between *will* and *would* as observed in New Englishes.

In future research the investigation of the Irish English material should receive a more solid base by investigating more different categories of text from ICE-IRL, and by comparing these with the corresponding categories especially in ICE-GB to ascertain whether the tendencies observed here may also be found in this 'most central' Inner Circle variety of English.

Notes

1 The modal *shall* did not form part of Deuber's (2010) investigation.

2 Thanks to the authors for letting me have a pre-publication of this study.

References

Collins, P. (2009a), 'Modals and quasi-modals in World Englishes', *World Englishes*, 28: 281-292.

Collins, P. (2009b), *Modals and Quasi-Modals in English*. Amsterdam: Rodopi.

Deuber, D. (2010), 'Modal verb usage at the interface of English and a related creole: A corpus-based study of *can*/*could* and *will*/*would* in Trinidadian English', *Journal of English Linguistics*, 38: 105-142.

Deuber, D., C. Biewer, S. Hackert and M. Hilbert (forthcoming), '*Will* and *would* in selected New Englishes: General and variety-specific tendencies', in: M. Hundt and U. Gut (eds.), *Mapping Unity and Diversity World-Wide: Corpus-Based Studies of New Englishes*. Amsterdam: John Benjamins.

Farr, F. and O'Keeffe (2002), '*Would* as a hedging device in an Irish context: An intra-varietal comparison of institutionalised spoken interaction', in: R. Reppen, S.M. Fitzmaurice and D. Biber (eds.), *Using Corpora to Explore Linguistic Variation*. Amsterdam: John Benjamins. 25-48.

Filppula, M. (1999), *A Grammar of Irish English*. London: Routledge.

Hickey, R. (2009), 'Modal verbs in English and Irish', in: E. Penttilä and H. Paulasto (eds.), *Language Contacts Meet English Dialects: Studies in Honour of Markku Filppula*. Newcastle-upon-Tyne: Cambridge Scholars Publishing. 259-274.

Huddleston, R. and G. Pullum (2002), *The Cambridge Grammar of the English Language*. Cambridge: Cambridge University Press.

Kachru, B.B. (2006), 'World Englishes: Agony and ecstasy', in: K. Bolton and B.B. Kachru (eds.), *World Englishes: Critical Concepts in Linguistics*. London: Routledge. 69-88.

Mair, C. and G. Leech (2006), 'Current changes in English syntax', in: B. Aarts and A. McMahon (eds.), *Handbook of English Linguistics*. Oxford: Blackwell. 318-342.

Mesthrie, R. and R.M. Bhatt (2008), *World Englishes*. Cambridge: Cambridge University Press.

Quirk, R., S. Greenbaum, G. Leech and J. Svartvik (1985), *A Comprehensive Grammar of the English Language*. London: Longman.

Ronan, P. (2000), *Tense and Aspect Systems in Irish English: Their Use and Development*. München: Grin.

“Talked the council out of adopting any resolution”: On the transitive *out of -ing* construction in American English

Juhani Rudanko

University of Tampere

Abstract

The transitive out of -ing *pattern, as in* Duffy talked the council out of adopting any resolution… *(COHA), has often been neglected in work on sentential complementation in recent English, but COHA, the new* Corpus of Historical American English, *affords an excellent opportunity to examine the incidence of the pattern and its syntactic and semantic properties on the basis of a large corpus of recent English. It is observed that the pattern was attested in the nineteenth century, but that its frequency was very low. Larger numbers of tokens are found from about the middle of the twentieth century onwards. It is argued that an analysis of the pattern as a type of the caused motion construction is helpful in explaining its semantics in that it makes it possible to invoke two subevents in analyzing sentences involving the pattern. Two force dynamic schemas are identified for the more specific interpretation of the construction. The analysis of the pattern as a construction is also helpful from a syntactic point of view in that it accounts for the occurrence of the pattern with verbs independently selecting different types of argument structures. For instance, the verb* laugh *generally occurs with only one argument, but is also attested with* out of -ing, *as in* I was laughed out of giving the place a fair trial *(COHA). In this case the construction supplies two of the arguments.*

1. Introduction

Consider sentence (1), from the *Corpus of Historical American English* (COHA):

(1) Duffy talked the council out of adopting any resolution directed to the legislature. (1950, NEWS)

In (1) *talk,* the verb of the main clause, selects three arguments. The first two are NPs, *Duffy* and *the council*. As regards the third, it is assumed here that *out of* is a complex preposition (Quirk et al. 1985: 678; see also Lindstromberg 1997: 33), and the third argument is therefore a PP, *out of adopting any resolution directed to the legislature*. The semantic roles of the three arguments are Agent, Patient or Undergoer, and Source. It is also assumed here, in line with traditional and more modern work, that the third argument is sentential, with the argument structure of the lower verb justifying the postulation of an understood subject for the lower clause. The higher subject *Duffy* receives a theta role from the higher verb and the structure of (1) is therefore one of control. In accordance with recent practice, the lower subject is represented by the symbol PRO. Adopting a traditional analysis of the lower clause, it is here termed a nominal clause, which means that it is a sentential constituent with a NP dominating the sentence. With these assumptions made, the structure of (1) may be represented as in (1′):

(1′) $[[\text{Duffy}]_{NP}$ $[\text{talked}]_{Verb}$ $[\text{the council}]_{NP}$ $[[\text{out of}]_{Prep}$ $[[[\text{PRO}]_{NP}$ $[[\text{adopting}]_{Verb}$ $[\text{any resolution directed to the legislature}]_{NP}]_{VP}]_{S2}]_{NP}]_{S1}$

In the pattern of (1) PRO is controlled by the higher object, and the pattern is one of object control. Since one of the arguments of the higher verb is a direct object, the pattern may be termed the transitive *out of -ing* pattern.

This article examines the incidence and grammatical analysis of the transitive *out of -ing* pattern in American English in the last two centuries. The database used is the new *Corpus of Historical American English*, COHA, developed by Mark Davis, and all examples and illustrations, except where noted otherwise, are from that corpus.

The pattern of (1) should be distinguished from the intransitive *out of -ing* pattern, as in (2):

(2) I guess I can't manage to wriggle out of accompanying my parents to Europe. (1953, FIC)

While (2) is also a control pattern, in this case there is no direct object in the higher sentence and PRO is controlled by the higher subject, realized by the NP *I*. In this connection, consider sentence (3):

(3) I get a positive bang out of marching through a village like this. (1962, FIC)

The pattern of (3) has an NP between the higher verb and the *out of -ing* complement, but the NP in question, *a positive bang* in (3), does not control the reference of PRO. Instead the controller of PRO is the higher subject *I*, and the pattern of (3) is one of subject control. The subject control patterns of (2) and (3) are set aside here, and this article focuses on the object control pattern of (1).

On the other hand, consider (4):

(4) Girls can be, have been, trained out of worrying about their lessons. (1891, NF)

Sentence (4) represents the passive version of (1), and its argument structure can be considered on the basis of the active version of the sentence, and such passives are included in the present treatment.

The transitive *out of -ing* pattern has often been neglected in work on the system of English predicate complementation. For instance, while Bridgeman and Householder (1965: 64ff.) offer a discussion of the transitive *into -ing* pattern, as in *Try to scare him into giving us names*, they do not include the transitive *out of*

-ing pattern in their treatment. Francis et al. (1996: 412-416) offer a discussion of a nonsentential pattern that they term the 'V n *out of* n' pattern, which in the terminology used here would be the pattern of 'Verb NP *out of* NP', as in *They were conned out of several hundred pounds*, and they also offer some remarks on the *out of* pattern with a following sentential complement, but do not discuss the latter in its own right. Because of the relative neglect of the pattern, it merits investigation, especially at this time because COHA provides a new resource for the purpose. (Rudanko 2011, Chapter 5 discusses the pattern on the basis of the *TIME Magazine Corpus*, COCA, and the BNC.) COHA is a suitably large and well structured database making a longitudinal study of the pattern over two centuries in a major variety of English possible for the first time.

2. The transitive *out of -ing* pattern as a construction: Evidence from COHA

The search string adopted for this study is 'out of [v?g*]', where the last symbol stands for the *-ing* form of a verb, with the additional specification that there is a lexical verb within four words to the left. Given that the *-ing* form is tightly connected to the preposition as a complement, this search string seems possible from the point of view of recall. This search string retrieves 1,148 tokens from the corpus. The large majority of them are irrelevant for various reasons, leaving us with 126 relevant tokens.

As regards tokens that need to be set aside, there are a number of duplicates among the relevant tokens, and these should be counted only once. Further, a major type to be excluded here are subject control structures of the type of (3). Still further, there are other types that are also irrelevant. For instance, consider (5a-b):

(5) a. [...] she had been given cold chicken, which in her opinion showed a certain levity out of keeping with the occasion. (1972, FIC)
b. [...] it won't be any more use than a toy fort made out of kindling wood. (1940, FIC)

The pattern of (5b), where the *-ing* form is a premodifier of a noun inside a NP, is of course set aside. The fixed phrase *out of keeping*, as in (5a) is also set aside.

Here are some illustrations of relevant tokens in (6a-c):

(6) a. I said you couldn't scare me out of telling who tried to blow up the school-house stove, [...] (1883, FIC)
b. [...] Mr. Moegan had his revenge and frightened the Governor out of making the nomination, [...] (1887, NEWS)
c. Don't let anybody kid you out of going to State. (1939, FIC)

The totals of relevant tokens for each decade of the corpus are given in Table 1.

The figures in parentheses given for some decades indicate the frequency per million words. The verbs selecting the pattern are listed under 'Matrix verbs', with the number in parentheses indicating the number of tokens in that decade. (The absence of a number after a verb means that only one token of the verb was found in that decade.)

Table 1. Occurrences of the transitive *out of -ing* pattern in COHA

Decade	Number of Tokens (frq. pmw)	Matrix verbs
1820s	1	frighten
1830s	0	
1840s	0	
1850s	0	
1860s	1	keep
1870s	2	keep, laugh
1880s	3	frighten, scare, talk
1890s	4	cajole, cheat, train, vote
1900s	1	talk
1910s	1	get
1920s	1	scare
1930s	5 (0.2)	bluff, frighten, kid, scare, talk
1940s	5 (0.2)	talk (4), bluff
1950s	16 (0.7)	talk (9), scare (2), joke, kid, persuade
1960s	17 (0.7)	talk (16), argue
1970s	11 (0.5)	talk (9), pressure
1980s	14 (0.6)	talk (12), argue, drive
1990s	17 (0.6)	talk (13), conflict, intimidate, laugh, price
2000s	27 (0.9)	talk (22), argue, scare
Total	126 (0.3)	

Table 1 shows that the transitive *out of -ing* pattern was very rare in nineteenth century American English. From the 1930s onwards tokens of the construction pattern begin to be found slightly more frequently, but even then the pattern remains quite rare. Table 1 also shows that the pattern becomes somewhat more frequent from the 1950s onwards, and then maintains its position in the subsequent decades. It is also observed that the increase in frequency from the 1950s onwards is above all due to the increasing prominence of the matrix verb *talk* with the pattern. *Scare* is the second most frequent verb with the pattern, but its frequency is nowhere near that of *talk*.

To achieve a theoretical analysis of the transitive *out of -ing* pattern, it is helpful to invoke Adele Goldberg's (1995) notion of a construction. The proposal is made here that the transitive *out of -ing* pattern represents a type of an argument structure construction, and, more specifically, that the construction in question is a caused motion construction. To understand the nature of a caused motion construction, it is helpful to bear in mind that there are two subevents involved, the constructional subevent and the verbal subevent, and that there is a specific relation between the two. Goldberg and Jackendoff (2004) provide a discussion of resultatives which is also relevant to the caused motion construction, because the term resultative is used by these authors in a broad sense. They write:

> [...] the meaning of a resultative sentence contains two separable subevents. One of them, the VERBAL SUBEVENT, is determined by the verb of the sentence. The other subevent, the CONSTRUCTIONAL SUBEVENT, is determined by the construction. A resultative sentence means more than just the conjunction of the verbal subevent and the constructional subevent. [...] That is, for the bulk of cases [...] the verbal subevent is the MEANS by which the constructional subevent takes place. (Goldberg and Jackendoff 2004: 538; the emphasis in the original)

Regarding the nature of the constructional subevent in the case of the transitive *out of -ing* pattern, there are two interpretations identified in a more general discussion in Goldberg (1995: 161f.) that are relevant. The first is the force dynamic schema of 'X causes Y to move Z'. This is relevant to sentence (4), for instance. The sentence may be turned into the active for the purpose of illustrating the construction, as in (4′):

(4′) Mother trained the girls out of worrying about their lessons.

Applying a construction grammar analysis to (4′) and taking advantage of the notion that there are two subevents involved, it is possible to say that part of the meaning of (4′) is along the lines of 'Mother caused the girls to move out of worrying about their lessons by training them'. This interpretation entails that prior to the event expressed by the sentence the state of affairs named by the lower clause existed. That is, in the case of sentence (4′), the girls were worrying about their lessons. However, it follows from the truth of the proposition expressed by sentence (4′) that they moved out of that state by means of the verbal subevent. Because of the movement involved, the interpretation may be termed the extraction interpretation. The lower predicate 'worry about one's lessons' is atelic, without any natural endpoint or culmination, and this kind of predicate goes well with an extraction interpretation.

There is also another force dynamic schema that is often relevant. This is 'X prevents Y from moving Comp (Z)'. To quote Goldberg's more general discussion of the caused motion construction:

> This class of expressions [...] can be described in terms of the force-dynamic schema of imposition of a barrier, causing the patient to stay in a location despite its inherent tendency to move. (Goldberg 1995: 162)

For instance, consider a somewhat simplified version of (6b) to illustrate the schema:

(6b′) Mr. Morgan frightened the Governor out of making the nomination.

Sentence (6b′) does not mean that the Governor ever made the nomination. However, the sentence suggests that he/she had a tendency or an inclination to make the nomination but that he/she was prevented from doing so. Taking advantage of the Goldberg-Jackendoff analysis, it is possible to say that part of the meaning of (6b′) is along the lines of: ‘Mr. Morgan prevented the Governor from making the nomination by means of frightening him/her’. The lower predicate in (6b′) is telic, expressing an endpoint, and this kind of predicate is natural with a prevention interpretation.

Examining the matrix verbs identified in Table 1 from a syntactic point of view, it is possible to provide further evidence for a construction grammar analysis of the pattern. The matrix verbs in question are of different syntactic types. There are some verbs among them that select three arguments independently of the transitive *out of -ing* pattern and independently of any other prepositional pattern of complementation. *Persuade* and *pressure* are among such verbs. Here are illustrations of these with *out of -ing*:

(7) a. She’d persuaded her father out of putting us in a dungeon until he thought of us again. (1959, FIC)
 b. one whole night with Murray Chotiner [...] who had a helluva job pressuring her out of threatening to leave me if I ran for the Vice Presidency [...] (1977, FIC)

Persuade and *pressure* of course also select *to* infinitive complements that exhibit object control, and (7a-b) might be compared with the invented sentences of (8a-b):

(8) a. She had persuaded her father not to put us in a dungeon until he thought of us again.
 b. [...] who had a helluva time pressuring her not to threaten to leave me if I ran for the Vice Presidency [...]

The *out of -ing* pattern is more specific in meaning than the *to* infinitive with these verbs. For instance, comparing (7a) and (8a), the former suggests that the father *had made a decision to put them in a dungeon*, which reflects the ‘tendency to move’ ingredient, and that she prevented this from happening by means of persuading him out of doing so. By contrast, (8a) is less restricted to such a specific scenario.

Another type of matrix verb that is found in Table 1 as selecting the transitive *out of -ing* pattern is exemplified in *kid* and *scare*. Here are illustrations of these with *out of -ing* in (9a-b):

(9) a. Don't let anyone kid you out of going to State. (1939, FIC)
b. I said you couldn't scare me out of telling who tried to blow up the school- house stove, [...] (1883, FIC)

These are verbs that are very commonly found with only two arguments, with meanings such as "to hoax, humbug, try to make (one) believe what is not true" (OED, *kid*$_4$) for *kid* and "to frighten, terrify" (OED, sense 1.a) for *scare*, as in (10a-b):

(10) a. You're not kidding her, but go ahead. (1951, FIC)
b. "Look here, you're scaring me. I'm timid." (1919, FIC)

When the transitive *out of -ing* pattern is analyzed as a caused motion construction, it is possible to make use of the two subevents involved and say that the construction supplies the third argument in (9a-b) and further that the verb retains its basic meaning even in these sentences. Part of the meaning of (9a) for instance is then along the lines 'don't let anyone prevent you from going to State by means of hoaxing you'.

Further evidence for viewing the transitive *out of -ing* pattern as a construction may be gleaned from verbs that are often intransitive, including *joke* and *laugh*. Here are illustrations of these with the transitive *out of -ing* pattern in (11a-b):

(11) a. SLEEP softly, my true love, and when you wake, this will be over and will joke you out of trying to learn details of the triste metier of war [...] (1950, FIC)
b. Also, I had had but little experience in mining; and, moreover, whenever I mentioned Red Ridge I was simply laughed at by my mates. I was laughed out of giving the place a fair trial. (1874, FIC)

Joke frequently has the sense of 'make a joke or jokes, jest' (Shorter OED, sense 1) and *laugh* has the basic meaning of 'make the spasmodic inarticulate sounds, the movements of facial muscles, shaking of the sides, etc., which are the instinctive expressions of lively amusement, scorn, exultation, etc.' (Shorter OED, part of sense 1). With these senses the verb often has only one argument, as in (12a-b):

(12) a. That first evening he had been extraordinarily talkative – interrupting her, joking with her, teasing her, begging her not to leave him [...] (1975, FIC)
b. She laughed deliriously, and shuddered, as her voice died away on her lips, [...] (1822, FIC)

Again, when the transitive *out of -ing* pattern is viewed as a caused motion construction, it is possible to invoke the two subevents and to say that the verb retains its basic meaning even in (11a-b). (11a) is of the extraction type, and part of the meaning of the sentence is along the lines 'I will cause you to move out of trying to learn details of [...] by means of making jokes'. For its part (11b) is of the prevention type, and part of its meaning is along the lines 'I was prevented from giving the place a fair trial by means of my mates laughing at me'.

It is a reflection of the comprehensiveness of the OED that that work of reference provides separate senses for *out of* usages. (These are admittedly restricted to *out of* NP complements.) For instance, in the case of *laugh*, sense 6 is given as "6. With obj and compl. Or advb. Phr.: To produce a specified effect upon (a person) by laughing". Illustrations of *laugh* with this sense include *Sure ye'd be laughed out of any hunting-field in Britain if ye took one of them things there*. (1891, Rolf Boldrewood, *Col. Reformer*)

The inclusion of a sense of the type of sense 6 in a dictionary that aims at a comprehensive coverage of the language is justified, and maybe illustrations can also come to include tokens of the sentential *out of -ing* pattern, which is related to the nonsentential *out of* NP pattern that is illustrated. At the same time, the definition of the sense is clearly of interest, since it confirms the MEANS relation used in the construction grammar account adopted here on the basis of Goldberg and Jackendoff (2004).

Turning to the matrix verb *talk*, here are two additional illustrations of this verb, the most frequent with *out of -ing* by a long way in (13a-b):

(13) a. Suppose you talk her out of marrying Leo now. (1953, FIC)
b. He had undoubtedly tried to talk her out of staying in a house where so many peculiar, possibly threatening things, had happened. (1986, FIC)

Prevention readings, as in (13a), with the telic lower predicate *marry Leo*, seem more frequent with *talk* than extraction readings, but the latter do not seem impossible either, as in (13b), where the lower predicate, *stay in a house*, is atelic, and suggests an extraction interpretation.

The verb *talk* is similar to *joke* and *laugh* in that it is often used with only one argument as in (14):

(14) Why, we sat down together, before a comfortable fire, and talked for a whole hour! (1823, FIC)

The use of the verb in the transitive *out of -ing* construction might therefore be accounted along similar lines, as with *joke* and *laugh*, with the construction supplying two of the arguments in the caused motion construction. However, there is an additional consideration. This is that this same verb is also found very frequently in the caused motion construction involving the preposition *into*, of the type *talk someone into doing something*. In some recent work on constructions, admittedly on the conative construction, it has been pointed out that constructions do not operate in a vacuum and that instead one construction may have an impact upon another (Perek 2010). In the present case the transitive *out of -ing* and the transitive *into -ing* patterns are both object control patterns, and while the third argument is a Source in the former and a Goal in the latter, these are both roles expressing Path, and the prepositions *into* and *out of* may be felt to have an antonymic relation, and these considerations may go some way towards explaining why the same matrix verb *talk* tends to be found frequently with both types of the caused motion construction. It may be added that most of the verbs listed in Table 1, including *bluff*, *cajole*, *frighten*, *intimidate*, *persuade*, *pressure*, and *scare*, are also prominently featured in lists of verbs selecting the transitive *into -ing* pattern (see Francis et al. 1996: 412-416; Rudanko 2000: Chapter 5). This further supports the idea that there is a connection between the two types of caused motion construction. At the same time, it also needs to be recognized, in view of earlier work, including Francis et al. (1996: 412-416) and Rudanko (2005), that the transitive *out of -ing* pattern is much less frequent as a caused motion construction than the transitive *into -ing* pattern. This statement holds for the overall frequencies of the patterns and for the types of matrix verbs selecting them.

3. Concluding observations

This study shows that the transitive *out of -ing* pattern was very rare in nineteenth century American English. It became slightly more frequent from the 1930s and especially from the 1950s onwards, but it has still not become anywhere near as frequent as the transitive *into -ing* pattern. The overall frequency of the pattern remains fairly low, and the types of matrix verbs that are attested with it do not have the variety that is found with the transitive *into -ing* pattern.

While the transitive *out of -ing* pattern is not very frequent, which may be a reason why it has sometimes been ignored in the literature, it is still helpful to analyze it as a construction. The view that it is a type of the caused motion construction is supported by semantic and syntactic considerations. From a semantic point of view, the construction grammar analysis makes it possible to invoke two force dynamic schemas to account for the constructional meaning of the pattern. The verbal subevent also regularly expresses the means by which the constructional subevent takes place, and the regularity of the relation lends support to the construction grammar analysis. From a syntactic point of view, it was seen that the transitive *out of -ing* construction may occur with verbs such as *joke* and *laugh* that are prototypically intransitive, and it is then possible to say that it is the caused motion construction that supplies the missing arguments for these verbs. Since the verbs come with one argument, the construction supplies two arguments in their case. Establishing a relation between the transitive *out of -ing* pattern and the transitive *into -ing* pattern may also serve to account, at least in part, why the same verb *talk* is so frequent in both constructions.

This study invites further work for instance on the transitive *out of -ing* pattern in British English in the last two centuries and on comparing the results with those obtained here for American English. Further, the suggestion made above that the transitive *out of -ing* pattern has a more specific meaning than the *to* infinitive, with verbs that select both, will merit further investigation, and it will be of interest further to explore the semantic properties of the two force dynamic schemas associated with the transitive *out of -ing* pattern here, and to compare them to schemas found for instance with *to* infinitive complements selected by verbs that select both types of complements.

References

Bridgeman, L.I. and F.W. Householder (eds.) (1965), *More Classes of Verbs in English*. Bloomington, IN: Indiana University Linguistics Club.

Brown, L. (ed.) (1993), *The New Shorter Oxford English Dictionary on Historical Principles*. Oxford: Clarendon Press. [Shorter OED]

Francis, G., S. Hunston and E. Manning (eds.) (1996), *Collins Cobuild Grammar Patterns 1: Verbs*. London: HarperCollins Publishers.

Goldberg, A. (1995), *Constructions*. Chicago, IL: Chicago University Press.

Goldberg, A. and R. Jackendoff (2004), 'The English resultative as a family of constructions', *Language*, 80: 532-568.

Lindstromberg, S. (1997), *English Prepositions Explained*. Amsterdam: John Benjamins.

Simpson, J. and E. Weiner (eds.) (1989), *The Oxford English Dictionary*. 2nd edition. Oxford: Clarendon Press. [OED]

Perek, F. (2010), 'Reappraising the role of alternations in construction grammar: The case of the conative construction'. Paper presented at the 3rd UK Cognitive Linguistics Conference, University of Hertfordshire, July 2010.

Quirk, R., S. Greenbaum, G. Leech and J. Svartvik (1985), *A Comprehensive Grammar of the English Language*. London: Longman.

Rudanko, J. (2000), *Corpora and Complementation*. Lanham, MD: University Press of America.

Rudanko, J. (2005), 'Lexico-grammatical innovation in current British and American English: A case study on the transitive *into -ing* pattern with evidence from the Bank of English Corpus', *Studia Neophilologica*, 77: 171-187.

Rudanko, J. (2011), *Changes in Complementation in British and American English*. Houndsmills: Palgrave Macmillan.

Tracking the evolution of vernaculars: Corpus linguistics and earlier Southern US Englishes

Edgar W. Schneider

University of Regensburg

Abstract

*The paper argues for the need to investigate vernacular speech forms diachronically as evidence of natural language change, largely untouched by standardization processes. It suggests letters written by semi-literate writers as an appropriate source of data, and after surveying earlier pertinent writings and approaches it pays some attention to methodological considerations which play a role specifically in compiling and analyzing nonstandard corpora. The principles considered are then applied in an investigation of black and white dialects from the Southern United States as reflected in diachronic sources. Under the umbrella heading of ReCAmED (*Regensburg Corpora of American English Dialects*), three pertinent corpus compilation and analysis projects are introduced and characterized: SPOC, a corpus of* Southern Plantation Overseers Letters, *by white nineteenth century writers; COAAL, a* Corpus of Older African American Letters, *from roughly the same period; and BLUR, a corpus of early twentieth century* Blues Lyrics compiled at the University of Regensburg. *The three corpora are compared in terms of their properties and usefulness for dialect analysis, including methodological decisions taken, and are illustrated by short sample texts. Subsequently, exemplary investigations based on them are presented. First, some erratic, quasi-phonetic spellings, some widely discussed nonstandard grammatical patterns, and the continuous use of the old English* 'for to + *infinitive' construction to express a purpose in these dialects are documented. Secondly, the corpora are employed to test hypotheses of earlier scholarship which claimed (a) a comparatively late post-Reconstruction origin of the southern dialect, and (b) the existence of fundamental grammatical differences between the races at earlier times (with the corpus data providing strong support for the former but not for the latter hypothesis).*[1]

1. Introduction

For a number of decades sociolinguistics and variationist linguistics have taught us that the traditional post-Saussurean assumption of language being a self-contained, neatly structured system, consisting of clearly delimitated units and their mutual relationships, is overly idealistic at best (and possibly simply mistaken). In contrast, recent theorizing (to which this paper implicitly subscribes) has come to view language as a complex self-organizing system (Larsen-Freeman and Cameron 2008), possibly with chaotic, nonlinear properties (Schneider 1997). Functional considerations are central to such a perspective, which gives priority to performance and language use, i.e. speech (Kretzschmar 2009), which emphasizes the importance of cognitive processes and frequency effects (Bybee 2007), or the importance of language contact effects via individual languages contributing to a 'feature pool' of available choices (Mufwene 2001).

While a closer consideration of these theories and assumptions would lead too far in the present context, the essential point that needs to be made here is the idea that language organization operates first and foremost on the vernacular level of real-life speech rather than on the level of standard forms and written or edited texts. By implication, obviously the same holds true for the diachronic perspective, i.e. principles of language evolution manifest themselves most directly in histories of dialectal varieties, not in language histories based on standard and literary sources. Such attempts, however, typically are faced with the 'bad data problem', given that for obvious reasons historical texts that have come down to us tend to represent formal text types and styles. Thus, obtaining reliable data and authentic evidence of earlier vernaculars is a fundamental problem in the study of real-life language change, and tracking the evolution of vernaculars is a desirable but difficult goal in historical linguistics, and also, obviously, in historical corpus linguistics.

The goal of this paper is to address this issue systematically and to characterize a research project which promises to come reasonably close to a solution with respect to a specific variety of English. In the following sections, I will first survey methodological problems and earlier approaches in the study of earlier vernaculars (2.), and then apply them to a specific case, the history of Southern US dialects, the investigation of which has been characterized by a few heated, and in part ideologically motivated, debates (3.). A set of electronic corpora of vernacular texts from the US South, covering the late eighteenth to the early twentieth centuries, will be presented, characterized and compared to each other (4.), also by illustrating how some of the methodological issues have been addressed in the compilation of these corpora (5.). Finally, some data and findings drawn from these projects will be documented (6.).

2. Theory and methodology: Survey

2.1 Earlier approaches: Some projects

Of course, the quest for detecting evidence of earlier speech (rather than writing) is not a new issue, and so the present paper ties in with and indirectly builds upon a number of earlier studies in this field. Notably, the earliest classic of historical corpus linguistics, the *Helsinki Corpus* itself, pursued similar goals via the representation of different text types and thus formal and relatively more informal styles and also, considering the "Older Scots" part, varieties. A selection of other comparable projects and studies needs to mention at least the following model studies: the *Corpus of Early English Conversations* (CEEC; Nevalainen and Raumolin-Brunberg 1996) with its more recent *Extension and Supplement* (Nurmi et al. 2009); the *Corpus of English Dialogues* (CED; Kytö et al. 2006; Culpeper and Kytö 2010), and Huber's *Old Bailey Corpus* (cf. Huber 2007 and the ICAME workshop 2010). Note, however, that in all these cases the emphasis was on the rendition of speech as against writing, and not primarily on vernacularity and the rendition of regional or social dialect.

A number of earlier studies, including publications resulting from the projects just mentioned, have developed theoretical insights and contributed to discussions surrounding the investigation of earlier speech and dialect. Schneider (2001) systematically discussed the investigation of linguistic variation and change on the basis of written sources, introducing a so-called 'Principle of Filter Removal' which employed text typology and considerations on the proximity of a given text type to a speech event represented by it to assess the reliability of a written record as a mirror of a speech event. Further problems and pitfalls in this growing discipline have been addressed in Taavitsainen et al. (2000), a volume with investigations of literary dialect samples and historical sources, Nevalainen and Tanskanen (2007), with a focus on letter writing and pragmatic issues, and Dossena and Tieken-Boon van Ostade (2008), also a volume on aspects of contemporary letter-writing with many relevant observations, though only marginally on vernacular styles. Hickey (2010) is a recent volume which specifically looks at the written representation of varieties of English, both diachronically and today. Amongst other pertinent contributions in this volume, Hickey (2010) provides a historical survey of discussions of speech, issues raised in this context, and earlier approaches towards a reliable assessment of vernacularity, and Claridge and Kytö (2010) discuss the notion of non-standardness in historical contexts, using CED examples. Of course, the Helsinki school and the VARIENG project context have produced a range of relevant sources, including some collective volumes (e.g. Nevalainen and Raumolin-Brunberg 1996, 2003; Nurmi, Nevala and Palander-Collin 2009) and several papers (e.g. Kytö and Walker 2003; Culpeper and Kytö 2010). Many of these writings have also discussed methodological issues (notably the role of dialogic genres), in addition to thoroughly investigating specific linguistic issues.

Several topics have turned out to be particularly fruitful or prominent in these research efforts. In recent years there has been a clear focus on pragmatics, looking at expressions of politeness, the use of address systems in earlier times, and so on. Also with respect to usage in context, subjects of research have included lexical bundles and other co-occurrence phenomena, the use of repetitions, and the function of specific linguistic forms as markers of sociolinguistic identity expressions. The latter approach, of course, ties in with historical sociolinguistics, the discipline which has attempted to trace variation by gender, class, region, and other parameters, especially at VARIENG in Helsinki (Nevalainen and Raumolin-Brunberg 1996, 2003; Nurmi et al. 2009). The process of standardization and, in contrast, the notion of 'nonstandard', looking at its definition, identification, and historical emergence have been investigated and discussed (e.g. Claridge and Kytö 2010). Most fundamentally, however, the issue which stands behind many of these approaches is the question of to what extent historical writing (including vernacular writing) really reflects any earlier vernacular speech event (cf. Culpeper and Kytö 2000; Kytö and Walker 2003).

2.2 Theory: Text categorization

The most promising way of assessing the vernacularity of (historical) texts operates via a categorization of established text categories and an investigation of their properties. As was mentioned before, Schneider (2002) categorized text types by their proximity to speech events which they are taken to represent; accordingly, Table 1 summarizes the most important options.

Table 1. Text types by proximity to speech event (Schneider 2001: 73)

Category	Reality of speech event	Speaker-writer identity	Temporal distance speech-record	Characteristic text types
Recorded	real, unique	different	immediate	interview transcripts, trial records
Recalled	real, unique	different	later	ex-slave narratives
Imagined	hypothetic, unique	identical	immediate	letters, diaries
Observed	usu. real, unique	identical	later	commentaries
Invented	hypothetic, unspecified	n.a.	unspecified	literary dialect

The table identifies some text types which have been widely used in the reconstruction of historical speech, with their respective pros and cons. Literary dialect is fairly widely available, but of questionable validity, given that not infrequently authors seek a desired effect via overusing salient, stereotypical forms of any variety. Trial records and witness depositions are certainly most promising and interesting in this context; Kytö and Walker (2003: 230) qualify them as "relatively faithful" but also never "equivalent to actual speech" (cf. also Huber 2007). The most widely employed source have certainly been letters, which have been "shown to be close to spoken language in many ways" and rated as the "best possible access to early phases of change in the history of a language" (Palander-Collin et al. 2009: 5). But even in projects where the goal of getting closer to earlier forms of speech has been pursued, there was usually relatively little emphasis on vernacularity in the narrow sense. Main topics of scholarly interest in this domain have been the social setup of societies in earlier times and corresponding modes of behavior, historical pragmatics and the rules of a polite society, and certainly also representations of an informal register via selecting letters to family and friends specifically. Still, the speakers investigated have tended to be representatives of the higher social strata – an assessment which is confirmed, for example, by the fact that the *Oxford Dictionary of National Biography* is offered as the relevant source for sociolinguistic speaker/writer assessments in the CEEC and CEEC+ projects. The speech of common folks, ordinary working class people, has hardly been investigated in these projects, perhaps because such evidence is much more difficult to come by. The point is simply that those who could read and write in earlier times were almost automatically members of higher social classes, and even amongst their writings the texts which have been handed down to the present day have been preserved because they were perceived as somehow important, and thus worthy of special attention and care, e.g. in the form of being archived. Typically down-to-earth natural speech was not recorded, and even if it had been there was no reason to preserve such a record.

2.3 Semi-literate letters as evidence

Thus, what we would be interested in as historical linguists is written records of the speech of those who could not read or write. While this certainly is somewhat paradoxical, there is a promising text type which comes reasonably close to such expectations, namely letters written by semi-literate writers, people who could barely read and write but did get their words onto paper for some important reason (and, ideally, this reason has supported the preservation of such letters). In a similar vein, Claridge and Kytö (2010) also recommend "pauper letters" as a recommendable source, and Fairman (2008: 193) labels such authors as "mechanically-letterate writers". Much valuable work along such lines has been carried out by Michael Montgomery of the University of South Carolina, notably on the history of Appalachian and Ulster dialects (but outside the corpus-linguistic tradition). The major advantage of semi-literate letters, following Montgomery (1999: 25), is their high authenticity – when writers just try to get words onto paper somehow they are not concerned with linguistic decorum. The limitations are equally obvious: on most of such writers there is usually no or hardly any biographic information available (which would be important for a sociolinguistic assessment of the speech recorded); and such letters are just simply difficult to find, and in the absence of information of the writer's skills and education their vernacularity is difficult to assess. We are interested in disclosing writers and their products, Montgomery (1997: 229) argued, who had "a compelling reason to write" and whose letters had an increased chance of preservation, for example because they were addressed to a government institution (with an established archiving procedure). Accordingly, he identified three types of writers (by motivation) where these conditions were likely to be fulfilled: "desperadoes" (who desperately pleaded for mercy, relief or help to some official institution), "functionaries" (who because of their role were required to report to someone else in writing on a regular basis), and "lonelyhearts" (people separated from their loved ones who tried to communicate nevertheless). Many of the texts investigated below fall into these categories.

Obviously, the research strategy of disclosing and investigating such letters raises a few specific methodological concerns. One central issue is that of identification: how do we recognize a semi-literate writer and his texts? Claridge and Kytö (2010: 34) point out that the fact that "a language user [is] unaccustomed to writing [...] is visible in the complete lack of punctuation and the uncertain orthography". Secondly, there is the issue of representativeness: do semi-literate writers really represent a lower-class social stratum? This is difficult to assess and impossible to answer on a general basis; it depends on the literacy rate or the amount of access to writing in a given culture, and probably simply also on idiosyncratic factors. An important sideline, obviously, is the problem of excluding the possible help of scribes or amanuenses: of course texts produced by untrained writers are of interest only if they wrote them themselves, and not if the texts were dictated to someone else. Finally, there is the fundamental issue of validity: do the texts really represent natural speech? Given the contexts of text production the interference of stylistic considerations on the side of the writers seems unlikely, but a point which does need consideration is the presence of (and, from the perspective of corpus compilation, the need to exclude) certain formulaic passages, such as openings and closings of letters, ritual greetings or expressions of deference.

2.4 Methodological issues

From the perspective of corpus-linguistic methodology, dealing with vernacular data poses special methodological questions. Some of these are briefly addressed here, and will be illustrated below when discussing the corpora used.

First, there is the issue of finding and assessing sources. Semi-literate letters are basically available in two forms and contexts. Some such texts have been published, for instance by historians as first-hand evidence in pertinent books, but usually without closer attention paid to linguistic form. Published texts clearly are easier to find and to handle (e.g. to scan), but their linguistic reliability may be questionable, so for a linguist the question of the editing strategies employed (e.g. the amount of faithfulness in manuscript transcription) needs to be reflected. In contrast, manuscript sources provide first-hand evidence, but getting hold of them requires substantial efforts (archival search and identification of pertinent texts on location), and so does an assessment of their usefulness, and also, not infrequently, the process of deciphering old handwriting.

Secondly, the type of source used has obvious consequences for corpus compilation and data input. Printed texts can be scanned; manuscripts need to be read and keyboarded; both types must be checked against originals and proofread. As with other corpora as well, decisions must be made as to the identification of specific components and the handling of problematic text parts, i.e. on mark-up, the structure and components of headers, and the handling of difficult parts and special components such as crossed-out words, superscripts, missing text, and so on. Decisions on the preservation and possibly distribution of corpus data are frequently faced with the need to consider copyright issues and constraints.

Thirdly, vernacular texts also pose special problems of corpus analysis, which may reduce the usefulness of the corpus-linguistic approach in general and corpus software in particular. Vernacular texts typically contain unpredictable orthographic variants of target forms, so variant and erratic spellings increase the search effort dramatically and decrease the reliability of the search return, because desired target forms may not be formally identifiable. For the comparable problem domain of historical texts the lists of variant spellings provided by the OED entries have commonly been used and accepted as a practicable yardstick. It remains questionable, however, whether these lists are complete and reliable, especially so for younger, vernacular texts (where the parameters that determine orthographic variation may be different from the ones reflected in the OED's diachronic orientation). Certain formal properties of informal texts are particularly problematic to identify, most notably all kinds of zero forms (omitted but understood words, or zero allomorphs of endings), which are known to be particularly common in colloquial speech but at the same time, given their very nature, formally unsearchable. A manual search may help to disclose many of them, but is clearly hugely inefficient and cumbersome: if a researcher needs to read an entire text anyhow, why compile and use an electronic corpus, then? One possible solution might be a process of 'normalization', the production of a parallel version in standard orthography; but again, this requires human input and is thus error-prone and time consuming. Compromise 'solutions' are conceivable and have sometimes been practiced, including structure-based searches (looking for typical environments of a target form) and lexically based searches (i.e. looking for the manifestations of a research issue in only a part of the corpus, e.g. restricted to some lexical items only). It seems that corpus work involving vernacular texts always requires a trade-off between the effort invested and the return hoped for, certainly more so than when we deal with standard language forms. Illustrations for these assessments and problem areas will be provided below.

3. The issue: Towards a history of Southern US dialects

The general considerations outlined above will now be applied to a corpus-based investigation of the history of Southern English in the US, the strongest and most stigmatized dialect of American English. Dialect geography has produced an immensely rich documentation of the language forms used in the South with the *Linguistic Atlas of the Gulf States* (LAGS; Pederson et al. 1986-1991), supplemented by much other work from the tradition of language variation and change research (for a recent survey see Nagle and Sanders 2003). Still, many debates have been left unresolved, and much research is still being carried out and also required. Most importantly, ethnic variation, the relationship between black and white speech in the South, has been a topic of long-standing controversy. Both the origin and the historical evolution of both ethnic varieties have been subjects of ongoing debates, and no consensus has been reached on these issues so far.

The best known and most widely documented topic of contention has been the debate on the origins of African American Vernacular English (AAVE), which essentially has been going on since the 1960s. In the early phase, two scholarly camps proposed and held competing positions as to the origin of AAVE which were vehemently opposed to each other. 'Anglicists', mostly coming from a dialectologist background, suggested that the forms characteristic of AAVE (called Black English in those days) can mostly be traced back to British dialectal roots, and have later been preserved more strongly in the black community because of social differences. In contrast, 'creolists' claimed that the dialect parallels Caribbean Creoles in having strong African roots and structural properties, later to be lost in part because of ongoing decreolization. In hindsight, one can state that these positions, as voiced between the Civil Rights Movement and Reagan's presidency, were strongly motivated by sociopolitical beliefs of their advocates but backed by only scant linguistic evidence, if any. The issue was revitalized in the 1990s and thereafter, however, when new types of evidence offered more thorough and also new insights, including slave narratives (Schneider 1989), audio recordings of former slaves (Bailey et al. 1991), diaspora dialects (Poplack and Tagliamonte 2001), old Hoodoo interviews (Kautzsch 2002), and others. Moderate compromise positions have been proposed (Winford 1997/98), and in general one can say that scholarly interests have changed and broadened to include trajectories of change in the black community (Wolfram and Thomas 2002) or the use of AAVE language forms for explicit identity projections, e.g. in hip hop (cf. Alim 2004); but in a so-called 'neo-Anglicist' camp and amongst some creolist contenders the controversial claims as to a dialectal or creole origin of AAVE are still vehemently contested (compare the positions voiced in Poplack (2000) or those in Rickford (2006), for instance).

Interestingly enough, the historical roots of not only the black but also those of the white dialects of the South have been contested (cf. Schneider 2003). A traditional view (e.g. Brooks 1935; Kurath 1972) claimed that the dialect of the South can be traced back to dialect input from different parts of the British Isles, and emphasized the importance of settlement streams; familiar manifestations of such thinking were Marckwardt's (1958) notion of 'colonial lag' and the popular myth, widespread in the South, of the 'Elizabethan' origin and character of the dialect (for documentation see Schneider 2003: 20). In contrast, Bailey (1997) claimed a relatively late origin of Southern English. He suggested that the variety is predominantly a product of the post-Reconstruction period when after the loss of the Civil War and under northern dominance it emerged as an identity marker signaling resistance to 'Yankee' dominance. His evidence suggests that the most distinctive characteristics of Southern English appear for the first time and then get linguistically established only in the late nineteenth and early twentieth centuries. Schneider (2004) suggested a compromise which makes both approaches reconcilable to a certain extent, arguing that there is a difference between two types (or rather, conceptualizations) of southern dialect: a 'Traditional Southern', marked by certain traditional and rural features which are increasingly getting archaic or have disappeared by today, as against a 'Modern Southern', characterized by innovative features preferred in modern, urban contexts. It is clear that for a final resolution of this issue better evidence is in need.

A third, equally disputed issue, known as the 'divergence controversy', concerns the direction of the changing relationship between black and white speech in the recent past. In the 1980s two research teams around Bill Labov in Pennsylvania and Guy Bailey in Texas independently of each other found that the difference between black and white dialects of a comparable socioeconomic stratum is increasing rather than decreasing. Obviously, the claim held a lot of sociopolitical conflict potential, and it invited some misinterpretations on the side of conservative contenders opposed to public funding of minority education. Evidence has been conflicting since then; apparently there are also a number of converging linguistic features where the linguistic behavior of blacks and whites becomes more alike; but there seem to be a few linguistic forms with respect to which the ethnicities increasingly differ from each other indeed (Butters 1989). Again, to achieve reasonable responses on all these issues, we need more evidence which is authentic and reliable and represents diachronically relevant vernacular dialect from earlier phases of the emergence of Southern English.

4. Sources: ReCAmED

New and pertinent evidence is being presented in this paper in the form of a set of data which together I have chosen to call ReCAmED (*Regensburg Corpora of American English Dialects*): a suite of three electronic corpora of diachronic sources of Southern American English vernacular dialects which has been compiled at the University of Regensburg over the last decade or more. As a linguistic data collection and project sequence, ReCAmED is meant to contribute to the above-mentioned issues but also to be of some interest in its own right as a source of data reflecting linguistic developments. Incidentally, the corpus collection is of course also of interest for cultural historians in some respects. The components of ReCAmED are three individual parts, originally separate corpora united by similarities in their compilation contexts, methodological approaches, and goals: the *Southern Plantation Overseers Corpus* (SPOC); the *Corpus of Older African-American Letters* (COAAL); and the *Corpus of Blues Lyrics compiled at the University of Regensburg* (BLUR).

4.1 Sources: SPOC

The *Southern Plantation Overseers Corpus* (SPOC) consists of letters written on a regular basis by plantation overseers to absentee plantation owners, reporting on ongoing activities and events on the plantation. These letters were collected in various southern archives by Michael Montgomery, and they were computerized between 1999 and 2001 at the University of Regensburg. These are classic instances of semi-literate letters, composed by white writers who were "functionaries" in the sense of Montgomery's (1997: 229) classification referred to above. The corpus consists of 536 letters, with a total of c. 155,000 words, written by 50 writers and stemming from 33 different family and archival collections; it covers the time span of 1794-1876.

Text 1. A sample letter from SPOC

<Collection: Thomas Ruffin Papers>
<Source: UNC-CH, Southern Historical Collection 641>
<Letter ID: Carter 69>
<From: Alexander Carter>
<To: Judge Thomas Ruffin>
<Date: 12 June May 1856>
June th 12 1856
Mr. Ruffin I Right you, we
are all wel, I finished planting tobacco
Saturday, with a fin Season, we Had a fine
Rain on thirs day Before, on Sunday we Had
Sum Rain & a Smart Hail, on munday we
Had a very Washing Rain washed out all
of my water gaps, on tusday we Had
a Still wors Rain, the Hiland is washed
very Bad, the Branch By the packing House
was very Rapid washed very Bad, Except
what Has washed up my tobacco Stands wel
corn on the Stiff Land Sufferd very much
Before the Rain is groing very fast now, I
Hav Bin over my corn twise, as Soon as the
Land get in aurder, I in tend Runing over
with my cultervato[r] Before Lay ing By,
my wheat is fine I am a fread the wet
will giv my wheat the Rust, if no dis as-
ter Be fauls my wheat I Shal make a Lage
crop, will git nearly threw striping this
weak, Hav deliverd Eight thousand twoo
hundred pounds Expect to Send off five thous
and pounds to morrow, will Send off what
part of the crop I Hav to Hall my Self
th in the morning I think their will Be a Bout
thirty thousand pounds
youre frend
Alexander Carter

It is introduced and characterized in two earlier publications which also present first results, Schneider and Montgomery (2001) and Trüb (2006). Text 1 presents a sample letter from the corpus, together with the header which precedes each of these papers and marks up some essential background information.

4.2 Sources: COAAL

Secondly, the *Corpus of Older African American Letters* (COAAL) consists of letters written by semi-literate African-Americans, mostly "desperadoes" or "lonelyhearts" (in Montgomery's scheme). This corpus has also been compiled in collaboration with Michael Montgomery of USC, and in association with Lucia Siebers of the University of Regensburg, who has served as Principal Investigator and has directed and carried out herself most of the ongoing work. The project was funded by the *Deutsche Forschungsgemeinschaft* (DFG, project number SCHN 388/12-1) between 2007 and mid-2010; at the time of writing this corpus collection is completed and much of the editing work has been done, but with some parts of the corpus editing is still going on. A total number of 1,530 letters is expected, produced by c. 900 writers.

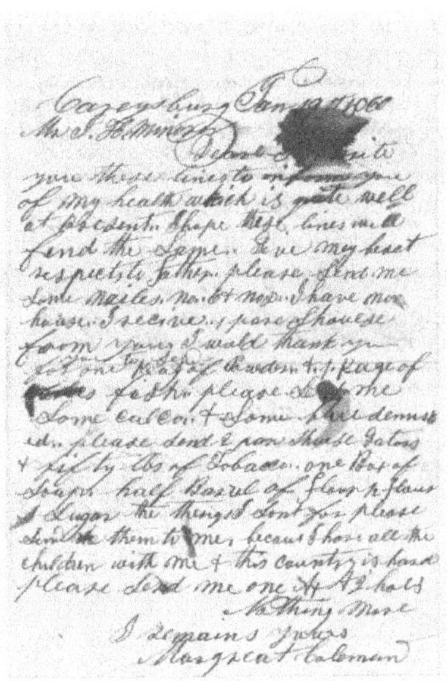

<Source: University of Virginia>
<Collection: Terrell letters>
<Letter ID: 419>
<From: Margreat Coleman>
<To: Dr. James H. Minor>
<Date: 19 Jan 1860>

Careysburg Jan 19th 1860
Mr. J. H. Minoror<xxq>
Deare Sir<xxq> iwrite
you these lines to inform you
of my health which is quite well
at present.. Ihope these lines will
find the Same.. Give me<yyq>y beset
respects to Father.. please Send me
Some nailes. no.. 6 & no 8.. I have nor
house.. I recive.. 1 pare Shouese
from you. I wold thank you
for [<raised insertion:> you to send]
one keag of Powder.. &. 1. kage of
<xx> fish.. please Send me
Some calco.. & Some blue denns
ed.. please Send 2 par Shuese Gators
& fifty lbs of Tobacco.. one Box of
Soap. half Barrel of flour 1/2 flour
& Sugar the thengs I Se<yyq>nt for please
Send [<crossed out: she<xxq>] them to me, becaus I
have all the
children with me & this country is hard
please Send me one Ax & 2 hoes
Nothing More
I remains yours
Margreat Coleman

Figure 1. COAAL mining: an exemplary facsimile letter and transcript from COAAL

About 35 per cent of the corpus stem from published and microfilm collections, while another 65 per cent go back directly to manuscripts collected in American archives. The time span covered is 1763-1919, though a large proportion of the letters dates from the 1860s. Figure 1 shows the reproduction of a facsimile letter together with its header and transcript as represented in COAAL.

4.3 Sources: BLUR

The *Corpus of Blues Lyrics compiled at the University of Regensburg* (BLUR) consists of transcripts of blues lyrics from the early phase of country blues recordings, i.e. mostly from the 1920s to the 1940s, assuming that during that period, before large-scale commercialization, the lyrics of blues songs were still fairly authentic and representative of African American speech at the time. The corpus mostly builds upon existing transcripts of traditional recordings which R.R. Macleod, a Scottish blues lover, had produced and published in 11 volumes. Compilation went on between 1997 and 2002. BLUR consists of 7,341 songs, and c. 1.48 million words altogether, subdivided into BLURsec (with secular texts) and BLURrel (with religious songs, a smaller fraction of about 10% of the total corpus). 776 solo singers from 16 states are represented, of whom 85% are males; in addition, there are 57 duets. Singers were born between 1867 and 1930, and the recordings were made between 1921 and 1969 (the vast majority before WW II). This project was funded by the DFG as well (SCHN 388/4-1, 4-2, 4-3). The Principal Investigator was Ulrich Miethaner, whose monograph (2005), based on his dissertation, presents a comprehensive description of the project and the corpus together with some sample results. Another article, Schneider and Miethaner (2006), investigates a peculiar syntactic pattern observed surprisingly frequently in this corpus. Text 2 presents a sample song, slightly abbreviated but illustrating typical components. Note that this corpus is marked up in *WordCruncher*, then still the leading corpus-linguistic program.

Text 2. Sample song in BLUR

```
|aKOKOMO_ARNOLD
[|mC-9656-A3 spaces|tBACK_DOOR_BLUES2 spaces|rDe_7156
|pChicago.2 spaces|d15_January_1935
Kokomo Arnold, v; acc. own g.]
|o1
|l1 (Ah, bring Kokomo another half a pint.)
|s1
|l1 Says the blues come down the alley, made it up to my back door.
|l2 Says the blues come down the alley, made it up to my back door.
|l3 Says I had the blues today, mama, just like I never had before.
|s2
|l1 Blues and trouble have been my best friends.
|l2 Blues and trouble have been my best friends.
|l3 I says when my blues leave me, my trouble just begin.
[OTHERS - Taft.]
[Source: R R Macleod, Document Blues 1 - DOCD 5037]
[|m91068-A  |tBACK_FENCE_PICKET_BLUES  |rDe_7306
|pChicago.  |d12_January_1937
Kokomo Arnold, v; acc. own g.]
```

4.4 Sources: comparison

Table 2 puts together some of the features and properties of the three corpora combined in ReCAmED for comparison. Much of the information is immediately transparent and needs no further commentary.

Table 2. Component corpora in ReCAmED, compared

	SPOC	COAAL	BLUR
Ethnicity of speaker/writer	white (most likely)	African-American	African-American
Text type	letters (narratives of plantation concerns and affairs)	letters (mostly requests or personal reports)	transcriptions of blues song lyrics from recordings (various topics)
Social status of speaker/ writer	plantation overseers, semi-literate	various; semi-literate	blues singers, largely non-commercial
Regional origin	South, various regions (some centers of documentation)	South, practically all regions	South, practically all regions
Period covered	1794-1876	1763-1919	1920-1940s/1969
Size: no. of texts	536	1,530 [int4_10: 1,291]	7,356
Size: no. of words	c. 155,000	int4_10: c. 465,500	c. 1.49 million
Style represented	relatively factual to informal, largely non-standard	relatively factual to informal, largely non-standard	informal, largely non-standard (but possibly influenced by verse structure)

Notice that SPOC and COAAL, both semi-literate letter corpora, can be viewed as directly comparable representations of informal black and white speech from the nineteenth century, respectively, whereas COAAL and BLUR, abstracting from genre differences, represent two subsequent stages of the development of black dialect, in the nineteenth and earlier twentieth century, respectively.

5. ReCAmED applied: Getting back to some of the issues

This section ties in with Section 2 above; it briefly describes and compares steps in corpus compilation in the three component corpora of ReCAmED and informs about how the methodological problems identified above have been tackled.

With respect to the identification of source texts, SPOC and COAAL are very similar. SPOC builds upon Michael Montgomery's searches in southern archives exclusively. COAAL combines two principal sources. Its core consists of c. 900 unpublished manuscript letters collected in archives. Montgomery's personal collection served as initial input and starting point, but the majority of texts were unearthed (and mostly secured with digital photography) by Lucia Siebers during a field tour of as many as 18 archives in the Southern and Eastern United States between February and April 2008. An additional 630 letters come from 6 published collections edited by historians. BLUR, in contrast, is mostly based on Macleod's transcripts of a systematic collection of re-issued original recordings, a "near-complete documentation of the audio-recorded pre-World War II (country) blues tradition" (Miethaner 2005: 138). In addition, these texts have been supplemented by some transcripts made by Ulrich Miethaner at the *Library of Congress*.

In terms of selection criteria, SPOC and BLUR were easy to handle, in fact, at least within the project environment: the selection of source texts had been carried out beforehand (by the original compilers, Montgomery and Macleod, respectively). Montgomery's selection of what ultimately would become SPOC, in various visits to southern archives, was guided by the presence of nonstandard orthography. BLUR builds on the recording collection used by the transcriber, which had aimed at comprehensive coverage of accessible source recordings from that culture and period. For COAAL, acceptance of any letter into the corpus was dependent upon two criteria. First, the African American ethnicity of the writer had to be guaranteed; usually this was identified by source information available for the respective collection, or on the basis of letter contents. Attention was given to the exclusion of dictated letters, and published letters were accepted only if either they could be checked against a manuscript original or they were described as having been edited from manuscript originals by a modern historian skilled in documentary editing. Secondly, the "semi-literate" status of a writer had to be established, and this had to be done through indirect clues. In such a case the criterion needs to be clear and consistent; it should have no relation to the linguistic features of the documents being analyzed (to avoid circularity); and it should represent an unambiguous indication of marginal literacy. We followed the guiding principles for such cases proposed by Claridge and Kytö (2010: 33) or Meurman-Solin (2000): minimal or lacking punctuation and unpredictable and inconsistent capitalization served as indicators of semi-literacy.

The procedure of corpus compilation essentially resulted from text selection and the nature of the samples chosen. Published letters (in COAAL) and printed song transcripts (in BLUR) were scanned; the files were then checked against the published versions; and if possible the texts were checked against manuscript or song originals (some but not all of these were available). For the COAAL published texts, editorial procedures (as spelled out in book prefaces, for instance) were considered, and letters were accepted only if the precision of transcripts was explicitly confirmed by the editor. In the case of BLUR, some attention was paid to details of the transcription procedure (see Miethaner 2005:

126-134). The manuscript letters (of SPOC and COAAL) were keyboarded by student helpers employed by the project, and then proofread and checked several times by staff members. We employed a set of explicit coding conventions concerning the format of headers and mark-up added. Assistance by experienced historians was sought to decipher difficult hands, to improve the accuracy of the transcripts and also to contribute to a proper understanding of the cultural and historical settings of the letters under scrutiny. This step was carried out by Michael Montgomery in the US; it turned out successful with SPOC but has been less so so far with COAAL (as many historians are busy pursuing their own projects, and their interests and standard procedures tend to be different from those of linguists).

With BLUR (with respect to songs and singers) and COAAL (for all letters in the corpus), databases were built to systematically monitor work progress and to identify relevant text properties (as identified in the headers). It is thus possible to identify and extract sub-corpora (say, texts from specific regions or periods only).

Authenticity assessment of the corpus samples is best carried out via looking at the respective text categories. SPOC and COAAL fully consist of semi-literate letters, which, in terms of Schneider's (2001) scheme reproduced above, represent 'Imagined' speech. The validity of these texts is high; their representativeness is certainly acceptable but needs to be assessed. The question is of which stratum of society these semi-literate writers are representative. SPOC writers are restricted to overseers, and in terms of contents the letters cover a rather narrow range of topics – two factors which restrict their representativeness. For COAAL, the question is to what extent the ability to write singled out a special stratum amongst the African-American population. BLUR texts, in contrast, are song transcripts throughout, and hence 'Recorded' genres. Their validity is reasonably high, given that the texts were transcribed directly from recordings. One consideration was the quality of transcripts, known to have increased over time; and so Macleod's first volume of transcripts was excluded (assuming that it still represented something like the author's 'training ground' in getting familiarized with and transcribing the blues lyrics). The representativeness of the texts seems acceptable but also needs to be assessed: what kinds of factors may have influenced the African American dialect produced in the songs? Singers are known to have come from across all social strata, and it is commonly assumed that the recording situation also had no significant effects on their performance. What may play a restricting role, however, is the fact that these are song lyrics tied to a given verse format with its obvious restrictions. There are both filler and deleted syllables, and the line format has an impact on utterance length, the potential for subordination, the representation of certain pragmatic functions, etc. Thus, some degree of reduced syntactic complexity and pragmatic versatility is to be expected, but detailed discussion and investigation of the issue (Miethaner 2005; Schneider and Miethaner 2006) has suggested that no serious impact on basic sentence structures and morphologically relevant syllables is to be expected.

With respect to mark-up and coding conventions, the manuscript letters (SPOC, COAAL) were keyboarded exactly as is, preserving letters, spaces, and line length (with a 'Carriage Return' at the end of each manuscript line). Missing or illegible text portions were explicitly identified by specific codes (<xx> for 'one word illegible'; <yy> 'part of a word illegible'; <xxq> 'one word, reading questionable'; <yyq> 'part of a word, uncertain'; <raised insertion:>; <crossed out:>). Attempts were made to weed out these insecurity markers in the long run by repeated checks and the contribution of handwriting experts. As was illustrated above, headers were added to each letter which systematically encode and identify the source (library or collection), a running letter ID, author, recipient, and date; and attempts were made to include some additional (and in part innovative) categories which were considered to be potentially helpful in future analyses (and are directly transparent: <lg_quality:>, <motivation:>, <contents:>). In BLUR, headers identify song numbers, singers, song titles, the recording context (place, time), record label, musicians and instrumentation; and often there is also a footer with additional source information and references to other transcripts (if applicable). The mark-up in texts shows spoken insertions, and doubtful or inaudible text segments. The line and stanza structure was also fully retained. BLUR was encoded in *WordCruncher* (dated today, but the program of choice at the time when corpus building was planned), so there is a specific, conventionalized tag set, including |a 'artist', |m 'matrix song number', |t 'song title', |p 'place of recording', |s 'sung stanza' |o 'spoken stanza', etc.

Text normalization (to ease searches) was not carried out with SPOC and COAAL, but BLUR exists in two parallel versions: BLURzero is the close dialect transcript, with inconsistent spellings as represented in the transcripts, while there is also a main version with mild normalization, in which g-dropping, r-dropping, th-stopping, and the reduction of allegro forms were removed but quasi-modals (like *gonna*) were retained (see Miethaner 2005 for justifying considerations and more information on this).

Encoding and distribution conditions were strongly determined by practical considerations. BLUR exists in *WordCruncher* format and a .txt version for in-house use only. SPOC exists in *WordCruncher* and SGML-encoded .txt versions. COAAL is still under construction and hence consists of .txt versions, though for the future encoding in SGML and/or XML is considered. As to accessibility, in May 2005 BLUR was offered to Knut Hofland at ICAME for distribution, but so far, BLUR has not been included in the archive of ICAME. Copyright concerns prevent a wider distribution of the corpus, but it has been made available to interested researchers after signing a copyright form. SPOC and COAAL are available on site (in Regensburg); for a wider distribution Michael Montgomery's consent would be needed. Future publication would be desirable but seems problematic as it is not clear to what extent the archives where the texts stem form originally have copyright. Whether a web interface with restricted access would be a possibility is being considered (but also seems problematic for various reasons). I suppose in an ideal world all these issues might seem rather trivial, but we have found that in a real-life project context, with restrictions of time, funding, and, for example, legal expertise they are difficult to handle and to decide on.

Finally, a word on analysis strategies: How can the problems of finding (all or at least a reasonable sample of) relevant tokens be overcome, given the problem of orthographic variability (for examples, see below)? In my view, a (limited but workable) solution is offered via the production of a wordlist, e.g. based on *WordSmith*'s 'Word list' tool, which will provide clues to likely variants of a target item (assuming that initial letter sequences will at least be similar and target word variants thus stand close to each other; educated guesses in this area are possible and called for). This strategy reaches its absolute limits, however, when, as is not infrequently the case in semi-literate writing, there are spaces within (!) words (e.g. in *Tues day*, in SPOC). For investigations of inflectional morphology, e.g. to study constraints on zero endings of verbs or nouns, and disregarding the cumbersome and inefficient option of manual tagging, the selection and investigation of a sub-set of high-frequency lexemes may offer easy access to a reasonably large and (hopefully) representative dataset. For example, Schneider (2007) documents the impact of the 'Northern Subject Rule' (known to be a complex set of constraints on verbal *-s* choice in many dialects) in BLUR based on forms of the verb *love* only (yielding, in line with the NSR, the illustrative example "My baby loves me, she love me"). So in some cases pragmatic and creative procedures are called for, in the absence of principled solutions.

6. Sample analyses

In this section I will be presenting some sample data and analyses, to test and illustrate the applicability of the corpora presented and procedures discussed in this paper. Given the principled interest of some of the above discussions, a view back to some methodological issues may be inserted at times. The COAAL results reported here are based on a preliminary version of the corpus as available in late April 2010 (hence in the above table I called it "int4_10"), consisting of 1,291 letters and c. 465,500 words.

I will start with a few illustrative examples (of spelling variability and some typical nonstandard patterns represented), will illustrate the possibility of tracing historical roots of these forms (based on the '*for to* + infinitive' construction), and will then approach two issue-driven cases of hypothesis testing, with respect to dating the origin of Southern English (testing Guy Bailey's hypothesis of a post-Reconstruction origin reported above) and the quest for ethnic differentiation, the issue of black-white speech differences in the nineteenth century (looking at the regularization of past tense verb forms and redundant noun pluralization as test cases).

6.1 Some illustrative examples

As was mentioned above, in the semi-literate letters amazingly variable spellings, which may or may not be indicative of pronunciation details, can be found. The examples under (1) show that spaces within words (not only at morpheme boundaries) are common. (2) illustrates quasi-phonetic spellings which correspond to 'eye dialect' in some literary dialect writing, i.e. seemingly odd spellings which, however, represent standard pronunciations. In the words in (3), postvocalic *r*'s are inserted without phonetic motivation, a hypercorrect habit which may be indicative of the writers' insecurity as to the phonetic interpretation of the letter <r> and thus of the non-rhotic character of their speech. The examples under (4) document the presence of consonant cluster reduction in earlier southern speech. (SPOC letters are identified by writers, and COAAL letters by their running IDs.)

(1) new monier 'pneumonia' (SPOC Carter), aulter raytion 'alteration' (SPOC Meadow), per mit 'permit' (SPOC Carter), sircum stance 'circumstance' (COAAL 1400), to day (passim), yester day (COAAL 215)
(2) chusday 'Tuesday'; yoused 'used', dide 'died' (SPOC Carter); rane 'rain' (COAAL 220), to 'two' (passim)
(3) gorn 'gone' (SPOC Carter, COAAL 193), Surpose 'suppose' (SPOC Carter, COAAL 7 times); ort 'ought' (SPOC Doyal, COOAL 815), borthard 'bothered' (COAAL 1142)
(4) hansome 'handsome' (COAAL 705), nex 'next' (COAAL 355), Coles 'colds' (COAAL 1143)

The following sets of examples illustrate the widespread presence of certain types of nonstandard morphology: lack of tense marking (5); double marking of past tense and past participle (6); and nonstandard verbal *-s* (7).

(5) I finnish planing planting then (SPOC Meadow)
he tell me that [...] when he come from down ther and he allso tell me [...] and I thought [...] (SPOC Meadow)
Henry arrive here on yesterday (SPOC Meadow)
I plow the next day (SPOC Carter)
Your Letter come to hand the 1 (COAAL 1059)
(6) it broked it down (SPOC Meadow)
as the rains has So lately brokened up (SPOC Meadow)
the Roap broked (COAAL 861)
now you done broked and run (DLUR)
gav'd, gaven, woken (COAAL)
(7) we wants this proved to Indian that the Colored People has got Here a few month a go (COAAL 1076)
here is the Main object that we Bases upon. (COAAL 1079)
we wants to no of you (COAAL 1081)

he hope [...] (COAAL 189)
he have Brought the waggen (COAAL 1434)

Common syntactic processes include nonstandard uses of *be* (8), zero copula (9), nonstandard negation, including multiple negation and occurrences of preverbal *no* and *ain't* (10), left dislocation (11), and the use of relative *what* (12).

(8) we is Deprived of A school here (COAAL 1060)
we is plenty wet at this time (SPOC Meadow)
whither you is Marred or not (COAAL 165)
if it be possible try to do som thing for us. (COAAL 528)
(9) and we [Ø] Not half Ready (SPOC Doyal)
the Rest of the Negros [Ø] well. (SPOC Doyal)
the Ballance [Ø] too wet (SPOC Doyal)
and so we [Ø] all lving an hap hards (COAAL 1058)
(10) she hasnot no help from any sorce for a Year (COAAL 872)
I don know no man by culler (COAAL 334)
I don't want no sugar stirred up in my tea (BLUR)
we no understand (COOAL 670)
I ain't gonna be your mule (BLUR)
(11) Suckey She is very poly (SPOC Carter 21)
patsy She is sick (SPOC Carter 26)
Rena Paralea she is also well (COAAL 708)
my baby she don't treat me right (BLUR)
(12) the bills what I paid (SPOC Johnson)
one thing what pleas me (COAAL 154)

6.2 Searching for historical roots: *for to* + infinitive

The construction '*for to* + infinitive' to express a purpose or intention can be traced back far in the history of English; for example, everybody who has read the introduction to Chaucer's *Canterbury Tales* will remember that the pilgrims got on their way "the hooly blisful martir for to seke". In present-day white or black dialects in the US this construction has no longer been found or commented on, however. Is there any evidence for its use in these dialects in earlier periods? The examples under (13) provide some illustration; Table 3 provides absolute and relative frequencies (i.e. number of occurrences per 10,000 words) in each of the three corpora.

(13) making me more anxious for to see you all (SPOC Moore)
[...] do not think that it is rite for to make other ingagements untill [...] (SPOC Bassett)
we shal make anof for to surply the plas (SPOC Bassett)
I Rite to you for to ask you [...] (COAAL 931)
Dear mis i Rite you A fuw lines for to Let you knoo (COAAL 307)

I enlisted for To do militarie duties (COAAL 862)
Oh, some go to church for to show their clothes (BLUR)
Swing low, sweet chariot, coming for to carry me home (BLUR)
I din't have nobody for to carry my troubles to (BLUR)

Table 3. Absolute and relative frequency of the *for to*-construction in the three corpora

	SPOC	**COAAL**	**BLUR**
n	10	56	133
***n*/10,000 wds**	.65	1.2	.89

The evidence from ReCAmED clearly shows that this Middle English construction continued to have been in use in American English dialects into the nineteenth and early twentieth centuries. In fact, we do get implicit information on its ethnically diagnostic value and its trajectory of change: apparently the construction was more common in black than in white dialect (cf. its relative frequency in SPOC vs. COAAL and BLUR); and it decreased in frequency in AAVE around the turn of the twentieth century (cf. the COAAL vs. BLUR values). In the light of the debate on the origins of AAVE this is a remarkable piece of evidence, documenting the continuity of some British ancestry forms in earlier AAVE which has been lost by today.

6.3 Hypothesis testing with ReCAmED: Dating the origin of Southern English

As diachronic evidence of southern dialect, ReCAmED should also be suitable to test Bailey's (1997) claim, introduced in Section 3, that several features considered hallmarks of Southern English originated only fairly late, during the Reconstruction period in the late nineteenth and early twentieth centuries. Table 4 presents a short summary of the evidence Bailey's claim is built upon. It lists the features which he discusses, each illustrated by a short example, and, in the last three columns it identifies the periods during which, following Bailey (1997), they were in existence in southern dialect. If Bailey is right, then the forms in the last six rows, from *yall* to *drug*, should not occur (roughly) before 1875, i.e. in SPOC and COAAL, while BLUR, by comparison, might have them.

A few methodological notes are in order here. Some forms are clearly identifiable and thus relatively easy to search. Lexical forms can be most effectively searched on the basis of word lists (including a check for likely spelling variants). Structural and phrasal units can be effectively searched using concord with wildcard searches (e.g. for the inceptive pattern, *get* to *ing*). Spelling variants were checked (and in some cases found not to be instances of the target item): *you-all* comes up as *youa* (SPOC), *youall* or *youal* (COAAL), or just *y'all* (BLUR); *fixin' to* was found via *fix**; for double modals, *might could* (known to be the most frequent one in the South today) and *may can* were searched for; and the word lists were checked for spelling variants first (e.g. *might*, *mite*, *mit*; *duv* 'dove') before running the concord search. And of course homographs had to be excluded (e.g. *dove* 'k.a. bird').

Table 4. Periods of use of hallmark features of Southern English, after Bailey (1997)

Feature	**Illustration**	**Period distribution of origin (Bailey)**		
		before 1875	**1875-1945**	**1945-1980**
a-verb(-ing)	he left a-running	+	+/-	-
plural verb -s	folks sits here	+	+/-	-
liketa	I liketa died	+	+/-	+/-
perf. done	she's done left	+	+	+
you-all/yall	we saw yall	-/+	+	+
fixin' to	I'm fixin' to eat	-/+	-/+	+
multiple modals	I might could do it	?	-/+	+
incept. get/got to	I got to talking	-	-/+	+
dove 'dived'	they dove in	-	-/+	+
drug 'dragged'	he drug it	-	-/+	-/+

A few pertinent examples from the corpora (including years of attestation from SPOC and COAAL) are illustrated below, showing *you-all* (14), *fixin' to* (15), double modals (16), inceptive *get/got to* V*-ing* (17), *dove* 'dived' (18) and *drug* 'dragged' (19). The quantitative distribution of the complete set of target data is provided in Table 5.

(14) If we never see youall no more (COAAL 707 [3 exx.]; 1848)
ginger for youal to plant (COAAL 943; 1866)
boy, y'all be careful (BLUR)

(15) we are now fixen to plant Rice (COAAL 409; 1858)
I'm fixing to leave your town (BLUR)
What's you fixing to do now? (BLUR)

(16) I might could be ashamed of it (BLUR)
brother, you may can't understand (BLUR)
Lord, I may can do something (BLUR)

(17) But will get to trashing again sune (SPOC Allston; 1865)
Man, my mind get to rambling (BLUR)
he get to flying and buzzing (BLUR)

I got to thinking, I got to wondering, do this freight train go by my home (BLUR)
And them blues got to running (BLUR)

(18) God's mercy dove down on them all (BLUR)

(19) Ain't you tired now being drug around? (BLUR)
where he drug his tail (BLUR)

Table 5. Frequency of target forms in the corpora

	SPOC	COAAL	BLUR
you-all	Ø	4	12
fixin' to	Ø	1	39
double modals	Ø	Ø	3
inceptive get/got to V-ing	1	Ø	40 get to 15 got to
dove 'dived'	Ø	Ø	1
drug 'dragged'	Ø	Ø	18

The results show that indeed all forms for which Bailey claims a late origin are unattested or very rare in the nineteenth century corpora (SPOC and COAAL) but common in twentieth century African American dialect as represented in BLUR. Thus, my evidence from ReCAmED largely confirms Bailey's hypothesis of a post-Civil War origin and twentieth-century diffusion of characteristically southern forms.

6.4 In search of ethnic differentiation: Black-white speech differences?

Given the heated debates (briefly outlined above) on whether black and white dialects of the South share British roots or have completely different (European vs. African, respectively) origins, sifting ReCAmED for pertinent evidence is a natural application of this corpus suite. As there is no twentieth century white match for BLUR, in this section I restrict myself to a comparison of SPOC and COAAL, both of which, representing nineteenth-century usage in letters by semi-literate writers, are uniquely comparable. I investigate two test structures, both of which have commonly been associated with black dialect, namely the regularization of verb forms (e.g. *knowed* for *knew*) and zero noun plural forms, especially redundantly after numerals (e.g. in *20 mile away*).

Again, this calls for a discussion of the methodological procedure first. Exhaustive searches for all relevant forms in the corpora would be highly inefficient and hugely laborious, going far beyond the scope of this paper. For instance, while it would be interesting to study the productivity of regularization, a wildcard search for **ed* yields 8,354 hits in COAAL only – too many to categorize in this context. Thus, I decided in favor of a selective procedure, based on the idea of studying a restricted set of predefined, representative lexemes. For verb morphology, a number of verbs known to vary in their past and past participle forms (e.g. from Schneider 1989) were selected, and their regular vs. irregular occurrences (after checking) were counted, and the frequencies compared. The test lexemes chosen were *know*, *blow*, *throw*, *blow*, *teach*, *dig*, *wake*, *bring*, and *give*. Similarly, for noun morphology a number of nouns (of measure) known to vary were selected (these were *acre*, *bale*, *bushel*, *cent*, *day*, *dollar*, *head*, *mile*, *month*, *pound*, *week*, and *year*) and checked for the presence or absence of an *-s*-plural suffix and of preceding quantifiers.

The results for verb past tense regularization need to be interpreted with some reluctance. Of the test verbs selected four proved to be inefficient, i.e. providing no instances of regularization (*teach*, *wake*, *bring*, *give*). For the others, Table 6 shows the frequency of tokens with regularization.

Table 6. Frequency of regularized verb forms

	SPOC	COAAL
knowed/node/noed	0	7
knew/known	10	104
blowed/blowd	4	2
blew/blown	9	2
digged/diged	0	2
dug	11	7
sum: regularized	4	11
irregular	30	113
% regularized	11.8	8.9

Roughly 10 per cent of all verb forms are regularized – a bit more frequently in texts written by white than those by black writers (at 11.8% vs. 8.9%), but the distribution is not significant (based on Fisher's Exact test), so no ethnic differentiation can be documented. Regularization occurs with three verb lexemes in black dialect as against only one in white speech, so the wider type range might imply greater productivity of the process in earlier AAVE, but the token numbers are too low to justify postulating a serious hypothesis along these lines. However, there is a second, slightly different observation which also, on in itself equally thin evidence, suggests greater affinity of black speakers with the regularization process, namely the fact that double formatives (notably, the forms *woken*, *gav'd*, and *gaven*) have been recorded in COAAL only and not in SPOC.

In the case of regular noun plural formation, the conventional claim is that a redundant *-s* is omitted more readily in AAVE. Methodologically, it turned out that the range of spelling variants found is fairly wide here, so I consult the corpus wordlist to identify spelling variants first and then use 'Concord' to look for premodifying quantifiers. The spelling variants recorded include: *acre*, *acr*, *acer*, *acker*, *ackor*; *bushal*, *bushall*, *bushel*, *bushell*, *busheles*, *bushils*, *bushiels*, *bushls*; *dollar*, *dolliar*, *dollars*, *dollares*, *dolliars*, *dollors*, *dollrs*, *dollas*, *doller(s)* (*great deal dollar*, twice in COAAL, was accepted as modified by a numeral); *mile*, *miles*, *mils*; *month*, *months*, *monts*; *wek*, *week*, *weks*, *weeks*; and similarly *year*(*e*)(*s*), *day*(*e*)(*s*) (and derivatives like *weekdays*, *Thursday*). Overall, token numbers of noun plural forms were fairly high; search and investigation were a bit tedious but feasible.

The presence of a premodifying numeral (and thus the semantically redundant status of the suffix), it turned out, constitutes almost a mandatory condition for suffix omission to occur at all. Plural nouns without preceding numerals were considered and investigated as well, but in this context suffix omission is practically not found; there is a single example: *mile from home* (COAAL 765). This is therefore not documented any further.

The examples in (20) illustrate the omission of redundant plural markers. The frequency of this process by corpus and lexeme is documented in Table 7.

(20) one hundred and 65 dolliar for nine months (SPOC Allston)
for ten doller (COAAL 762)
it was some 15 month old (SPOC Long)
he think in some to or 3 week can have her (SPOC Long)
200 Bushills more (COAAL 641)
eight or ten day since (COAAL 426)
we were gone fifteen day and only Lost one man in the Battle (COAAL 157)
Six monthe i have sirved in the U.S.A. (COAAL 783)

Table 7. Omission of redundant plural suffixes by corpora and lexemes

	SPOC			COAAL		
Numeral	+NUM			+NUM		
Suffix	*-s*	-Ø	%-Ø	*-s*	-Ø	%-Ø
acre	21	9	30	58	1	2
bale	78	5	6	14	1	7
bushel	192	11	5	15	8	35
cent	29	3	9	43	5	10
day	283	37	12	302	8	3
dollar	121	4	3	212	11	5
head	5	45	90	2	7	78
mile	12	-	0	119	4	3
month	15	3	17	148	22	13
pound	63	2	3	20	10	33
week	53	7	12	119	1	1
year	30	1	3	303	7	2
sum	902	127	12.3	1,355	85	6.0

The results fail to suggest a general or strong tendency. The overall deletion rate is actually stronger, contrary to the initial hypothesis, in white than in black dialect. Table 7 shows that the process is strongly lexically bound: it is important to consider lexical tendencies and idiosyncracies. A high deletion rate is found with *head* in both dialects, and with *acre* and *week* in white but *bushel* and *pound* in black dialect.

So, to sum up the issue of black-white speech differences in the nineteenth century: in the test cases considered here, primarily the data seem to be determined by a high degree of variability from one lexeme to another; apart from that, and secondarily, a fairly high level of similarity between the two corpora can be observed. Thus, the data presented here provide no evidence of substantial differences between black and white speech in the nineteenth century (at least with respect to the features of verb and noun morphology investigated here).Summary and conclusion

In this paper I have argued that tracking language change in vernacular varieties is a worthwhile goal in linguistics, requiring an interdisciplinary approach between historical linguistics and dialectology. It was shown that semi-literate letters are a promising and useful tool for that purpose. From a corpus-linguistic perspective, they pose specific methodological problems which can be overcome to some extent, though limitations remain, quite unavoidably, and methodological awareness and reluctance is thus of central importance. The ReCAmED corpus set, consisting of the SPOC, COAAL and BLUR corpora of nineteenth and twentieth century black and white dialect sources, was introduced, and it was argued that this corpus group constitutes a useful tool for investigating the evolution of black and white dialects in the Southern US. The results have shown, amongst other things, that both dialects are highly variable and show many common nonstandard features; that there is evidence indeed for a late (post-Reconstruction) origin of some characteristic features of the Southern English dialect; and that, contrary to widespread assumptions and claims, there is no evidence for the existence of systematic ethnic dialect differences at that period.

Notes

1 Obviously, the work reported here has been a collaborative effort to which a number of colleagues and helpers have contributed important parts. Most explicitly, my sincere thanks are due to: Prof. Michael Montgomery, University of South Carolina, for his input (also in the form of many letter photocopies), constant support and stimulation; Dr. Lucia Siebers, principal researcher on COAAL, for her work related to COAAL and for providing substantial input to this presentation; Dr. Ulrich Miethaner for his earlier work on BLUR; and Sabrina Mintschke and Stephanie Bestle, student workers on COAAL who carried out much of the keyboarding, scanning and proofing of the texts. The support of the *Deutsche Forschungsgemeinschaft* (DFG) (project numbers SCHN 388/4-1, 4-2, 4-3 and SCHN 388/12-1) is gratefully acknowledged.

References

Alim, H.S. (2004), *You Know My Steez: An Ethnographic and Sociolinguistic Study of Styleshifting in a Black American Community*. Raleigh, NC: Duke University Press for the American Dialect Society.

Bailey, G. (1997), 'When did Southern English begin?', in: E.W. Schneider (ed.), *Englishes Around the World. Volume 1: General Studies, British Isles, North America*. Amsterdam: John Benjamins. 255-275.

Bailey, G., N. Maynor and P. Cukor-Avila (eds.) (1991), *The Emergence of Black English: Text and Commentary*. Amsterdam: John Benjamins.

Brooks, C. (1935), *The Relation of the Alabama-Georgia Dialect to the Provincial Dialects of Great Britain*. Baton Rouge, LA: Louisiana State University. Repr. 1972, Port Washington, NY: Kennikat Press.

Butters, R.R. (1989), *The Death of Black English: Divergence and Convergence in Black and White Vernaculars*. Frankfurt am Main: Peter Lang.

Bybee, J. (2007), *Frequency of Use and the Organization of Language*. Oxford: Oxford University Press.

Claridge, C. and M. Kytö (2010), 'Non-standard language in earlier English', in: R. Hickey (ed.), *Varieties of English in Writing: The Written Word as Linguistic Evidence*. Amsterdam: John Benjamins. 15-42.

Culpeper, J. and M. Kytö (2000), 'Investigating nonstandard language in a corpus of Early Modern English dialogues. Methodological considerations and problems', in: I. Taavitsainen, G. Melchers and P. Pahta (eds.), *Writing in Nonstandard English*. Amsterdam: John Benjamins. 171-187.

Culpeper, J. and M. Kytö (2010), *Early Modern English Dialogues: Spoken Interaction as Writing*. Cambridge: Cambridge University Press.

Dossena, M. and I. Tieken-Boon van Ostade (eds.) (2008), *Studies in Late Modern English Correspondence: Methodology and Data*. Frankfurt am Main: Peter Lang.

Fairman, T. (2008), 'Strike-throughs: What textual alterations can tell us about writers and their scripts, 1795-1835', in: M. Dossena and I. Tieken-Boon van Ostade (eds.), *Studies in Late Modern English Correspondence: Methodology and Data*. Bern: Peter Lang. 193-212.

Hickey, R. (2010), 'Linguistic evaluation of earlier texts', in: R. Hickey (ed.), *Varieties of English in Writing: The Written Word as Linguistic Evidence*. Amsterdam: John Benjamins. 1-14.

Hickey, R. (ed.) (2010), *Varieties of English in Writing: The Written Word as Linguistic Evidence*. Amsterdam: John Benjamins.

Huber, M. (2007), 'The Old Bailey Proceedings, 1674-1834. Evaluating and annotating a corpus of 18th- and 19th-century spoken English', in: A. Meurman-Solin and A. Nurmi (eds.), *Annotating Variation and Change*. <http://www.helsinki.fi/varieng/journal/volumes/01/index.html> (12.09. 2011)

Kautzsch, A. (2002), *The Historical Evolution of Earlier African American English: An Empirical Comparison of Early Sources*. Berlin: de Gruyter.

Kretzschmar, W.R., Jr. (2009), *The Linguistics of Speech*. Cambridge: Cambridge University Press.

Kurath, H. (1972), 'Relics of English folk speech in American English', in: L. Davis (ed.), *Studies in Linguistics in Honor of Raven I. McDavid, Jr.* Tuscaloosa, AL: University of Alabama Press. 367-375.

Kytö, M., J. Culpeper and T. Walker (2006), *A Corpus of English Dialogues 1560-1760*. Uppsala: Uppsala University Press.

Kytö, M. and T. Walker (2003), 'The linguistic study of Early Modern English speech-related texts: How "bad" can "bad" data be?', *Journal of English Linguistics*, 31: 221-248.

Larsen-Freeman, D. and L. Cameron (2008), *Complex Systems and Applied Linguistics*. Oxford: Oxford University Press.

Marckwardt, A.H. (1958), *American English*. New York, NY: Oxford University Press.

Meurman-Solin, A. (2000), 'Letters as a source of data for reconstructing Early Spoken Scots', in: I. Taavitsainen, G. Melchers and P. Pahta (eds.), *Writing in Nonstandard English*. Amsterdam: John Benjamins. 305-322.

Miethaner, U. (2005), *I can look through muddy water: Analyzing AAVE with BLUR*. Frankfurt am Main: Peter Lang.

Montgomery, M. (1997), 'A tale of two Georges: The language of Irish Indian traders in colonial North America', in: J. Kallen (ed.), *Focus on Ireland*. Amsterdam: John Benjamins. 227-254.

Montgomery, M. (1999), 'Eighteenth-century Sierra Leone English: Another exported variety of African American English', *English World-Wide*, 20: 1-34.

Mufwene, S.S. (2001), *The Ecology of Language Evolution*. Cambridge: Cambridge University Press.

Nagle, S.J. and S.L. Sanders (eds.) (2003), *English in the Southern United States*. Cambridge: Cambridge University Press.

Nevalainen, T. and H. Raumolin-Brunberg (eds.) (1996), *Sociolinguistics and Language History: Studies Based on the Corpus of Early English Correspondence*. Amsterdam: Rodopi.

Nevalainen, T. and H. Raumolin-Brunberg (2003), *Historical Sociolinguistics: Language Change in Tudor and Stuart England*. London: Longman.

Nevalainen, T. and S.-K. Tanskanen (eds.) (2007), *Letter Writing*. Amsterdam: John Benjamins.

Nurmi, A., M. Nevala and M. Palander-Collins (eds.) (2009), *The Language of Daily Life in England (1400-1800)*. Amsterdam: John Benjamins.

Palander-Collin, M., M. Nevala and A. Nurmi (2009), 'The language of daily life in the history of English. Studying how macro meets micro', in: A. Nurmi, M. Nevala and M. Palander-Collin (eds.), *The Language of Daily Life in England (1400-1800)*. Amsterdam: John Benjamins. 1-23.

Pederson, L. et al. (eds.) (1986-1991), *Linguistic Atlas of the Gulf States*. 7 volumes. Athens, GA: University of Georgia Press.

Poplack, S. (ed.) (2000), *The English History of African American English*. Malden, MA: Blackwell.

Poplack, S. and S. Tagliamonte (2001), *African American English in the Diaspora*. Malden, MA: Blackwell.

Rickford, J. (2006), 'Down for the count? The Creole Origins Hypothesis of AAVE at the hands of the Ottawa circle, and their supporters', *Journal of Pidgin and Creole Languages*, 21: 97-155.

Schneider, E.W. (1989), *American Earlier Black English*. Tuscaloosa, AL: The University of Alabama Press.

Schneider, E.W. (1997), 'Chaos theory as a model for dialect variability and change?', in: A.R. Thomas (ed.), *Issues and Methods in Dialectology*. Clevedon: Multilingual Matters. 22-36.

Schneider, E.W. (2001), 'Investigating variation and change in written documents', in: J.K. Chambers, P. Trudgill and N. Schilling-Estes (eds.), *The Handbook of Language Variation and Change*. Malden, MA: Blackwell. 67-96.

Schneider, E.W. (2003), 'Shakespeare in the coves and hollows? Toward a history of Southern English', in: S.J. Nagle and S.L. Sanders (eds.), *English in the Southern United States*. Cambridge: Cambridge University Press. 17-35.

Schneider, E.W. (2004), 'The English dialect heritage of the Southern United States', in: R. Hickey (ed.), *Legacies of Colonial English. Studies of Transported Dialects*. Cambridge: Cambridge University Press. 262-310.

Schneider, E.W. (2007), 'My baby loves me, she love me: verbal *-s* variability in the history of black and white dialects of the southern United States', in: U. Smit, S. Dollinger, J. Hüttner, G. Kaltenböck and U. Lutzky (eds.), *Tracing English Through Time: Explorations in Language Variation*. Wien: Braumüller. 345-358.

Schneider, E.W. and U. Miethaner (2006), 'When I started to using BLUR: Accounting for unusual verb complementation patterns in an electronic corpus of Earlier African American English', *Journal of English Linguistics*, 34: 233-256.

Schneider, E.W. and M. Montgomery (2001), 'On the trail of early nonstandard grammar: An electronic corpus of Southern U.S. antebellum overseers letters', *American Speech*, 76: 388-410.

Taavitsainen, I., G. Melchers and P. Pahta (eds.) (2000), *Writing in Nonstandard English*. Amsterdam: John Benjamins.

Trüb, R. (2006), 'Nonstandard verbal paradigms in earlier white Southern American English', *American Speech*, 81: 250-265.

Winford, D. (1997/98), 'On the origins of African American Vernacular English a creolist perspective. Part I: The sociohistorical background. Part 2: Linguistic features', *Diachronica*, 14: 305-344; 15: 99-154.

Wolfram, W. and E. Thomas (2002), *The Development of African American English*. Malden, MA: Blackwell.

Methodological issues in a television news corpus: Discourse and annotation

Stefania Spina

University for Foreigners of Perugia

Abstract

This paper describes some of the methodological issues concerning the creation of the Corpus di Italiano Televisivo, *'Corpus of Italian Television Language' (cf. Spina 2005). The data considered in this paper comes from the news subsection, which includes news programmes transcribed in electronic form, annotated and POS-tagged. The aim of the corpus is to provide a balanced and consistent collection of data which may be utilized in research in the field of the language used in television. However, the process of data annotation has raised a number of both methodological and theoretical issues on the structure of TV news, on its discoursive features and on its status as a television genre. The emergence of these issues from corpus annotation demonstrates that corpus-based methodologies can shed light on the linguistic specificity of TV news.*

1. Background and motivation

The starting point of this study is the observation that there is a substantial lack of corpus-based studies on the language of television. Corpus-based methodologies have been applied to a wide range of linguistic subfields, and have made remarkable advances in many of them; in discourse analysis, for example, in recent years "many studies within corpus linguistics address discourse-level concerns, many showing association patterns on the interaction of variables that would not be apparent without corpus-based techniques" (Conrad 2002: 86).

There are many general research questions concerning the language of television that corpus-based methodologies could help to answer, and these include: "Is there a great divide separating the language of television and the language of other media?", "Are there specific linguistic features associated with different functions, corresponding to specific television genres?", "Is there a single, homogeneous language of television, or is it a diversified, genre-specific language?" (Hassanpour 2005: 1317). The availability of large corpora of television programmes could shed light on these and many other questions and provide researchers with a solid basis of structured data to analyze.

However, this potential has been largely neglected in studies on the language of television that often rely on the impressionistic and casual observation of a few television programmes rather than on balanced and consistent collections of TV data.[1]

One of the reasons for this shortage of data-oriented studies is almost certainly that building a TV corpus is a long, complex and expensive process (Spina 2005), which consists of having to deal with programme selection, tape recording and transcription. In addition, the mixed nature and the articulated structure of television texts require a number of complex decisions to be taken in the process of data annotation (see Section 4).

Although television conveys a number of different genres (Swales 1990; Bhatia 1993; Montgomery 2007), the scarcity of corpus-based studies is particularly evident in one of the genres which is, ironically, especially dominant in television, both in terms of audience and space within the daily coverage: the news.

All these considerations have led to the creation of the *Corpus of Italian Television Language* (CIT),[2] the aim of which is to provide a balanced and consistent collection of data which may be utilized in research in the field of the language used in television.[3]

2. Data

2.1 Description of the corpus

The CIT is composed of transcripts of TV programmes, for a total number of 1 million words, POS-tagged and lemmatized.[4] Its two main sections are closely connected to the two main functions that are typically ascribed to television (Tannenbaum 1980): information and entertainment.

Each of the two sections has distinct sub-sections, corresponding to TV genres with the greatest audience,[5] as shown in Table 1.

Table 1. The CIT composition

Information	**Entertainment**
news	talk shows
current affairs	fiction
	sport
	variety shows
500,000 words	500,000 words

The digital texts of the TV programmes included in the CIT have two possible sources: the direct transcription of a recorded version of the programme, or a text file with the subtitles provided by the broadcasting company, both from live and pre-recorded programmes. With regard to the second source, each subtitle text has been checked and revised and, in the case of discrepancies or cuts, the missing text has been incorporated. The subtitles, in fact, typically omit proto-typical features of spoken texts, such as discourse markers, and tend to capture mainly the propositional content of the broadcast talk (Biq 1993: 351).

2.2 The news sub-section

The news sub-section includes news programmes transcribed in electronic form, both from general (public and private) channels and from specialised, thematic channels. The data discussed in this paper comes from general news channels; more specifically, it includes 35 complete news programmes (21 from *RAI* and 14 from *Mediaset*, a private company). The resulting news sub-corpus on which this study is focused includes 200,000 words total.

3. Features of TV news

3.1 A popular genre

On the 3rd of January 1954, when the Italian public broadcasting company officially began to transmit its television programmes, news was one of the first ones that a small number of people had the chance to watch (Menduni 2004). Since then, news has increasingly enlarged its space in the daily TV schedule and watching it, particularly the evening edition, has become a sort of routine habit for many Italian families.

News programmes have certainly evolved over the course of the last few decades (Erhardt 2008); the structure and the organization of news programmes, however, remain much the same as fifty years ago. Moreover, news still has a central position within the daily programme schedule, and retains a high number of viewers: the seven evening news editions of the major public and private Italian networks have an average daily audience of more than 20 million viewers (see Note 5).

The language of TV news has attracted the attention of academics, in particular, on account of its ideological issues about the construction of audiences (Hartley 1982; Bell 1991; Scannell 1991; Conboy 2007), and for its relationship with standards and norms (Ennaji 1995; Nacci 2003; Alfieri and Bonomi 2008). A corpus-based methodology could give rise to other interesting perspectives in the study of the language of TV news, with regard to the mixed types of discourse it conveys (Marriott 1997; de Araujo 2003; Montgomery 2007).

3.2 A mixed genre

While its final recipients perceive it as a spoken text, news is probably the most 'written' genre on TV. In fact, not only is the text of a news broadcast written: furthermore, its composition is strongly rooted in a series of editorial activities, such as selection, deletion, and the combination of different materials, which are typical of written media. The production of a news broadcast is a complex and cyclical process whereby many authors with different functions constantly interact with each other, drawing on written as well as spoken sources. The result is a final, written text, linked to other media such as pictures, audio, video (Goodman and Manners 1997), which incorporates different layers of other pre-existing texts (Bell 1991: 41) and which is read as a spoken text to the audience (Rossini Favretti 1988). Despite the fact that it is spoken, a news programme is perceived by the audience as a complete media product rather than as an ongoing talk-oriented process (Ilie 2001: 212).

News texts therefore exhibit a mixture of characteristics pertaining both to written and spoken language; one of the most interesting research questions raised by this combination of features is: to what extent does this communication hybrid reproduce existing discourse patterns, and to what extent does it create a new 'news style', broadcasted by TV?

3.3 A constructed genre

The non-homogeneous nature of TV news language can also be ascribed to its textual and functional organization: a news broadcast demands the use of several discourse types at the same time (reported information, interviews, fragments of public speech, live talk, etc.). Due to the strict time restrictions of news programmes, these fragments, with variable functions and size, are continuously merged and assembled, based on a mechanism of juxtaposition.

Thus, TV news can be regarded as a mixed discourse, which integrates heterogeneous text types (Montgomery 2007). This form of intertextuality can be compared to the interdiscursivity described by Fairclough, who distinguishes between embedded intertextuality "where one text or discourse type is clearly contained within the matrix of another", and mixed intertextuality "where texts or discourse types are merged in a more complex and less easily separable way" (Fairclough 1998: 118). News programmes, in fact, incorporate both singular discourse types embedded in others (a fragment of public speech embedded in a news report, for example) and mixed discourse types, juxtaposed with each other. As a consequence, news programmes are among the most 'constructed' television texts, whereby the process of selection of elements plays an essential role (Hartley 1982). This selection takes place in two different steps: firstly, the selection of news (which of the stories brought by press agencies will effectively become a TV news item?); secondly, the selection of fragments of discourse types to be included in each news programme (a live interview, a fragment of public speech, a spokesman's statement, the comment of an expert, etc.).

4. Annotation of news programmes

The process of annotation of the news programme transcriptions clearly displays this characteristic of intertextuality. The structure of each of the 35 broadcasts included in the corpus has been represented using a TEI-compliant XML annotation (Text Encoding Initiative Consortium 2002). Accordingly, each news programme encompasses a primary division into its two main sub-parts: the headlines and the news stories.

The headlines are the most homogeneous part of the news, from a functional and linguistic point of view; the same is not true for news stories, which include the mixed group of discourse types described in the previous section. Therefore, the structural level of the annotation 'news story' can, in turn, contain different sub-levels, for example: lead-ins, interviews, statements, pre-recorded and live reports. Each of these sub-levels is associated with different functions and has unique textual features, as shown in Table 2.

Table 2. Features and functions of TV news sub-sections

Section	**Function**	**Textual features**
headlines	summarize the news	short, written to be read, monologic
lead-in	introduce the news (in studio)	short; written to be read (occasionally spoken, prepared), monologic
pre-registered report	report the news	written to be read, longer (from 40 seconds to 2 minutes), monologic
live report	report the news in real time	spoken, prepared, monologic
interview	comment on the news	spoken, often prepared, dialogic
statement	illustrate the news	written to be read or spoken, prepared; monologic

The extract (1) below is an example of how fragments belonging to different discourse types are selected and juxtaposed in a TV news edition, and clearly shows a mixed type of broadcasting discourse;[6] in the interview section, in particular, the remark of the witness is an answer to the probable question of the journalist "What happened?", but the audience does not hear this question.

(1) <div1 type="news_story">
<div2 type="lead_in"><u who="journalist">
Adesso la cronaca. Un tragico incidente alle porte di Roma.
</u></div2>
<div2 type="report"><u who="journalist">
Non era la prima volta che guidava. A 17 anni, senza patente. Ha ucciso così, per un sorpasso azzardato.
</u></div2>
<div2 type="interview"><u who="witness">
Un forte boato e basta. Come una bomba.
</u></div2>
<div2 type="report"><u who="journalist">
Roberto stava tornando a casa quando il furgone gli è piombato addosso a grande velocità.

</u></div2>
</div1>

5. Example of variation of linguistic features in TV news

As a consequence of this annotation of TV news, it becomes possible to search for specific linguistic features, associated with specific functions, within the different discourse types included in the news.

Although a systematic description of the data extracted from the CIT is beyond the scope of the present study, some preliminary, quantitative data already shows the variation across the different corpus sections: Table 3 presents their respective size and number of words per sentence. Reports are by far the largest section, and produce the longest sentences, while headlines are the smallest section and their sentences are around half the length in terms of number of words.

Cross corpora comparison allowed us to look at how these figures vary across different media: if compared to the mean number of words per sentence in newspaper articles, that is 22.6 (Spina, forthcoming), broadcast news presents a lower value (15.8 mean number of words per sentence). The use of shorter sentences in broadcast news seems more suited to the on-line report of events in progress, which is distinctive of television programmes.

Table 3. Token distribution and words per sentence in the news corpus

	% of tokens	words per sentence
headlines	3.40	10.68
lead-ins	16.23	14.46
reports	58.54	20.22
interviews	13.74	15.04
statements	4.46	16.51
live reports	3.63	18.4

Another example of the variation of linguistic features, using a frequency-based, grammatical approach, is the part-of-speech distribution across the different discourse types of the news programmes. Figure 1 shows the respective distribution of verbs, nouns and subordinators.

Headlines have few verbs, very few subordinators (less than one every 100 words) and the highest number of nouns compared to the other sections; they are made of short, coordinated sentences with dense packages of information, consistent with their function of briefly summarizing the news.

At the other extreme, interviews and statements, the spoken sections in which the news is illustrated and commented on, have a very similar distribution, with longer and more hierarchically articulated sentences and an almost equivalent distribution of nouns and verbs.

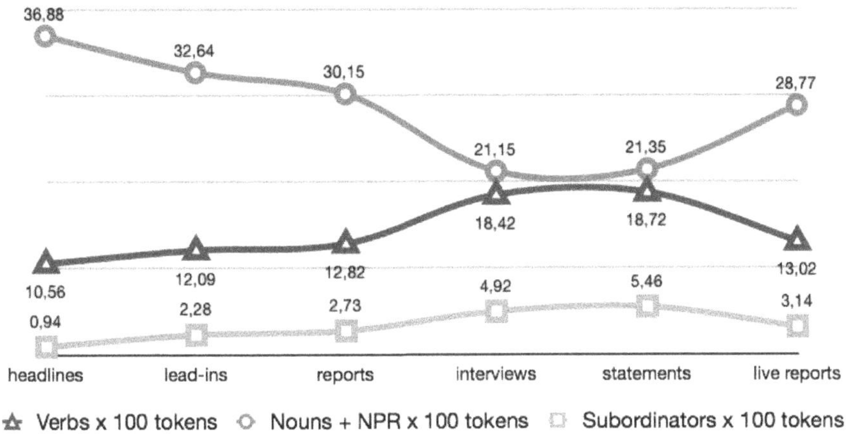

Figure 1. Common and proper nouns (NRP), verbs and subordinators in the news sections

Lead-ins are positioned halfway between headlines and reports, with an intermediate distribution of the three parts-of-speech, in accordance with their function of briefly introducing the news, which follows the summarization of headlines and precedes the more articulated description of reports.

Reports, finally, have the purpose of giving details of events actually in progress; in their pre-recorded versions, a team of journalists is expected to have gathered information from a range of sources and to report this information to the viewers. Consequently, reports are supposed to present a great proportion of informational and narrative features (Biber 1988), and an elaborated structure.

Our first data demonstrates that, while reports exhibit a high occurrence of nouns, they do not show a widespread use of subordination, and the number of verbs is lower if compared to interviews; for more than 40%, in addition, verbs occur in the present tense.

Again, the function of reporting with spoken words events which are in progress seems to reduce some of the informational and narrative features of TV news reports, such as the number of subordinators; as Montgomery puts it, "prevalent characteristics of television news reports include: common use of the present tense to refer to an ongoing reality, parts of which may be interpreted as visible in the visual track" (Montgomery 2007: 104).

6. Concluding remarks

By focusing on the annotation of a corpus of TV news, this study tries to highlight the effectiveness of a corpus-based approach in drawing attention to the deep differentiation within TV news discourse. As it has been pointed out, "despite the potential difficulties of automatizing data retrieval and analysis, researchers interested in discourse have started to adopt corpus-linguistic methods more seriously over the past few years" (Ädel and Reppen 2008: 1).

It is suggested that a news programme is a sort of patchwork, whereby fragments of texts belonging to different discourse types, with variable functions and size, are assembled, mixed and juxtaposed. News programmes can be considered a structured sequence of nested fragments of discourse; they are among the most 'constructed' television texts, whereby the selection of single portions of discourse plays a key role in the construction and transmission of information.

Notes

1 There are remarkable exceptions to this statement: just to give two examples, the corpus-based analysis of sitcom dialogues (Quaglio 2009) and the comparison between American, British and Italian TV reports on Iraqi war (Haarman and Lombardo 2008).

2 Detailed information on the CIT is available at the following web site: <http://elearning.unistrapg.it/corpora/cit.html> (24.11.2011).

3 The CIT project was started at the end of the 1990s, and it was interrupted after a couple of years, precisely because of the complexity and length of the task. It was, however, resumed at the end of 2009 due to an agreement between the University for Foreigners, Perugia and RAI, the Italian public television network. RAI agreed to provide us with the digital version of the subtitles of a number of programs. The CIT is now one of the 8 sub-sections of the larger *Perugia Corpus*, a reference corpus of Italian (<http://elearning.unistrapg.it/corpora/pec.html>) (24.11.2011).

4 The POS-tagging has been carried out using *TreeTagger* (Schmid 1994), trained with ad-hoc resources.

5 Data on Italian TV program audiences is provided by Auditel, and can be found at the company web site (<http://www.auditel.it>) (24.11.2011).

6 The extract has been taken from a news broadcast from 7th February 2010; the following is the English translation: "And now for the news headlines. There has been a tragic accident on the outskirts of Rome. It wasn't the first time he had driven. 17 year-old, without a licence. He killed someone because he overtook dangerously. A loud bang and then silence. Like a bomb. Roberto was on his way home when the van hit him at high speed".

References

Ädel, A. and R. Reppen (2008), 'The challenges of different settings: An overview', in: A. Ädel and R. Reppen (eds.), *Corpora and Discourse*. Amsterdam: John Benjamins. 1-6.

Alfieri, G. and I. Bonomi (eds.) (2008), *Gli Italiani del Piccolo Schermo*. Florence: Franco Cesati.

Bhatia, V.K. (1993), *Analysing Genre: Language Use in Professional Settings*. London: Longman.

Bell, A. (1991), *The Language of News Media*. Oxford: Blackwell.

Biber, D. (1988), *Variation Across Speech and Writing*. Cambridge: Cambridge University Press.

Biq, Y.O. (1993), 'From TV talk to screen caption', *Text*, 13: 351-369.

Conboy, M. (2007), *The Language of the News*. London: Routledge.

Conrad, S. (2002), 'Corpus linguistics approaches for discourse analysis', *Annual Review of Applied Linguistics*, 22: 75-95.

de Araujo, D.L. (2003), 'A língua falada na TV. Texto falado ou escrito?', *Linguagem & Ensino*, 6: 57-76.

Ennaji, M. (1995), 'A syntactico-semantic study of the language of news in Morocco', *International Journal of the Sociology of Language*, 112: 97-111.

Erhardt, E. (2008), 'Come cambia l'italiano dei telegiornali dagli anni '60 ad oggi', Pergunia University for Foreigners, <http://elearning.unistrapg.it /dspace/bitstream/2447/87/1/erhardt.pdf> (13.09.2011).

Fairclough, N. (1998), *Discourse and Social Change*. Cambridge: Polity Press.

Goodman, S. and P. Manners (1997), 'Making it "real": Words and pictures in television news', *Language and Communication*, 17: 53-66.

Haarman, L. and L. Lombardo (eds.) (2008), *Evaluation and Stance in War News: A Linguistic Analysis of American, British and Italian Television News Reporting of the 2003 Iraqi War*. London: Continuum.

Hartley, J. (1982), *Understanding News*. London: Methuen.

Hassanpour, A. (2005), 'Language and television', in: H. Newcomb (ed.), *Encyclopedia of Television*. Chicago, IL: Fitzroy Dearborn Publishers. 1313-1318.

Ilie, C. (2001), 'Semi-institutional discourse: The case of talk shows', *Journal of Pragmatics*, 33: 209-254.

Marriott, S. (1997), 'The emergence of live television talk', *Text*, 17: 181-198.

Menduni, E. (2004), *La Televisione*. Roma-Bari: Laterza.

Montgomery, M. (2007), *The Discourse of Broadcast News: A Linguistic Approach*. London: Routledge.

Nacci, L. (2003), 'La lingua della televisione', in: I. Bonomi, A. Masini and S. Morgana (eds.), *La Lingua Italiana e i Mass Media*. Rome: Carocci. 67-92.

Quaglio, P. (2009), *Television Dialogue: The Sitcom* Friends *vs. Natural Conversation*. Amsterdam: John Benjamins.

Rossini Favretti, R. (1988), 'L'oralità del testo televisivo', *Studi Italiani di Linguistica Teorica ed Applicata*, XVII: 203-218.

Scannell, P. (ed.) (1991), *Broadcast Talk*. London: Sage.

Schmid, H. (1994), 'Probabilistic part-of-speech tagging using decision trees', in: *Proceedings of the International Conference on New Methods in Language Processing*. <http://www.ims.uni-stuttgart.de/ftp/pub/corpora/tree-tagger1.pdf> (13.09.2011).

Spina, S. (2005), 'Il corpus di Italiano televisivo (CIT): Struttura e annotazione', in: E. Burr (ed.), *Tradizione & Innovazione. Il Parlato: Teoria Corpora Linguistica dei Corpora. Proceedings of the VI SILFI Conference*. Florence: Franco Cesati. 413-426.

Spina, S. (forthcoming), 'Changing trends in Italian newspaper language. A diachronic, corpus-based study', in: *Proceedings of CLAVIER 2009 Conference*. Amsterdam: John Benjamins.

Swales, J. (1990), *Genre Analysis: English in Academic and Research Settings*. Cambridge: Cambridge University Press.

Tannenbaum, P.H. (ed.) (1980), *The Entertainment Functions of Television*. Hillsdale, NJ: Lawrence Erlbaum.

Text Encoding Initiative Consortium (2002), *Guidelines for Electronic Text Encoding and Interchange: Volumes 1 and 2 (Edition P4)*. Charlottesville, VA: University of Virginia Press.

Corpora and texts: Lexis and text structure

Michael Stubbs

University of Trier

Abstract

Corpus studies have shown that words in texts have two strong tendencies: they occur in clusters and they occur in partly fixed phrases. These features have text-management and evaluative functions, and therefore provide the basis of a theory of how lexis contributes to textual organization. Although there are many excellent individual case studies of these topics, they have not yet been systematically integrated into a functional theory of lexis.

1. Introduction

In the last few years an increasing number of case studies have used corpus data to study textual organization, including the characteristics of specific genres (e.g. academic and legal) and their different conventions (Aijmer and Stenström 2004; Connor and Upton 2004; Partington et al. 2004; Baker 2006; Biber et al. 2007; Ädel and Reppen 2008; Adolphs 2008; Flowerdew 2008). It follows that none of the facts which I discuss are very original, but I will argue that much work requires to be done before these case studies can be synthesized and integrated in a way which would reveal their full significance for a general theory of language.

I begin with a simple point. Corpora are artificial sets of data, which are produced by linguists, whereas texts are real language events, which are produced by language users. So, it is really texts – spoken and written – which should be the focus of attention. Corpora are one or two levels of abstraction away from real language events. In particular, concordances, one of the main tools of corpus study, encourage the analysis of small fragments of language, which are extracted from a cross-section of texts.

I will divide my examples into three main sets, which go from more concrete to more abstract:

1. word distribution: word-forms and semantically related words
2. word classes: what have been called general nouns and shell nouns
3. phraseology: particularly extended lexical units.

2. Word distribution

I will start with the contribution of word distribution to text structure, and give just one example of each of two cases: the distribution of mere word-forms, where the analysis can be automatic and knowledge-free, and then the distribution of words in semantic fields, where the analysis depends on semantic interpretation.

The concept of knowledge-free text analysis famously goes back to work by Zellig Harris (1952). Although his specific proposals have rarely been directly developed, frequency and distribution are the features *par excellence* studied in corpus linguistics, and some text analysis makes either very simple assumptions about common-sense knowledge of the world or none at all. In an early quantitative analysis of word distribution in texts, Alford (1971) studied content words in Russian texts about physics: he pointed to an important difference between general high-frequency vocabulary and local high-frequency vocabulary, calculating that "once a general low-frequency word has occurred in a text, its immediate future text-coverage is likely to be more than ten times that predicted by [a] general count".

Church and Mercer (1994) make a similar point about the "burstiness" of lexical distribution. They note that content words in texts behave like buses in New York. You can wait for ages for a bus and none arrives, then several arrive together. I've never been to New York, so I can't confirm this, but I can corroborate the generalization from independent observations of buses in London: it may be an omnibus universal. Manning and Schütze (1999: 547) put it more formally: "[m]ost content words are much more likely to occur again in a text once they have occurred once". Kilgarriff (1997) calls it the "whelks problem". The lemma WHELK occurs over 70 times in the 100 million words of the BNC (*British National Corpus*), but around 40 of the occurrences are from one single article. In terms of text analysis, of course, it is not a problem, but a predictable and probabilistic feature of lexical cohesion.

One way of operationalizing a knowledge-free text analysis has been proposed by Youmans (1991). He calculates the type-token ratio in texts within a moving span of word-tokens: e.g. 1 to 35, 2 to 36, etc. For each new span, the software identifies "old" words (that is, words which have already occurred in the text) and "new" words (words occurring for the first time in the text). The changing type-token ratio is one indication of text structure. Figure 1 is an illustrative example from Joseph Conrad's short novel *Heart of Darkness*. This shows the first half of the text, with the type-token ratio measured over a moving span. The ratio tends to decline over the text as a whole, as more and more words are repeated, but the ratio rises at points in the story when something new is happening: new characters are introduced or there is some new incident. For example, there are clear spikes in the ratio at points A and B. These spikes have been found with no prior assumptions about meaning, but of course their significance requires human interpretation. If we go back to the text, we discover that something new is, indeed, happening at points A and B. At A, a group of people arrive, and the main character, Marlow, clearly disapproves of them: they are "an invasion, an infliction, a visitation". At B, Marlow makes an "extraordinary" and "amazing" find, an old book in the middle of the jungle. If you have read *Heart of Darkness*, you will know that this is an important symbol in the story. The software has successfully identified significant points in the text. The “new” words are here marked with “>”.

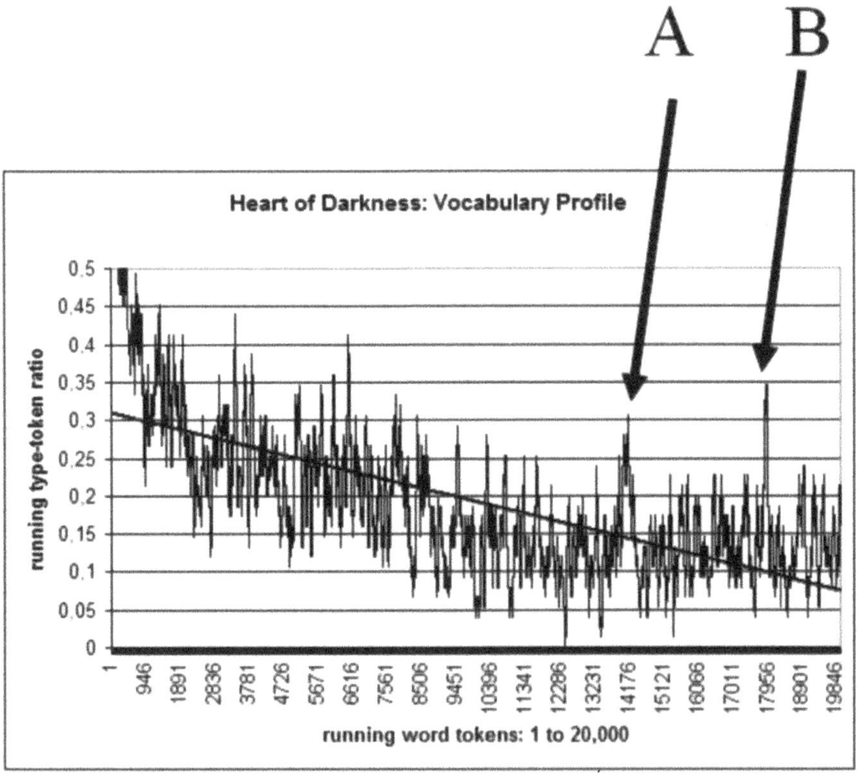

Figure 1. The moving type-token ratio across the first half of Conrad’s novella

Point A:

> ... It was an >inextricable >mess of things decent in >themselves but that human folly made look like >spoils of >thieving. This devoted band called itself the >Eldorado >Exploring >Expedition and I believe they were >sworn to >secrecy. Their talk however was the talk of sordid >buccaneers, it was >reckless without >hardihood, >greedy without >audacity, and >cruel without >courage; there was not an >atom of >foresight or of >serious intention in the whole >batch of them ...

Point B:

> ... I >picked up a >book. ... It was an extraordinary find. Its >title was *An >Inquiry into some >Points of >Seamanship* by a man, >Tower,

>Towson – some such name – >Master in his >Majesty's >Navy. ... I >handled this amazing >antiquity with the greatest >possible >tenderness, >lest it should >dissolve in my hands ... Not a very >enthralling book; but at the first glance you could see there … an >honest concern for the right way of going to work ... I couldn't believe my eyes. ... It was an >extravagant mystery. ...

Other studies show that the uneven distribution of words from given semantic fields signals text structure. Here the analysis is clearly not knowledge-free, but depends on a semantic interpretation of the words. For example, Bondi (2007) studies economics articles and shows that different words are preferred in opening paragraphs (examples in (1) and (2) below) and in the main body of the text (examples in (3)):

(1) debate, economics, research, studies, theory
(2) developed, modern, popular, rapid, seminal
(3) coefficient, equation, increases, negative, parameter(s), rate, regression, total

In the opening paragraphs of such articles, there are frequent references to the discipline (often nouns) and evaluative words (often adjectives), whereas in the main body of the text there are statistical and logical expressions. As is often the case, this may seem rather obvious in retrospect, but such findings are not evident to introspection.

3. Word classes

Many studies have shown the contribution of word classes to textual cohesion. I will give brief examples of what have been called general nouns and shell nouns.

The top nouns in the *British National Corpus* (BNC) by descending frequency are illustrated in (4):

(4) time, people, way, years, year, work, government, £#, day, man, world, life, part, mr, number, house, children, system, case, place, end, group, things

These words are not a random set. A couple (e.g. *government*, *£#*, where # represents any number) imply something about the design of the BNC (possible over representation of topics common to newspaper texts). However, several have to do with time, place and people, and one or two have very vague meanings (*things*). That is, almost all are "general nouns", in the sense of Mahlberg (2005). In a recent article (Stubbs 2007), I studied why one of these words, *world*, is so frequent. The answer is that it occurs in many semi-fixed phrases.

(5) from all over the world; in many parts of the world; the other side of the world
(6) World War, Second World War, World Cup, Third World, World Bank
(7) one of the world's most gifted scientists; the most natural thing in the world

Those in (5) refer literally to the external world: they are idiomatic and conventional but semantically transparent. Those in (6) are not entirely compositional, and those in (7) are evaluative phrasal constructions which have the function of emphasising something in the text.

In summary: high frequency nouns are frequent because they occur in frequent phrases, and many of these phrases are frequent because they structure and evaluate information. In addition, as Mukherjee (2007: 143) points out, high frequency is usually taken as a criterion of typicality. But the most frequent nouns in the language are not typical of the class of nouns: they do not denote categories of things in the external world, but have text-internal functions. In order to explain lexical frequency data, we require to show how lexis is used in texts.

Several studies go a step further and classify words functionally, according to their metalinguistic contribution to text structure: they encapsulate, interpret and evaluate a piece of information in the text. Many different terms have been used to label such lexis: vocabulary 3 (Winter 1977), procedural vocabulary (Widdowson 1983), prospective vocabulary (Tadros 1994), shell nouns (Francis 1994; Schmid 2000), signalling nouns (Flowerdew 2006), unspecific anaphoric nouns (Yamasaki 2008), and probably others. Shell nouns refer to something spoken or written (see example (8) below), or to thought processes (see example (9) below), and encapsulate a piece of information in the text, and thereby make a metalinguistic contribution to text structure (Hunston and Francis 2000).

(8) accusation, boast, claim, demand, excuse, forecast, guess, hint, implication, etc.
(9) agreement, belief, concept, desire, fear, hunch, illusion, judgement, etc.

Mahlberg (2009) gives an example which relates a genre-specific shell noun to text structure. In news stories, the noun *move* summarizes previous text, and the phrase *The move follows* often occurs at the beginning of the second paragraph of news stories. In the BNC there are 50 examples, all from spoken or written news media. Example (10) is one example from BNC file CBF (periodical, world affairs).

(10) The BBC is to be stripped of responsibility for the Queen's annual Christmas TV broadcast ... The move follows ... claims that a BBC employee leaked the speech to a newspaper.

Hoey (2005) calls this tendency of certain words and phrases to occur at particular positions in texts "textual collocation" and "textual colligation".

4. Phraseology

Finally, there are also many case studies of the text management functions of extended lexical units. In informal discourse, several constructions are used both to close a segment of narrative and to signal speaker attitude. The END UP VERB-ING construction (Louw 2000: 51) expresses irritation at a situation which leaves someone's image or status impaired (*you may end up looking a bit foolish*; *it ended up costing a fortune*; *we might end up regretting it*). The END UP IN construction signals a boundary in a story, often about something which started well but has gone wrong (*landing downwind and ending up in a hedge*). The most frequent collocates are *prison, jail, court* and *hospital.* It is not surprising that the lemma END occurs in phraseology which signals a narrative boundary, but the phraseology is conventional, not entirely compositional, and signals speaker attitude. The PAR FOR THE COURSE construction (Channell 2000) is a way of complaining that things have turned out disappointingly, but in rather the way you expected, and that there is nothing further to be said (*it didn't take* [*her*] *long to realize that this sort of thing was par for the course ... and that you have to learn to live with it*).

The WENT AND VERB-ED construction also signals the end of a segment of narrative, and often in addition expresses the speaker's surprise and/or disapproval of what has happened, as illustrated in (11)-(16).

(11) he put the phone down and went and got himself a whisky
(12) so I went and toddled off to find somebody
(13) then he went and jumped out of a plane
(14) Paul Bodin then went and missed a penalty
(15) then she went and spoiled everything by behaving as if pissed
(16) and then, would you believe it, she went and married him

Again, it is important to relate such observations back to texts. Example (16) is from BNC file BN6 (non-academic prose and biography), illustrated in (17).

(17) ... a sad and curious story ... it concerns my great-aunt [and] a man ... called John Bell ... he was as mad as a hatter, and really no good at all ... and then, would you believe it, <u>she went and married him</u> ... the match was a disaster ... he made a lot of trouble ... and the family wanted nothing to do with him ...

5. Conclusions

I have used a few individual examples to make just one main point. Although there are many valuable individual case studies of the textual functions of lexis, they would contribute more convincingly to an overall functional theory of language use, if they were better synthesized and integrated.

There are many attempts to list and classify discourse markers of various kinds, but these taxonomies will never fully explain textual cohesion. This is because text structure is signalled by general mechanisms, including the uneven distribution of word-forms and of words which have been semantically and functionally classified. In addition, much frequent phraseology signals textual boundaries and/or evaluates a section of text. Much about lexical frequency is explained by textual function. The most frequent nouns are not typical nouns: they have text-internal functions. High frequency words are frequent because they occur in frequent phrases, and many phrases are frequent because they structure and evaluate information. It follows that implicit coherence (which relies on extra-linguistic knowledge) has been over-estimated, whereas explicit cohesion has been correspondingly under-estimated.

If we ignore the functions of lexis in texts, we miss the opportunity to make interesting generalizations. If we invent isolated sentences, and speculate about what is possible in theory (a Chomskyan view of things), then lexis appears chaotic. If we study attested texts, and look at what is probable in practice (a Firthian view of things), then lexis is much more predictable. This point reverses the classic Saussurian assumption. If we look at lexis as part of the language system (*langue*), many of its functions remain obscure. If we look at lexis as part of language in use (*parole*), many of its functions become much clearer.

References

Ädel, A. and R. Reppen (eds.) (2008), *Corpora and Discourse*. Amsterdam: John Benjamins.

Adolphs, S. (2008), *Corpus and Context*. Amsterdam: John Benjamins.

Aijmer, K. and A.B. Stenström (eds.) (2004), *Discourse Patterns in Spoken and Written Corpora*. Amsterdam: John Benjamins.

Alford, M.H.T. (1971), 'Computer assistance in language learning', in: R.A. Wisbey (ed.), *The Computer in Literary and Linguistic Research*. Cambridge: Cambridge University Press. 77-86.

Baker, P. (2006), *Using Corpora in Discourse Analysis*. London: Continuum.

Biber, D., U. Connor and T. Upton (eds.) (2007), *Discourse on the Move*. Amsterdam: John Benjamins.

Bondi, M. (2007), 'Historical research articles in English and Italian', in: M.B. Papi, G. Cappelli and S. Masi (eds.), *Lexical Complexity*. Pisa: Pisa University Press. 65-83.

Channell, J. (2000), 'Corpus-based analysis of evaluative lexis', in: S. Hunston and G. Thompson (eds.), *Evaluation in Text*. Oxford: Oxford University Press. 38-55.

Church, K.W. and R.L. Mercer (1994), 'Introduction', in: S. Armstrong (ed.), *Using Large Corpora*. Cambridge, MA: MIT Press. 1-24.

Connor, U. and T.A. Upton (eds.) (2004), *Discourse in the Professions*. Amsterdam: John Benjamins.

Flowerdew, J. (2006), 'Use of signalling nouns in a learner corpus', *International Journal of Corpus Linguistics*, 11: 345-62.

Flowerdew, L. (2008), *Corpus-Based Analyses of the Problem-Solution Pattern*. Amsterdam: John Benjamins.

Francis, G. (1994), 'Labelling discourse', in: R.M. Coulthard (ed.), *Advances in Written Text Analysis*. London: Routledge. 83-101.

Harris, Z. (1952), 'Discourse analysis', *Language*, 28: 1-30.

Hoey, M. (2005), *Lexical Priming*. London: Routledge.

Hunston, S. and G. Francis (2000), *Pattern Grammar*. Amsterdam: John Benjamins.

Kilgarriff, A. (1997), 'Putting frequencies in the dictionary', *International Journal of Lexicography*, 10: 135-155.

Louw, B. (2000), 'Contextual prosodic theory', in: C. Heffer, H. Saunston and G. Fox (eds.), *Words in Context*. Birmingham: University of Birmingham. 48-94.

Mahlberg, M. (2005), *English General Nouns*. Amsterdam: John Benjamins.

Mahlberg, M. (2009), 'Local textual functions of *move* in newspaper story patterns', in: U. Römer and R. Schulze (eds.), *Exploring the Lexis-Grammar Interface*. Amsterdam: John Benjamins. 265-287.

Manning, C.D. and H. Schütze (1999), *Foundations of Natural Language Processing*. Cambridge, MA: MIT Press.

Mukherjee, J. (2007) 'Corpus linguistics and linguistic theory' [Review of Mahlberg 2005], *International Journal of Corpus Linguistics*, 12: 131-147.

Partington, A., J. Morley and L. Haarman (2004), *Corpora and Discourse*. Bern: Peter Lang.

Schmid, H.-J. (2000), *English Abstract Nouns as Conceptual Shells*. Berlin: de Gruyter.

Stubbs, M. (2007), 'Quantitative data on multi-word sequences in English', in: M. Hoey, M. Mahlberg, M. Stubbs and W. Teubert (eds.), *Text, Discourse and Corpora*. London: Continuum. 163-189.

Tadros, A. (1994), 'Predictive categories in expository text', in: R.M. Coulthard (ed.), *Advances in Written Text Analysis*. London: Routledge. 69-82.

Widdowson, H.G. (1983), *Learning Purpose and Language Use*. Oxford: Oxford University Press.

Winter, E. (1977), 'A clause relational approach to English texts', *Instructional Science*, 6: 1-92.

Yamasaki, N. (2008), 'Collocations and colligations associated with discourse functions of unspecific anaphoric nouns', *International Journal of Corpus Linguistics*, 13: 75-98.

Youmans, G. (1991), 'A new tool for discourse analysis: The vocabulary management profile', *Language*, 67: 763-89.

On the persistence of ambiguous linguistic contexts over time: Implications for corpus research on micro-changes

Elizabeth Closs Traugott

Stanford University

Abstract

Most instances of grammaticalization have been shown to arise in restrictive contexts (cf. Bybee et al. 1994). The persistence (Hopper 1991) of linguistic contexts raises theoretical and methodological issues for historical corpus research. What is the appropriate unit of linguistic context? How long do contexts remain relevant in the history of specific constructions? In quantitative work should "bridging contexts" (Heine 2002) and "critical contexts" (Diewald 2002) that enable grammaticalization be counted after grammaticalization has set in? I argue that ambiguous contexts ('co-texts' broadly defined to include prior and following discourse), if attested, should be counted (contra Eckardt 2006), because they persist as part of the ecology of a newly grammaticalizing construction and should therefore be considered an integral component of diachronic corpus research. Data discussed involve the development of motion-with-a-purpose BE going to *V into an auxiliary of the future as evidenced by the Early Modern English part of* Helsinki Corpus, *and by the first fifty years of* Proceedings of the Old Bailey.

1. Introduction

Contexts for grammaticalization have been the topic of several papers in recent years (e.g. Diewald 2002, 2006; Heine 2002; Himmelmann 2004; Traugott, forthcoming). In this paper I focus on ambiguous contexts that 'persist', i.e. originally enabling ambiguous contexts that continue to be used after grammaticalization has set in, and some of the implications of such contexts for corpus work.

It has been suggested that once grammaticalization has taken place the status of enabling contexts has changed since they either do not continue to exist (Diewald 2002, 2006) or, if they do continue to exist, they no longer enable change, and therefore should not be counted (Eckardt 2006). My main argument will be that if ambiguous contexts occur and persist, as is often the case, they should be counted since they are an essential part of the ecology of the generalization and further development of the new grammatical construction.[1]

'Grammaticalization' is understood here as the development of grammatical markers such as markers of tense, aspect, modality, and mood, case, connectives, and Topic/Focus markers. The definition is a functional one seeking to answer the question "How do expressions change with respect to morphosyntactic function" (Kiparsky, forthcoming; Traugott 2010), as opposed to a formal one that seeks to answer the question "How do internal dependencies change" (e.g. Lehmann 1995; Haspelmath 2004).[2]

By 'context' I mean linguistic environment, including pragmatic inferences, larger discourses in both written and spoken mode (see similarly Himmelmann 2004). Crucially, 'context' is not limited to the clause in which an expression appears. It is linguistic (co-text broadly defined) and does not refer to the setting, or such factors as speaker-hearer roles, important though these are. Furthermore, I assume that the clause or intonation unit (not the sentence) is the chief linguistic unit relevant to change. Meanings arise in discourse contexts; change cannot be understood by studying decontextualized examples.

"Persistence" as defined by Hopper (1991) refers to retention in a newly grammaticalized form of traces of the semantics of the source. This is a well-known notion in the grammaticalization literature, and is summarized in "details of [a form's] lexical history may be reflected in constraints on its grammatical distribution" (Hopper 1991: 22). Here I extend the concept to retention of pragmatic ambiguities that may be among the enabling contexts for grammaticalization.

Section 2 provides a brief overview of prior work on contexts for grammaticalization. Section 3 discusses in some detail the persistence of motion-with-a-purpose BE *going to* as evidenced by the *Early Modern English Corpus* within the *Helsinki Corpus* (1500-1720, cf. Rissainen et al. 1991), and the first fifty years of the *Proceedings of the Old Bailey* (1674-1723, cf. Huber 2007), a period shortly after the grammaticalization of the auxiliary. In Section 4 I briefly comment on the uniqueness of BE *going to* in English from the perspective of micro-changes, and Section 5 serves as a conclusion.

2. Prior work on contexts for grammaticalization[3]

It has been a truism of work on grammaticalization at least since Bybee et al. (1994) that grammaticalization occurs only in context: "[e]verything that happens to the meaning of a gram happens because of the contexts in which it is used" (ibid.: 297) (see also recently Fried 2009). However, how context is to be defined continues to be a matter of debate.

Three proposals for defining contexts specifically for grammaticalization are mentioned here: those by Diewald (2002, 2006), Heine (2002) and Himmelmann (2004). In all three context crucially includes pragmatics, i.e. "invited inferences" (Traugott and König 1991) or "context induced interpretation" (Heine et al. 1991) in the flow of speech. In Heine's and Diewald's proposals there is a "stage" of enabling ambiguous contexts before grammaticalization can set in (however, such enabling contexts do not necessarily lead to change), and a sharp distinction is made between contexts before and after grammaticalization has set in. In Himmelmann's proposal the focus is on grammaticalization and extension/ generalization after onset.

Diewald (2002) posits three context stages:

I. "Untypical contexts": the development of implicatures in contexts "which show clusters of contextual features that had not been customary before" (ibid.: 109).

II: "Critical contexts" with "multiple structural and semantic ambiguities" or opacities that invite "several alternative interpretations, among them the new grammatical meaning" (ibid.: 103).

III: "Isolating contexts": "specific linguistic contexts that favor one reading to the exclusion of the other" (ibid.: 103). This is a stage of reorganization and differentiation.

Note that "critical contexts" are defined morphosyntactically and semantically as well as pragmatically. Diewald (2006: 4f.) points out that, unlike untypical contexts which may persist after grammaticalization has taken place, critical contexts cease to be critical once isolating contexts appear. This is true in the trivial sense that they can no longer be 'critical'. In the case she discusses, the verbal morphology of the German premodals, the morphosyntax changes significantly and therefore cannot persist. This is, however, a relatively rare phenomenon, and is not a necessary feature of critical contexts, as the example of BE *going to* shows: motion-with-a-purpose constructions and the morphosyntactic contexts in which they originally appeared still flourish today.

Heine (2002: 86) posits four context stages:

I. "[T]here is an expression with a 'normal' or source meaning occurring in an array of different contexts".

II. "[T]here is a bridging context giving rise to an inference to the effect that, rather than the source meaning, there is another meaning, the target meaning, offering a more plausible interpretation of the utterance concerned".

III. There is a switch context that no longer allows for old interpretations.

IV. Finally, there is a conventionalized context; the item is fully grammaticalized.

While the term "bridging" refers to pragmatic ambiguity (Evans and Wilkins 2000), a new stage of pragmatic ambiguity logically presupposes some kind of change in morphosyntactic distribution, hence morphosyntactic context. In Heine's article examples include metaphor and some distributionally atypical uses, so "bridging" contexts are clearly not intended to be pragmatic only.

Himmelmann's (2004: 33) three contexts for grammaticalization concern primarily the moment of onset of grammaticalization (Heine's "switch" contexts) and, more importantly, expansion/generalization after grammaticalization (Heine's "conventionalization" contexts). Himmelmann's examples are from the development of the definite article in German; here I use examples from the history of BE *going to*. He distinguishes:

I. Host-class expansion. This concerns expansion of collocations, e.g. in the case of auxiliary BE *going to*, the switch context of appearance with a verb that is implausible in a motion-with-a purpose construction, e.g. *read,* and then further collocational expansion, e.g. to *like.*

II. Syntactic expansion, e.g. in the case of auxiliary BE *going to*, use in raising constructions, such as *There is going to be an ugly election this year.*

III. Semantic-pragmatic expansion, e.g. in the case of auxiliary BE *going to*, the pragmatic implicature of future was taken to be salient in such contexts as passives, and at the onset of grammaticalization a new polysemy arose.

Himmelmann hypothesizes that in grammaticalization all three types of context expansion are necessary. By contrast lexicalization may or may not involve any of them.

It is often thought that pragmatic or structural ambiguity is a prerequisite to grammaticalization at the stage of critical contexts. However, as Diewald's definition of these contexts shows, this is in fact not necessary. Opacities that invite several alternative interpretations are sufficient (Diewald 2002: 103). This is a point made by Harris and Campbell (1995: 51): "reanalysis depends upon a pattern characterized by surface ambiguity or the possibility of more than one analysis". The exclusive "or" is crucial here. Harris and Campbell insist that (semantic) "opacity is not a prerequisite to reanalysis" (ibid.: 71), only the possibility of multiple structural analyses (ibid.: 72).

Standard examples of grammaticalization like BE *going to* do illustrate pragmatic ambiguity, in this case for about 130 years of textual history. Example (1) is the first example of a possible precursor of the future construction known to me:

(1) Also ther passed a theef byfore alexandre that ***was goyng to*** be hanged whiche saide … (1477, Mubashshir ibn Fatik, Abu al-Wafa', 11th C; *Dictes or sayengis of the philosophhres* [EEBO])
'Also a thief who was going to be hanged passed before Alexander, who said …'

(1) is passive as is the second known example from 1482 (see Danchev and Kytö 1994), but (1), unlike that example, has no *by*-phrase. Passive downgrades agency, especially when there is no *by*-phrase, but the general context suggests the motion meaning (*passed before*). It should be noted that (1) is 'untypical' in several ways: the *-ing* form of the progressive was relatively new and rare at the time; the use of the passive purposive is also rare; in most motion-with-a purpose constructions a directional prepositional phrase appears between BE *going to* and the verb.

However, not all developments that lead to grammaticalization illustrate pragmatic ambiguity, for example the development of BE/HAVE *like* from main verb > modal (Kytö and Romaine 2005). This has been partially replaced by BE *likely to* in Modern Standard English. In the fifteenth century, in the context of *to*-infinitives, past tense, and apodoses of counterfactuals, BE/HAVE *like* became saliently associated with an implicature of "action narrowly averted" (Kuteva 2001). An example is (2):

(2) Henry Ingloses men have slayn ij men … and if he had abedyn at hom ***he had lyke to have*** be fechid owte of his owyn hows
'Henry Inglos's men have slain nine (sic) men … and if he had been at home, he would have come close to being fetched out of his own house' (1453, *Paston Letters* [Kytö and Romaine 2005: 3])

Kytö and Romaine (2005) suggest the meaning of the counterfactual context became absorbed into the semantics of BE/HAVE *like to* in the sixteenth century, and the phrase was reanalyzed as an avertive modal auxiliary (see Kuteva 2001 on "context-absorption" and on avertive modals in Bulgarian). For example, (3) has no prior counterfactual clause, and the counterfactual semantics is expressed by *had like to*:

(3) Boy, shut ye door, for I rem'ber this time 4 yeares we ***had like to have*** been killed by thunder & lightning (1666, *Danforth Diary* [Kytö and Romaine 2005: 5])

On this analysis there are no ambiguous examples of BE/HAVE *like to*, only specialized pragmatic and morphosyntactic discourse contexts (i.e. "critical contexts") that enable grammaticalization. It is of course possible that individual speakers might have perceived ambiguity, but historical data can give us evidence only of what appears in texts that survive.

The question of interest for this paper is: if a case of grammaticalization such as BE *going to* provides textual evidence of pragmatic ambiguity, how should one think about that ambiguity if it is still attested once conventionalization sets in? In her study of BE *going to*, Eckardt (2006: 97) decided that such ambiguous contexts should no longer be counted. This is presumably because their status changed with the onset of grammaticalization. They are no longer pragmatic but semantic because a polysemy has arisen between the older motion construction and newer future. Furthermore, the contexts are no longer enabling.

There are problems with this approach. One is that when to stop counting depends heavily on what is considered to be the first switch example. Eckardt cites 1646, the date when a grammarian (Poole) equates *I am going to read* with *be about to* and calls it "the signe of the Participle of the future" (Eckardt 2006: 94 drawing on Danchev and Kytö 1994). However, Garrett (forthcoming) cites two probably earlier examples, the first of which is attested thirty-five years, i.e. more than a generation, earlier, cf. (4) and (5):

(4) So, for want of a Cord, hee tooke his owne garters off; and as he ***was going to*** make a nooze, I watch'd my time and ranne away. (1611, Tourneur, *The Atheist's Tragedie* [EEBO; Garrett, forthcoming])

(5) and all this they did of purpose to affright and distract me, and to make me believe I ***was going to*** be racked again, to make me confess an untruth. (1632, Lithgow, *Travels & Voyages* [ibid.; modern spelling])

In these examples host-class expansion to verbs implausible in a motion-with-a-purpose context appears to have occurred.

Another problem is that deciding to stop counting on the basis of particular example privileges innovation by an individual over change. Change involves spread within the system and within the community (Milroy 2003; Traugott and Trousdale 2010). Poplack and Tagliamonte (1999: 319) cite a grammarian (Ward 1765/1967) over a century after Poole who says BE *going to* is equivalent to BE *about to* "only in conversation". If Ward's assessment is correct, should one stop counting *BE going to* in texts that represent speech, but not in 'literate' written data?

For a contemporary speaker of English, auxiliary BE *going to* is deeply entrenched and it is all too easy to read an example with BE *going to* as an auxiliary construction with hindsight especially if only the immediate context is excerpted. In contemporary English there is no polysemy, since various changes have led it to diverge from the motion construction, e.g. the development of use in raising constructions and especially, in speech, the development of reduced forms which begin to appear in historical texts represented in the *Oxford English Dictionary* (OED, cf. Simpson and Weiner 2009) as *gonna* around 1910 (Mair 2004).[4] At the time it came into being, however, auxiliary BE *going to* was still a polysemy, not yet highly entrenched, and therefore less likely to be accessed easily.

As will be argued below, I recommend continuing to count both the semantic-pragmatic and morphosyntactic contexts that appear to have enabled grammaticalization to determine how they affect the use of the construction, especially later meanings and distributional patterns.

3. Data for persistence of motion BE *going to* in two corpora

In this paper I discuss evidence for persistence of the motion-with-purpose BE *going to* in two corpora. The first is the *Helsinki Corpus of Early Modern English* (HC), a corpus of c. 500,000 words for the period 1500-1720, the period during which the grammaticalization of the future use took place. The second is the first fifty years of the *Proceedings of Old Bailey* (POB 1674-1723), the period shortly after the grammaticalization of the future use, i.e. one of clearly conventionalizing and conventionalized contexts. This is a subset of the larger *Old Bailey Corpus* that has been used for linguistic analysis (POB 1674-1834) which contains over 100,000 trials, totaling about fifty million words (Huber 2007).[5] The trials are fairly representative of speech in interaction, even in the early period, in which most reports are in third person (first person reports dominate after the 1720s). It has been shown that trials of the seventeenth and eighteenth centuries in Britain (e.g. POB) and America (e.g. Salem Witch Trials, Rosenthal 2009) are good sources of data for interaction (see e.g. Culpeper and Kytö 2000; Archer 2006, 2007; Kryk-Kastovsky 2006, 2007). Archer outlines key differences from current Anglo-American legal practice: there was no presumption of innocence; the 'prosecution' was usually the plaintiff; there were no defense or prosecution lawyers. Therefore defendants, witnesses as well as judges negotiated turns, and legal discourses were therefore highly interactional.

The criteria used for identifying the relevant strings in the two corpora are:

a) a finite form of *be* followed by *going to* V

b) paraphrasability by 'be on one's way with the purpose of V-*ing*' (motion-with-a-purpose)

c) paraphrasability by 'be about to V/intend to V' (future)[6]

An unambiguous example of the auxiliary must be incompatible or at least implausible with a motion reading. This is an issue of host-class expansion. The criterion of use in a syntactic raising construction is irrelevant at the time as this is a later development after conventionalization (the earliest example I am aware of is dated 1725).

3.1 BE *going to* in the Helsinki Corpus of Early Modern English

The HC is divided into three seventy-year sections. In the first, 1500-1570, there are no examples with the relevant morphosyntactic structure: finite form of *be*, *go* in the progressive, and immediate adjacency to V. There are also no examples in the first period of *going to* V without a finite copula (e.g. *he going to strike*...),[7] or of *go to* V-*ing* with a gerund (e.g. *go to washing*), both construction types that Garrett (forthcoming) proposes were key to the development of the auxiliary.[8] There is, however, one possible example of the former in the second period, 1570-1650, cf. (6):

(6) [about drinking] I pledge you sir, quoth she, and ***going to*** fil more. Na, quoth the man, pay for yt first (1582 Maddox, *Diary*)

This occurs in a diary, and appears to have been ellipted. It probably means 'as she was going to fill [the tankard], "No" said the man'. The only instance of a *go*-gerund has a modifier (before hee ('horse') *goe to* his morning watring, and before hee *goe to* his euening watering, 1615, Gervase, *Countrey Contentments*) and is therefore not an immediate context for the development of the auxiliary.

In the third EModE period of HC (1650-1720) there are five examples of BE *going to* V. Of these three are plausibly ambiguous, two with foregrounded motion as in (7a, b).

(7) a. 5 or 6 days since, and when we ***were going to*** fight the Dutch, I had such a paine in my right arme that could not use it but very litle. (1672, Hatton, *Letters*)

b. (^Ma.^) Even now departed to hold forth amongst the Congregation of the Righteous, in the full Assembly of the Righteous… [in response to a question about where the referent of "now departed" was going] she answered and said, ***she was going to*** instruct our Friends. (1685, Pepys, *Penny Merriments*)

(7b) is very plausibly about going somewhere to do a linguistic act.

There are two examples which do not plausibly suggest motion, and can be analyzed as examples of the future, cf. (8a, b):

(8) a. but no creditor coming about the house, they on Tuesday published his being thus lost. The council sat upon it, and ***were going to*** order a search of all the houses about the town (1683 Burnet, *History of my own Time*)

b. he swore, that happy man whom she ***was going to*** name shou'd die, though it were even Oroonoko himself. (1688 Behn, *Oroonoko*)

A third example, (9) is undecidable. *This week*, occurring after the finite *be*, seems to favor a temporal reading. However, such a reading is not required, as contemporary English shows. Since Hatton is writing about Mr. Enis's travel plans, a motion reading is plausible ('is this week leaving to try…') as well as a future 'about to' meaning:

(9) Worthy Mr Ennis, who being turned out of his living here for not swearing … ***is*** this weeke ***going to*** try whither he cannot more quietly live among ye heathens in America. (1690 Hatton, *Letters*)

These data suggest that by the end of the seventeenth century possible ambiguity between the original motion construction and the future was part of the ecology of the polysemy, and that motion contexts may have favored motion readings. On the other hand, there are no unambiguous examples of the motion construction (however, *go to* V without the BE-*ing* is attested, e.g. *You goe to seeke him?* 1630, Middleton, *Chaste Maid in Cheapside*).

3.2 BE *going to* in the OBP 1674-1723

There are possibly seventy-eight relevant examples of BE *going to* V in POB 1674-1723 ('possibly' because in some cases whether a collocating lexeme is a verb or a noun is undecidable). Of these four are fairly unambiguously motion constructions. Two involve *see* in the sense 'visit', one *see after*, and one *look upon*, all activity verbs, e.g. (10):

(10) the Mare was found to be one Mr. Linvil's, who was killed in Abingdon Road at Nettlebed, as he ***was going to*** see his Friends in the Countrey. (t16940711-13, Trial of Thomas Hill)

Another eight precede the word *work* in a context that favors a motion reading, e.g. (11):

(11) on Thursday Morning, she and some more ***were going to*** work, and two Women told them there was a Woman murdered in the Ditch between Hyde-Park and Chelsea. (t17030707-1, Trial of John Dromett)

In (11) *work* may be a verb but it may equally well be a noun (cf. *was going to bed/church*, etc.).[9] In two of the examples *work* is capitalized. While capitalization suggests *Work* is a nominal, it is not a necessary sign of nominal status as some verbs are capitalized (e.g. *as he was going to Ride away with it* (t16891211-8, Trial of Ben Hall)).

In sum, there are only four clear examples of the motion construction in the first fifty years of POB, and maximally a total of twelve if those with *work* are included. There are four types among these twelve tokens: *see*, *see after*, *look upon*, and *work*.

Forty of the seventy-eight examples appear to be of the auxiliary, i.e. to have the future meaning. Three of these involve *marry/be married*, but none of the other verbs are repeated. This gives us thirty-eight types, including *work upon it*, among forty tokens, precisely the kind of type-token ratio that one might expect when conventionalization has taken place and host-class expansion is occurring. Examples include (12):

(12) a. L. C. J. Hold, what are you doing now? ***Are*** you ***going to*** arraign his whole Life? Away, away, that ought not to be. (t16920406-1 Trial of Henry Harrison)

b. he thought he ***was going to*** bilk ('cheat') him of his Fair. (t17180423-48 Trial of Bartholomew Coats)

(12a) records the Lord Chief Justice speaking. This suggests that when Ward said in 1776 that *be going to* was used "only in conversation" (see Section 2), he must have meant "conversation" in the sense of 'spoken interactions, formal or informal'.[10]

A particularly interesting example is (13):

(13) Seale told him that he ***was going to*** work, and bade him get him gone to the Door, or to some Alehouse, for he must not see him work. (t16940830-18, Trial of John Wild, John Stephens)

Online parsing of 'Seale told him that he was going to work' might lead to interpretation of *work* as either a noun, or a verb. In the latter case, the expected reading would be motion-with-a-purpose. But the clauses that follow suggest (13) is actually an example of future BE *going to*, since it appears that Seale will work *in situ*, not at some other location. Otherwise the addressee would not be told to go to the door or alehouse so that he could not see Seale working.

The remaining twenty-six examples allow for an ambiguous interpretation. In most, motion is salient because it is mentioned in preceding or following clauses, as in (14a, b):

(14) a. declared that he came from Park Hall in Essex and set up his Horse in White Chappell, and took his Bags, and ***was going to*** pay the Money to the Countess; but coming down Leaden-hall street … (t16970224-29 Trial of William Thomas)

b. he was there accidentally, having been out with his Wife with Packthread … and hearing that a Boy was shot ***was going to*** see him, but as he went was shot in the Leg himself. (t17190708-56 Trial of John Humphreys, Sam Bains, George Picket, Thomas Hardy, Charles Child)

Although BE *going to marry*/BE *married* has arguably future readings in three other examples, in (15) the groom unquestionably went to Knightsbridge to be married (bigamously), and the example appears to be ambiguous between motion and intention:

(15) but she having some mistrust that he was going to be married to a second Wife followed him to Knights-bridge in a Coach, where he was married a second time before she came. (t17021014-11 Trial of Simon Johnson)

In this set of twenty-six ambiguous tokens there are five in which BE *going to* collocates with *carry*, three with *do*, two with *buy*, and two with *see* 'visit'. In other words there are eighteen types. The type-token ratio raises an interesting question – was the motion-with-a purpose construction itself becoming conventionalized without a directional intervening between *going to* and V? In other words, was the new auxiliary influencing its source? This is the kind of question that would hardly come up if one were not to take persistent ambiguous motion contexts that support the original reading into consideration.

4. The uniqueness of BE *going to* in English from the perspective of micro-changes

The abstract schema 'motion verb > future' is a staple of work on grammaticalization. Bybee et al. (1994) and Heine and Kuteva (2002), among others, have shown that it occurs in many languages world-wide. Bybee et al. further specify that the change occurs only if *go* is imperfective, and if V is immediately adjacent. At the micro-level of host-class expansion and other types of expansion, there may, however, be significant differences in the later developments of the newly conventionalized construction.

For example, Hilpert (2008) investigates changing selectional restrictions on English BE *going to* V with a quantitative diachronic collostructional analysis and compares them with their equivalent in the Dutch cognate *gaan*. While the focus is primarily on semantic changes, the investigation of selectional restrictions has much in common with the phenomenon that Himmelmann called host-class expansion – changes in the lexical exponents of V. Hilpert shows while both BE *going to* and *gaan* are examples of 'motion verb > future' they have very different local trajectories after grammaticalization, and hence very different current uses. At first both languages show intentional future meanings. In contemporary English agentivity, transitivity, telicity are key, but light verbs (*do*, *get*, *have*) are preferred collocational contexts. In Dutch over time there was a shift to atelicity and less intentional meanings. Currently cognitive response verbs are preferred (e.g. *benimen* 'love', *denken* 'think'). This implies persistence of the original semantic context in English (agency, intention associated with motion), but no persistence of the original motion context in Dutch. It highlights the importance of identifying whether persistence occurs, and also the extent to which it is a language-specific phenomenon.

One question raised by the present study is how significantly the weighting of individual collocations that is key to collostructional analysis would be affected by taking into consideration the extent to which ambiguity may persist, at least in the early years after the onset of grammaticalization. Some issues of ambiguity in synchronic collostructional analysis have been explored in Zeschel (2008); they deserve to be explored diachronically as well. While collostructional analysis focuses on immediate context, and therefore ambiguity may not appear to be a particularly important issue, here I have been concerned to show that more distant discourse context may be relevant to an understanding of the changes undergone as a grammaticalization becomes conventionalized.

5. Conclusion

The data discussed here suggest that five types of context need to be distinguished in accounting for grammatical micro-changes, and therefore in corpus work. Of these the third to fifth are the most important for understanding grammaticalization:

1) Normal use.
2) Untypical use.
3) Critical contexts. These are the truly enabling contexts; they may be pragmatically ambiguous, but this is not a necessary criterion for grammaticalization.
4) Switch contexts. These are contexts that show a reanalysis has occurred (e.g. collocations that would not have been possible before; a meaning that was originally pragmatic has come to be coded and semantic).

5) Conventionalization contexts that lead to generalization and increased productivity of the new construction. These are of three types: host-class, pragmatic-semantic, and syntactic expansion.

The kind of persistence discussed here presupposes a critical stage in which pragmatic polysemies are associated with the original construction, and their use after the new grammatical constructions has come into being, but now as semantic polysemies. Ambiguity may or may not occur, but if it does it is significant for ways in which the construction in question develops. Presence or absence of persistence needs to be accounted for, identified, and measured. By hypothesis it may affect collostructional weighting.

Persistence can be identified only by paying attention to discourse contexts, mainly prior to but also following the relevant clause or intonation unit. Pragmatic discourse contexts are not easy to operationalize (but see e.g. Hinterhölzl and Petrova 2009; Taylor and Pintzuk, forthcoming, for analyses of information structure using electronic corpora).

One question for further research arising from this study is whether there is evidence in other cases of grammaticalization that the newly grammaticalized expression may itself serve as a model to which its source comes to be aligned, as suggested at the end of Section 4. Another is to what extent other types of enabling context, e.g. morphosyntactic distributions, persist.

Notes

1 By 'construction' I mean a form-meaning pairing, as defined in construction grammar terms, see e.g. Goldberg (2006). However, nothing in this paper depends crucially on this definition.

2 For detailed discussion of the two views of grammaticalization, see Traugott (2010).

3 This section is largely a summary of Traugott (forthcoming).

4 Nicolle (1998) proposes a monosemous account of the semantics of both BE *going to*'s, based on Relevance Theory. However, their syntactic and phonological differences are not addressed; these differences render a monosemous account problematic.

5 The full proceedings range from 1674-1913.

6 Using the *Early English Books Online* (EEBO) *Corpus* Garrett (forthcoming) argues for paraphrasability by incipient action or "turning or preparing to do an action". I have not used this criterion because HC does not yield the types of enabling contexts that Garrett identifies.

7 (i) is not an example as *going* and *to go* are split by a directional phrase.

(i) after the dancing and sporte was almoste ended, he *going* into his chamber *to* goe to bed, on ('one') as he thoughte stroke him in the necke. (1552-1602, Forman, *Autobiography and Diary*)

8 Different corpora may suggest different contexts were relevant, see Note 6.

9 We find 'and I was going to my Work' with a determiner in t17380906-5, Trial of Joseph Upton. Here *work* is unquestionably a noun.

10 For an analysis of what 'conversation' meant in the eighteenth century, see e.g. Brewer (1997).

References

Archer, D. (2006), '(Re)initiating strategies: Judges and defendants in Early Modern English courtrooms', *Journal of Historical Pragmatics*, 7: 181-211.

Archer, D. (2007), 'Developing a more detailed picture of the English courtroom (1640-1760): Data and methodological issues facing historical pragmatics', in: S. Fitzmaurice and I. Taavitsainen (eds.), *Methods in Historical Pragmatics*. Berlin: de Gruyter. 185-217.

Brewer, J. (1997), *The Pleasures of the Imagination: English Culture in the Eighteenth Century*. London: Harper Collins.

Bybee, J, R. Perkins and W. Pagliuca (1994), *The Evolution of Grammar: Tense, Aspect, and Modality in the Languages of the World*. Chicago, IL: University of Chicago Press.

Culpeper, J. and M. Kytö (2000), 'Data in historical pragmatics: Spoken interaction (re)cast as writing', *Journal of Historical Pragmatics*, 1: 175-199.

Danchev, A. and M. Kytö (1994), 'The construction *be going to* + infinitive in Early Modern English', in: D. Kastovsky (ed.), *Studies in Early Modern English*. Berlin: de Gruyter. 59-77.

Diewald, G. (2002), 'A model for relevant types of contexts in grammaticalization', in: I. Wischer and G. Diewald (eds.), *New Reflections on Grammaticalization*. Amsterdam: John Benjamins. 103-120.

Diewald, G. (2006), 'Context types in grammaticalization as constructions', *Constructions*, SV1-9. <http://elanguage.net/journals/index.php/constructions/article/viewFile/24/29> (8.12.2011)

Eckardt, R. (2006), *Meaning Change in Grammaticalization: An Enquiry Into Semantic Reanalysis*. Oxford: Oxford University Press.

Evans, N. and D. Wilkins (2000), 'In the mind's ear: The semantic extensions of perception verbs in Australian languages', *Language*, 76: 546-592.

Fried, M. (2009), 'Construction grammar as a tool for diachronic analysis', *Constructions and Frames*, 1: 262-291.

Garrett, A. (forthcoming), ‘The historical syntax problem: Reanalysis and directionality’, in: D. Jonas, J. Whitman and A. Garrett (eds.), *Grammatical Change: Origins, Nature, Outcomes*. Oxford: Oxford University Press.

Goldberg, A.E. (2006), *Constructions at Work: The Nature of Generalization in Language*. Oxford: Oxford University Press.

Harris, A. and L. Campbell (1995), *Historical Syntax in Cross-Linguistic Perspective*. Cambridge: Cambridge University Press.

Haspelmath, M. (2004), ‘On directionality in language change with particular reference to grammaticalization’, in: O. Fischer, M. Norde and H. Perridon (eds.), *Up and Down the Cline: The Nature of Grammaticalization*. Amsterdam: John Benjamins. 17-44.

Heine, B. (2002), ‘On the role of context in grammaticalization’, in: I. Wischer and G. Diewald (eds.), *New Reflections on Grammaticalization*. Amsterdam: John Benjamins. 83-101.

Heine, B., U. Claudi and F. Hünnemeyer (1991), *Grammaticalization: A Conceptual Framework*. Chicago, IL. University of Chicago Press.

Heine, B. and T. Kuteva (2002), *World Lexicon of Grammaticalization*. Cambridge: Cambridge University Press.

Hilpert, M. (2008), *Germanic Future Constructions: A Usage-Based Approach to Language Change*. Amsterdam: John Benjamins.

Himmelmann, N.P. (2004), ‘Lexicalization and grammaticization: Opposite or orthogonal?’, in: W. Bisang, N.P. Himmelmann and B. Wiemer (eds.), *What Makes Grammaticalization: A Look from its Fringes and its Components*. Berlin: de Gruyter. 19-40.

Hinterhölzl, R. and S. Petrova (eds.) (2009), *Information Structure and Language Change: New Approaches to Word Order Variation in Germanic*. Berlin: de Gruyter.

Hopper, P.J. (1991), ‘On some principles of grammaticization’, in: E.C. Traugott and B. Heine (eds.), *Approaches to Grammaticalization*. Amsterdam: John Benjamins. Volume 1: 17-35.

Huber, M. (2007), ‘The Old Bailey Proceedings, 1674-1834: Evaluating and annotating a corpus of eighteenth- and nineteenth-century spoken English’, in: A. Meurman-Solin and A. Nurmi (eds.), *Annotating Variation and Change*. <http://www.helsinki.fi/varieng/journal/volumes /01> (13.09.2011).

Jonas, D., J. Whitman and A. Garrett (eds.) (forthcoming), *Grammatical Change: Origins, Nature, Outcomes*. Oxford: Oxford University Press.

Kiparsky, P. (forthcoming), ‘Grammaticalization as optimization’, in: D. Jonas, J. Whitman and A. Garrett (eds.), *Grammatical Change: Origins, Nature, Outcomes*. Oxford: Oxford University Press.

Kryk-Kastovsky, B. (ed.) (2006, 2007), *Historical Courtroom Discourse*. Special issues of *Journal of Historical Pragmatics*, 7, 8.

Kuteva, T. (2001), *Auxiliation: An Enquiry into the Nature of Grammaticalization*. Oxford: Oxford University Press.

Kytö, M. and S. Romaine (2005), '"We had like to have been killed by thunder & lightning": The semantic and pragmatic history of a construction that like to disappeared', *Journal of Historical Pragmatics*, 6: 1-35.

Lehmann, C. (1995), *Thoughts on Grammaticalization*. Munich: LINCOM EUROPA. 2nd edition. 2002 version available at <http://www.christianlehmann.eu/> (13.09.2011).

Mair, C. (2004), 'Corpus linguistics and grammaticalisation theory: Statistics, frequencies, and beyond', in: H. Lindquist and C. Mair (eds.), *Corpus Approaches to Grammaticalization in English*. Amsterdam: John Benjamins. 121-150.

Milroy, J. (2003), 'On the role of speakers in language change', in: R. Hickey (ed.), *Motives for Language Change*. Cambridge: Cambridge University Press. 143-157.

Nicolle, S. (1998), 'A relevance theory perspective on grammaticalisation', *Cognitive Linguistics*, 9: 1-35.

Old Bailey Proceedings Online (2011), *Proceedings of the Old Bailey 1674-1913*. <http://www.oldbaileyonline.org/>. (25.11.2011) [POB]

Poplack, S. and S. Tagliamonte (1999), 'The grammaticization of *going to* in (African American) English', *Language Variation and Change*, 11: 315-342.

ProQuest LLC (ed.) (2011), *Early English Books Online 1450-1700*. <http://eebo.chadwyck.com/home> (13.09.2011). [EEBO]

Rissanen, M. et al. (1991), *Helsinki Corpus of English Texts, Diachronic Part*. University of Helsinki. <http://icame.uib.no/> (13.09.2011). [HC]

Rosenthal, B. (ed.) (2009), *Records of the Salem Witch-Hunt*. Cambridge: Cambridge University Press.

Simpson, J. and E. Weiner (2009): *The Oxford English Dictionary*. Oxford: Oxford University Press. [OED]

Taylor, A. and S. Pintzuk (forthcoming), 'Rethinking the OV/VO alternation in Old English: The effect of complexity, grammatical weight, and information status', in: T. Nevalainen and E.C. Traugott (eds.), *The Handbook of the History of English*. Oxford: Oxford University Press.

Traugott, E.C. (2010), 'Grammaticalization', in: S. Luraghi and V. Bubenik (eds.), *Continuum Companion to Historical Linguistics*. London: Continuum. 269-283.

Traugott, E. C. (forthcoming), 'The status of onset contexts in analysis of micro-changes', in: M. Kytö (ed.), *English Corpus Linguistics: Crossing Paths*. Amsterdam: Rodopi.

Traugott, E.C. and B. Heine (eds.) (1991), *Approaches to Grammaticalization*. 2 volumes. Amsterdam: John Benjamins.

Traugott, E.C. and E. König (1991), 'The semantics-pragmatics of grammaticalization revisited', in: E.C. Traugott and B. Heine (eds.). *Approaches to Grammaticalization*. Amsterdam: John Benjamins. Volume 1: 189-218.

Traugott, E.C. and G. Trousdale (2010), 'Gradience, gradualness and grammaticalization: How do they intersect?', in: E.C. Traugott and G. Trousdale (eds.), *Gradience, Gradualness, and Grammaticalization*. Amsterdam: John Benjamins. 19-44.

Ward, W. (1765/1967), *An Essay on Grammar*. Menston: The Scholar Press.

Wischer, I. and G. Diewald (eds.) (2002), *New Reflections on Grammaticalization*. Amsterdam: John Benjamins.

Zeschel, A. (2008), 'Introduction: Usage-based approaches to language processing and representation', *Cognitive Linguistics*, 19: 345-355.

Premodifying *-ing* participles in the parsed BNC

Turo Vartiainen and Jefrey Lijffijt

University of Helsinki and Aalto University

Abstract

In this article we will focus on premodifying -ing *participles in English. By premodifying* -ing *participles we refer to NP-internal* -ing *forms, such as the ones found in* a charming man *or* a barking dog. *Our first goal is to see how these participles are used in four registers of Present-Day English: academic prose, newspaper articles, fiction and conversations. Furthermore, we will attempt to find corpus evidence for Vartiainen (forthcoming), where it was suggested that there are solid grounds for dividing the class of premodifying* -ing *participles into adjectival and verbal* -ing *participles. Our hypothesis is that if this division is evident in the syntactic behaviour of the participles, then it might also be reflected in the way* -ing *participles are used in different registers.*

1. Introduction

Earlier research has indicated that premodifiers are used in very different ways in different registers. For example, Biber et al. (1999: 65) and Biber (2007: 135) found that adjectival premodifiers (including prenominal *-ing* participles) are used more often in newspaper texts and academic prose than in fiction or conversations. This tendency has been explained by the fact that attributive premodifiers are related to the "informational production" of the text (Biber 1998: 128f.). By this analysis, nominals with complex premodifiers are seen as densely packaged information units, the function of which is to allow the author to express their message in an economical way (Biber and Clark 2002; Biber 2007).

Although we find this idea sensible, we also believe that different kinds of premodifiers may have different functions and that these functions may not be observable if the modifiers are lumped together too coarsely. In the aforementioned literature, for example, the way word classes have been categorised is somewhat questionable. For instance, Biber and Clark (2002: 46) provide *detecting* in *detecting devices* as an example of a "participial adjective". In our opinion, *detecting* is not an adjective in this phrase; it is ambiguous between a noun and a verb ('devices for detecting' or 'devices that detect'). Similarly, in the workbook to *The Longman Student Grammar of Spoken and Written English* (Conrad et al. 2002: 14) the authors argue that *coming* in the phrase *the coming weekend* is an adjective, because "it precedes and modifies the noun weekend, and the meaning is 'the weekend which is coming'". In our view, it does not seem satisfactory to claim that a participle is an adjective because in a closely synonymous clause the corresponding meaning is expressed by a finite verb. Consequently, we would call *coming* in *the coming weekend* a verbal participle.

The problems in the categorisation of premodifying *-ing* participles have previously been discussed by Huddleston (1984), Laczkó (2001) and Vartiainen (forthcoming). From a morphosyntactic standpoint, it seems clear that the strategy of lumping all kinds of *-ing* forms into one 'adjective' category is quite problematic indeed. For example, the *-ing* forms in *an interesting article* or *a fascinating experience* behave very similarly to central adjectives, whereas those in *the approaching aircraft* or *the laughing man* do not (see e.g. Vartiainen, forthcoming, for some distributional tests for categoryhood). Because of limitations of space we can only provide some cursory remarks to the matter here, but suffice it to say that in this paper we adopt the stance that premodifying *-ing* participles may be divided into adjectival and verbal *-ing* participles based on their morphosyntactic properties.

It should also be pointed out that the word class of the participle is not predetermined. Rather, the verbhood or the adjectivehood of the participle always emerges in context as a result of the relationship between the head and the modifier. Consequently, it is practically impossible to device scripts that would be automatically able to categorise participles into adjectival and verbal participles in corpora, which also means that each participle + head construction needs to be analysed by the linguist. Table 1 illustrates the way *-ing* participles can be used as adjectives and as verbs:

Table 1. Adjectival and verbal participles

Adjectival participle	**Verbal participle**
An irritating habit	An irritating substance
A stimulating lecture	A stimulating electrode
A glowing review	Glowing coal
Freezing water ('very cold water')	Freezing water ('the water's temperature is decreasing towards its freezing point')
Sparkling results	Sparkling quartz

The relevance of the above discussion for our study is two-fold. First, the division of *-ing* participles into adjectival and verbal participles allows us to study the differences in the four registers in more detail (see Section 3). Second, the problems in the categorisation of the *-ing* participle are not only theoretical; they also result in problems on a more practical level of linguistic research, the annotation of corpora and data retrieval. In the BNC-XML, for example, word classes are annotated with the CLAWS-5 tagger, which categorises nearly all premodifying *-ing* participles as adjectives. However, the parsed version of the *British National Corpus* (BNC) (see Andersen et al. 2008), which is also used in this study, applies a modified version of the CLAWS tagset, and consequently, there is much more variation in the way the premodifying *-ing* participles are annotated. Here, some premodifying *-ing* participles are tagged as adjectives, while others have been tagged as verbs. We will discuss the specific details of the way these corpora are annotated below, but at this point it should be pointed out that the theoretical problems related to the categorisation of words into word classes often result in varying and messy POS annotation, which not only makes the retrieval of relevant forms more difficult but also complicates data comparison across corpora (and across different studies). Moreover, these theoretical issues imply that POS annotation may not be a very useful or reliable tool for retrieving relevant word forms from a corpus, as the annotation scheme always reflects the theoretical stance of its makers, and this stance may not be shared by the linguist using the corpus.

Let us conclude this section on a practical note. Even though we believe that there are good grounds for dividing *-ing* participles into two categories, adjectival and verbal participles, this fine-grained division may in fact turn out to be rather problematic for the corpus compiler. As it happens, if no parsing information is available, the retrieval of the premodifying *-ing* forms may actually be more efficient when the annotation scheme regards all premodifying *-ing* participles to be adjectives. However, this is not to say that all premodifying *-ing* forms *are* adjectives: it merely goes to show that the label *adjective* is very often used for words that occur in the typical *function* of the adjective, i.e. as a modifier to a term. This leads into a simplified situation where the POS category (i.e. the word class, *adjective*) in fact includes syntactic and functional information (modifier + head relations). Therefore, the confusion between the form class and the word's function may be convenient for the purpose of making corpus queries, but it nevertheless amounts to confounding different levels of analysis and including parsing information in the POS tag (see Pullum 2009 for an excellent discussion on the confusion of different levels of analysis in linguistics; also see Denison 2007 for the problems related to the POS annotation of categories that are undergoing change).

We will now turn to the description of the corpora we have used in our research. The details of the corpora and the script that we have used to extract the relevant *-ing* forms are discussed in Section 2. The results of our study are introduced in Section 3, which is followed by a discussion of our findings in Section 4.

2. BNC-XML and the parsed BNC, instance retrieval

The data for our study comes from the BNC, both from its XML version (BNC-XML) and a parsed version which is currently under development at the University of Cambridge (see Andersen et al. 2008). The BNC contains almost a hundred million words of Present-Day English, with c. 90 million words from the written and 10 million words from the spoken domain. All word tokens in the BNC-XML have been automatically annotated using the CLAWS-5 tagger.[1] The tagger uses a *hidden Markov model* for deciding the class of a word. The result is accurate, but not perfect, because the word class cannot always be decided by using only the adjacent words. Indeed, there may even be cases where human interpretations may differ. In the parsed BNC, a different POS-tagger has been used, which is incorporated in the *Robust Accurate Statistical Parser* (RASP). The set of tags is also slightly different. For brevity, we do not discuss the parser in detail. For our purposes it is enough to know that there are 22 relations. Each represents a relationship between a head word and a dependent word, except for the *passive*, which takes only one argument. The most relevant relation for us is *ncmod*, which states that one word is a non-clausal modifier of another word. Accuracy estimates for CLAWS-5 tagger can be found in the BNC manual and accuracy estimates for RASP in Briscoe et al. (2006).[2] To summarize, the following data is available to us in the parsed BNC: each word has both a CLAWS-5 tag and a RPOS (RASP POS) tag and each sentence has a variable number of grammatical relationships.

To find all instances of premodifying *-ing* participles in the parsed BNC, we need to write a query on the database, similar to writing a query in BNCweb. The problem is that we do not know in advance how the premodifying *-ing* participles have been annotated, and there are probably many other words matching such a straightforward query. For example, the BNCweb query **ing* gives about 2.75 million words, of which very few are premodifying participles. Using the more restrictive query *{*ing/ADJ}|{*ing/VERB}*, we can cut this down to about 400 thousand, but still the percentage of premodifying participles is very low. Clearly, a more sophisticated method to retrieve the relevant information is desirable.

The problem of retrieving words that are subject to intrinsic and grammatical constraints (premodifying *-ing* participles) can be viewed as a problem of building a classifier that *predicts* which words are interesting. We shall base this classifier on a set of rules. In this view, *{*ing/ADJ}* is a classifier which predicts that all words tagged as adjective and ending with *-ing* are positive instances and all other words are negative instances. If the parser works perfectly, it will be very straightforward to construct such a classifier. A rule such as '*the POS tag is adjective AND the word is a non-clausal modifier of a later word*' would give us a perfect prediction if both the POS tag and the parser were flawless. Unfortunately, we know that they are not (see Briscoe et al. 2006 and Burnard 2007).

We will construct a model that consists of a set of rules that accurately predicts the class. We restrict our search space to words that end with *-ing*. To choose the final set of rules, we need an estimate of the precision and recall of those rules. To do so, we have constructed a data set that we can use to *train* the model. We picked three texts from the written part of the BNC at random and extracted all words ending with *-ing*, including the full sentence as context. We then annotated all words as being a premodifying *-ing* participle or not. Table 2 lists the statistics of the training data.

Table 2. Statistics for the training data set based on texts A6G, B06 and C8A

#words	**#-*ing* words**	**#ambiguous cases**	**#premodifiers**	**#other forms**
110,990	2,902	12	351	2,539

We have checked the tag distributions for the C5 and RPOS tags and observe that the tags are quite similar for *-ing* words in general, but the CLAWS-5 tagger categorizes marginally more words as adjectives. Alarmingly, for the premodifying *-ing* participles the two taggers produce completely different results. The CLAWS-5 tagger assigns nearly all (93%) to the class of adjectives (AJ0), but the RASP tagger assigns roughly two thirds of the premodifying *-ing* participles as *-ing* verbs (VVG), while one sixth of the participles are tagged as adjectives (JJ) and one sixth as nouns (NN1).

The approach we take to construct a set of rules is simple. We choose the variables that our model is allowed to use and then we run a simple algorithm to incrementally add rules to the model:

1. Compute for each possible rule an estimate of precision
2. Sort all rules according to their estimated precision
3. Start with an empty set of rules
4. For *i = 1 to number of rules*
5. Include the rule with highest precision
6. Compute and store current precision and recall
7. End

The set of possible rules is spanned by a conjunction over all variables, such that each rule covers a most specific set of instances and the rules have no overlap. Because there are only a few variables, the number of possible rules is quite limited. Hence, the computation is fast and straightforward.

We now have everything we need to construct a good set of rules for retrieving premodifying *-ing* participles from the parsed BNC. We run our algorithm for combinations of the variables corresponding to the part-of-speech tags and the grammatical relations. Figure 1 gives the results in terms of precision and recall for different sets of variables. The best possible performance would be to return all 351 premodifying participles and no other *-ing* forms. As expected, including all variables gives the best performance, but the performance is only marginally better than using only the CLAWS-5 tags. The results obtained using the RASP POS tags and grammatical relations are worse than expected: the CLAWS-5 tags give more information with respect to locating premodifying *-ing* participles. Note that each point on any of the lines corresponds to a set of rules.

When we want to pick a good set of rules, we are left with a trade-off between precision and recall. Low precision is bad because we get many false positives and have to do more manual post-processing. Low recall is bad because it produces more false negatives and that may cause bias in the final results. For further analysis we require that the recall should be above 90%. A reasonable trade-off seems to be the simple and straightforward rule to include all words categorized by the CLAWS-5 tagger as adjective and exclude all other *-ing* words. This model results in an estimated recall of c. 92% and precision of c. 67%, i.e. about one third of the final results are not premodifying *-ing* participles. An alternative that would allow automated processing of the results is based on using both tags and the grammatical information and gives 99% precision, but only 38% recall. However, the latter seems to be a poor choice for our purposes.

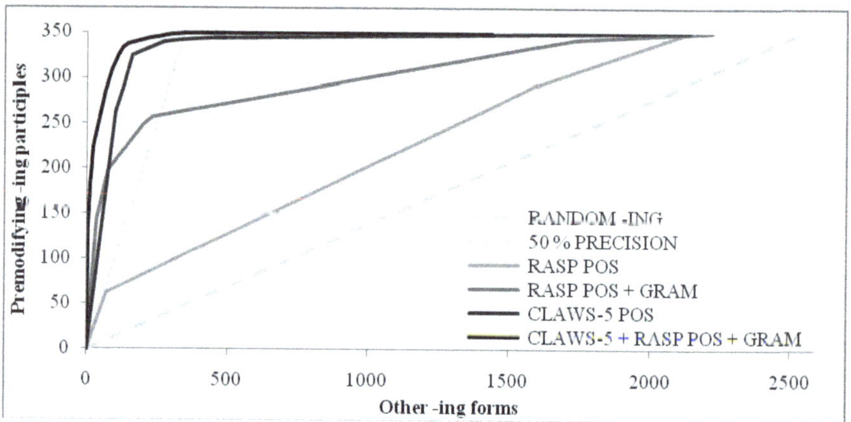

Figure 1. Precision vs. recall trade-off for different variables. (The y-axis represents the number of returned premodifying *-ing* participles. The x-axis gives the number of other *-ing* forms recalled. Each line represents a set of variables)

3. Premodifying *-ing* participles in the BNC

As described in the section above, we chose to retrieve the *-ing* forms relevant for this study by using a script that had very high recall and a reasonably high precision. The script was applied to the four registers we were interested in, after which each participle was analysed manually. After completing the analysis, we were left with 3,434 NPs with a premodifying *-ing* participle. These NPs were divided across the four registers in the following way, as illustrated in Table 3.

Table 3. Data included in the study

Register	**Files**	**Words**	**Nouns**	***-ing* pcpls**
Academic prose	15	595,380	152,802	1,490
Conversations	15	195,757	20,348	31
Fiction	15	603,199	106,971	1,519
Newspaper	10	187,632	46,889	394
Total	**55**	**1,581,968**	**327,010**	**3,434**

The files chosen to represent each register were selected randomly. For academic prose, we chose eight texts from the domain of social sciences and seven texts from natural and hard sciences. Although the selection process was indeed random in the sense that we did not study the data beforehand, we did try to choose texts of roughly equal length to ensure that the length of the text would have as little bearing on the overall results as possible. However, this could not be achieved for conversation data, as the conversation files in the BNC tend to be quite short. Therefore, the conversations in our data range from 2,161 words (file KPC) to 31,141 words (file KBG), the average number of words being 13,050. Moreover, the newspaper articles included in this study are actually collections of articles, which means that it is not sensible to compare lexical variation within the texts for this register (see Figure 4 below).

Before studying the use of adjectival and verbal *-ing* participles in more detail, let us take a look at the overall frequency of premodifying *-ing* participles in the four registers studied. Earlier research has indicated that conversations include more pronouns and fewer nouns than the other three registers, whereas academic prose and news contain more nouns and fewer pronouns (Biber et al. 1999: 92). As premodifying *-ing* participles by definition occur only before nouns, we have compared the number of *-ing* participles against the number of nouns instead of the number of words. Figure 2 illustrates the participle/noun ratio in the four registers.

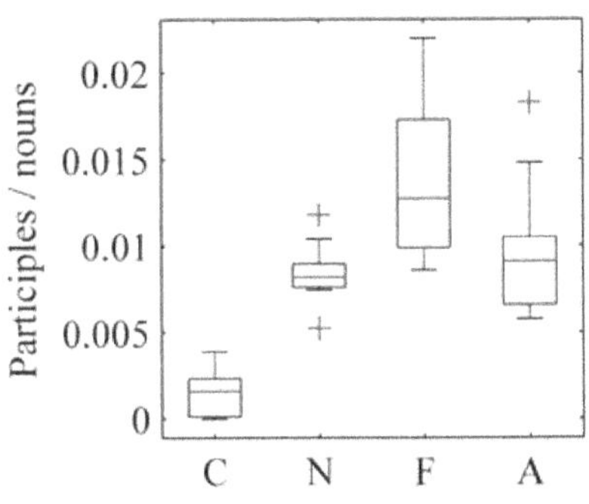

Figure 2. The frequency of the premodifying *-ing* participle in different registers

We may first observe from Figure 2 that conversations are indeed markedly different from the other three registers: of the 20,347 nouns that have the potential of occurring with a premodifying *-ing* participle, only 31 actually do so (see Table 3). As previous studies (e.g. Biber et al. 1999) have indicated that prenominal modifiers are rare in conversations, this is an expected result.

Less expected may be the fact that premodifying *-ing* participles are used more frequently in fiction than in academic prose or newspaper articles. This is contrary to earlier claims (e.g. Biber et al. 1999: 65), according to which *-ing* adjectives (a class in which other premodifying *-ing* participles are also included) are much more common in newspaper texts and in academic prose than in fiction.

In order to obtain a clearer picture of the use of premodifying *-ing* participles in the four registers, we annotated each participle as a verbal participle or an adjectival participle according to the distributional properties of the participle (see e.g. Vartiainen, forthcoming, for these distributional tests). Figure 3 shows the frequency of verbal participles in the four registers.

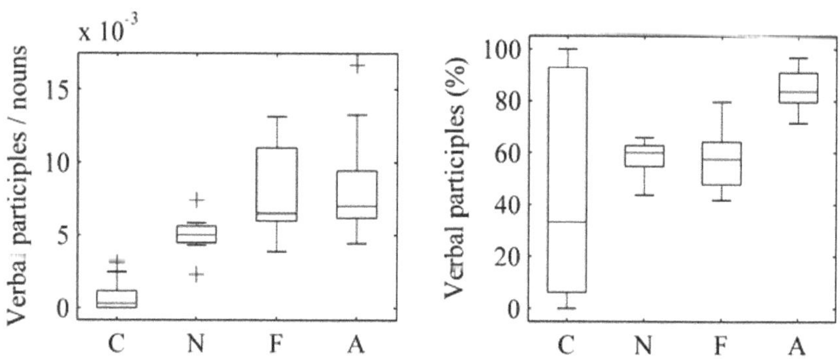

Figure 3. The frequency of verbal participles in different registers (left) and the proportion of verbal *-ing* participles of all premodifying *-ing* participles (right)

We can see from Figure 3 that, on average, the number of verbal participles is slightly larger in academic prose than in fiction or newspaper texts. However, the most significant difference across the four registers can be seen when the proportion of verbal and adjectival participles are compared: over 80 percent of all premodifying *-ing* participles are verbal participles in academic prose, while the corresponding proportions for newspaper texts and fiction are at around 60 percent. Clearly, the more fine-grained division of *-ing* participles into adjectives and verbs reveals a difference in the use of premodifying *-ing* participles.

The large proportion of verbal participles in academic prose can be explained in part by the use of certain frequently occurring participles, such as *following*, *preceding* and *succeeding*. Compared to fiction, where words like *following* almost always have a temporal function (e.g. *the following morning*), the function of these participles in academic prose is textual (e.g. *the following examples*). We suggest that in academic prose these participles offer the author a way to guide the reader's attention to a particularly significant or illustrative passage in a text (e.g. *the following examples*), or to re-introduce a previously mentioned referent into the reader's mind (e.g. *the preceding sections*). In other words, these participles are used as *foregrounding elements* in academic discourse. Moreover, their use is very specific to the academic register: 11.4 percent of all premodifying *-ing* participles in academic prose are foregrounding participles, whereas in newspaper articles only one percent of the participles have similar function. We found only one single foregrounding participle in our fiction data, while there were no occurrences in the conversation data.

However, the use of foregrounding participles cannot by itself explain why the proportion of verbal participles is so large in academic prose. Another reason for the frequent use of verbal participles is that topical phrases including a premodifying *-ing* participle are often repeated in academic prose. For example, the file CS3, a text about social classes and different kinds of government, includes 160 premodifying *-ing* participles. Of these, the participle *ruling* occurs 54 times, while *governing* occurs 23 times. The use of foregrounding participles and the repetition of topical phrases also mean that there is much less lexical variation in academic prose than in fiction, for example. This difference is depicted in Figure 4. Quite strikingly, the two registers can be distinguished with very high precision by this single parameter (each data point represents a text file in the BNC).

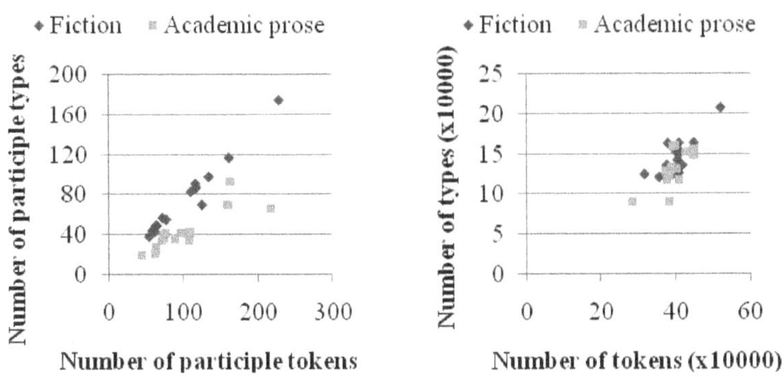

Figure 4. The number of unique participles in academic prose and fiction (left) and the type/token ratio in academic prose and fiction (right)

Importantly, the variance between the two registers described in Figure 4 is independent of the type/token ratio of the texts, which indicates that the difference in the lexical variation of *-ing* participles is not motivated by a more general lexical tendency.

4. Discussion and conclusion

In this article, we have concentrated on a single group of nominal premodifiers: *-ing* participles. We studied the frequency and use of the *-ing* participle in four registers, and our results can be seen as largely corroborating earlier research, while also presenting novel ideas. First, contrary to earlier research (Biber et al. 2002; Biber 2007), we found that in our data, premodifying *-ing* participles are most frequently used in fiction. This suggests that there is more to the use of NP-internal participial modifiers than just economy of expression or information packaging (see e.g. Biber and Clark 2002; Biber and Gray 2010). Second, we found that the division of *-ing* participles into verbal and adjectival participles is not motivated only on morphosyntactic grounds; rather, the differences in the syntactic behaviour of the participle classes have an impact on language use as well: while both adjectival and verbal participles are common in novels and newspaper articles, academic prose strongly favours verbal participles. This tendency can be explained by the repetition of topical phrases (e.g. *the ruling elite*), on the one hand, and the frequent use of foregrounding participles, such as *following*, on the other. The foregrounding function of this subclass of *-ing* participles can also be seen as a means of (re-)introducing a discourse referent. Thompson (1988) already noted that premodifying (attributive) adjectives often introduce a new discourse referent, while predicative adjectives typically have a characterising function (see also Englebretson 1997; Ford et al. 2003). Our data complements these findings, indicating that not only adjectival but also verbal premodifiers may have such referent-introducing function. We also suspect that adjectival participles can be used to express the author's attitude or stance more readily than verbal participles. This may also contribute to their relative infrequency in academic prose, which tends to be written in a more formal and more objective tone than novels and newspaper texts.

To conclude, we find that the differences in the morphosyntactic behaviour of adjectival and verbal *-ing* participles imply that the debate over the categorisation of the participle is not just a theoretical concern but that it is actually relevant for language users and is part of linguistic reality. This observation may present difficulties for the automatic (and often overly simplified) annotation of corpora, and it may also be inconvenient for the linguist who is trying to retrieve the relevant *-ing* forms from a corpus. On the other hand, mislabelled and miscategorised modifiers may create a false picture of the way language is used in different registers both synchronically and diachronically.

Notes

1 <http://ucrel.lancs.ac.uk/bnc2/bnc2autotag.htm> (15.09.2011)

2 <http://www.natcorp.ox.ac.uk/docs/URG/posguide.html> (15.09.2011)

References

Andersen, Ø., J. Nioche, E.J. Briscoe and J. Carroll (2008), 'The BNC parsed with RASP4UIMA', in: N. Calzolari, K. Choukri, B. Meagaard, J. Mariani, J. Odijk, S. Piperidis and D. Tapias (eds.), *Proceedings of the Sixth International Language Resources and Evaluation Conference (LREC08)*, Marrakesh: ELRA. 865-869.

Biber, D. (1998), *Variation across Speech and Writing*. Cambridge: Cambridge University Press.

Biber, D. (2007), 'Compressed noun-phrase structures in newspaper discourse', in: W. Teubert and R. Krishnamurthy (eds.), *Corpus Linguistics: Critical Concepts in Linguistics*. London: Routledge. 130-41.

Biber, D., S. Johansson, G. Leech, S. Conrad and E. Finegan (1999), *The Longman Grammar of Spoken and Written English*. Harlow: Pearson Education.

Biber, D. and V. Clark. (2002), 'Historical shifts in modification patterns with complex noun phrase structures: How long can you go without a verb?', in: T. Fanego, M.J. López-Couso and J. Pérez-Guerra (eds.), *English Historical Syntax and Morphology*. Amsterdam: John Benjamins. 43-66.

Biber, D. and B. Gray (2010), 'Challenging stereotypes about academic writing: Complexity, elaboration, explicitness', *Journal of English for Academic Purposes*, 9: 2-20.

Briscoe, T., J. Carroll and R. Watson (2006), 'The second release of the RASP system', in: *Proceedings of the COLING/ACL on interactive presentation sessions*. <http://delivery.acm.org/10.1145/1230000/1225423/p77-briscoe.pdf?ip=84.58.235.186&acc=OPEN&CFID=55361924&CFTOKEN=36146067&__acm__=1322326824_c0016fcbf2bf46ee3d6c98159df79373> (26.11.2011).

Burnard, L. (2007), *Reference Guide for the British National Corpus XML Edition*. Oxford: Oxford University Computing Services. H. Stroudsberg: ACM Digital Library, 77-80. <http://www.natcorp.ox.ac.uk/URG/> (15.09.2011).

Conrad, S., D. Biber and G. Leech (2002), *The Longman Student Grammar of Spoken and Written English: Workbook*. Harlow: Pearson Education.

Denison, D. (2007), 'Playing tag with category boundaries', in: A. Meurman-Solin and A. Nurmi (eds.), *Annotating Variation and Change*. Helsinki: Research Unit for Variation, Contacts, and Change in English (VARIENG). <http://www.helsinki.fi/varieng/journal/volumes/01/denison/> (15.09.2011).

Englebretson, R. (1997), 'Genre and grammar: Predicative and attributive adjectives in spoken English', *Berkeley Linguistics Society*, 23: 411-421.

Ford, C.E., B.A. Fox and S.A. Thompson (2003), 'Social interaction and grammar', in: M. Tomasello (ed.), *The New Psychology of Language: Cognitive and Functional Approaches to Language Structure*. London: Erlbaum. 119-144.

Huddleston, R. (1984), *Introduction to the Grammar of English*. Cambridge: Cambridge University Press.

Laczkó, T. (2001), 'Another look at participles and adjectives in the English DP', in: M. Butt and T. Holloway King (eds.), *Proceedings of the LFG01 Conference*. Stanford, CA: CSLI Publications. 201-220. <http://cslipublications.stanford.edu/LFG/6/lfg01.pdf> (15.09.2011).

Pullum, G. (2009), 'Lexical categorization in English dictionaries and traditional grammars', *Zeitschrift für Anglistik und Amerikanistik*, 57: 255-273.

Thompson, S.A. (1988), 'A discourse approach to the cross-linguistic category "adjective"', in: J. Hawkins (ed.), *Explaining Linguistic Universals.* Oxford: Basil Blackwell. 167-85.

Vartiainen, T. (forthcoming), 'Telicity and the Premodifying *-ing*-participle in English'. Proceedings of the 30th ICAME conference, Lancaster, May 2010.

www.ingramcontent.com/pod-product-compliance
Lightning Source LLC
LaVergne TN
LVHW020635300926
849161LV00004B/709

* 9 7 8 9 0 4 2 0 3 4 9 5 2 *